Richard Garnett, John Milton

Prose

Richard Garnett, John Milton

Prose

ISBN/EAN: 9783337370183

Printed in Europe, USA, Canada, Australia, Japan

Cover: Foto ©Thomas Meinert / pixelio.de

More available books at **www.hansebooks.com**

Prose of Milton: Selected and Edited, with an Introduction, by Richard Garnett, LL.D.

LONDON: WALTER SCOTT, LTD.
24 WARWICK LANE.

CONTENTS.

	PAGE
INTRODUCTION	vii
AREOPAGITICA: A SPEECH FOR THE LIBERTY OF UNLICENSED PRINTING	1
ON EDUCATION	48
FROM "THE TENURE OF KINGS AND MAGISTRATES"	61
PREFACE TO "EIKONOKLASTES"	92
FROM "THE SECOND DEFENCE OF THE PEOPLE OF ENGLAND"	101
THE READY AND EASY WAY TO ESTABLISH A FREE COMMONWEALTH	130
FROM "REFORMATION IN ENGLAND, AND THE CAUSES THAT HITHERTO HAVE HINDERED IT"	160
FROM "ANIMADVERSIONS UPON THE REMONSTRANT'S DEFENCE AGAINST SMECTYMNUUS"	182
FROM "THE REASON OF CHURCH GOVERNMENT URGED AGAINST PRELATY"	194
FROM "AN APOLOGY FOR SMECTYMNUUS"	220
DEDICATION TO "THE DOCTRINE AND DISCIPLINE OF DIVORCE"	227
DEDICATION TO "A TREATISE ON CHRISTIAN DOCTRINE"	251

INTRODUCTION.

THE excerpters from Milton's prose are now a numerous body, but the saying is by no means applicable to them, *tot homines quot sententiæ;* rather may we remark the agreement in things fundamental which Sydney Smith observed to prevail between Pythagoras and Mrs. Trimmer. They all have eyes for the purple patches, and originality in this department of editorship must absolutely declare in favour of drab. No future editor is likely to be so ultra-original and at the same time so ultra-foolish; and nothing short of this will lead him far from the path of Mr. Ernest Myers, the latest and the most tasteful anthologist. We, at all events, have deemed that it would be injurious to depart from it except as regards the order of the pieces and the inclusion of translations from Milton's Latin writings, which we shall hereafter endeavour to justify. Nor can much be added to Mr. Myers' critical appreciation of his author; though something may be subtracted if we dispute, as we must, his assertion that, among the good prose of good English poets, Milton's alone has preserved any considerable power. Surely Mr. Myers would admit that Coleridge's prose has influenced the national mind far more profoundly than Milton's. It may also be questioned whether a fallacy does not lurk in the comparison: whether because Milton exercised his pen upon matters of greater concern than most other poets who have written prose, we do not glide insensibly into the notion that he must have produced greater results; whether, too, we do not confound the admiration which his prose writings have justly received from a later age with an imaginary influence which it is inferred that they must have exerted on their own. In truth, the influence of Milton's English prose writings seems to have been very slight. In his attacks upon prelacy he went with the stream, and his voice mingled with the universal shout. When he took an independent line, when he pleaded for liberty of divorce, or, with a heroism of which even he might not have been capable if his infirmity had not severed him from the world, launched pamphlets against monarchy on the very vigil of the Restoration, he produced absolutely no effect whatever. Nor can we perceive that his "Areopagitica" hastened the liberty of the press by a day, though, when this had come about by wholly different agencies, it was rightly adopted as the gospel of the new dispensation: as the newly-discovered Venus of Milo might be made the goddess of a classical revival inaugurated while she yet slept under the sod. The only prose production of Milton to which a considerable contemporary effect can be justly ascribed is not an English but a Latin one, his defence of the English people against Salmasius; and of all his writings this at present concerns us least. Hence Milton is not to be reckoned among those who have most directly influenced his countrymen, and, as a prose-writer, he survives rather by his literary than his historical greatness. The effect produced in criticism by Dryden, Wordsworth, Matthew Arnold, has been more profound than any that Milton could achieve in theology and politics. Nor is it easy to balance his literary achievement against that of writers so unlike him as Coleridge and the three just named, or with the epistolary mastery of Gray and Cowper, Shelley and Byron.

We must therefore agree with Mr. Myers that Milton in a measure exemplifies the maxim, "Prose is for an age, poetry for all time." Yet this maxim is not of universal application. It notoriously does not apply to the greatest prose-writers of antiquity, nor to some of modern date. Still, upon deeper consideration, it seems justified to a certain extent even in these by the fact that, unlike the poets, they owe their immortality to their matter rather than their manner. The manner is indeed of great importance; few or none have obtained abiding fame without first-rate excellence of style, unless, like Aristotle and Polybius, they have had a monopoly of their subjects. But that that style is not the preservative is evident from the fact that an equal opulence of merely literary endowment fails to preserve an inferior subject, or one with which the writer is less qualified to deal. Hume lives by his essays, not by his history; Gibbon by his history, not by his essays. Here Milton comes short, his claims are the splendour of his style and the wonderful elevation of his mind; his matter, save in the "Areopagitica" and the "Treatise on Education" (the "Treatise on Divorce" might have been a grand exception but is not), is derived from the transient controversies of his day, and has little significance for ours. But this merely enhances our admiration for the literary genius displayed in these writings. To have invested the ecclesiastical and political disputes of the seventeenth century with interest for the nineteenth in any other way than as subjects of historical or philosophical investigation is a wonderful feat of eloquence, and the wonder is augmented when it is considered that Milton's style was becoming old-fashioned in his own day, and soon afterwards became obsolete. The sonorous grandeur which captivates us was a positive offence to the eighteenth century, whose mission, a most important one, was to free the language from the tautology and obscurity incidental to its age of grandeur, and render it an exact instrument of thought. The poetry and music of prose diction necessarily went overboard; it has been the mission of our own age to reintroduce them without sacrificing the lucidity, the polish, the cultured grace for which we are indebted to the eighteenth century. We are thus in a position to admire both, but, however we may stare at some of the literary judgments of Hume, for instance, we must not blame the eighteenth century for seeing little merit in what it was its business to abolish, and we shall find in what must have seemed Milton's uncouthness a better explanation of the comparative neglect which has befallen him than that which has commended itself to his most enthusiastic editor, Mr. J. A. St. John. Mr. St. John, whose glowing appreciation of Milton's merit has enabled him to imbibe not a little of Milton's manner, inquires how it was that while the scarcely more majestic eloquence of Demosthenes and Cicero took rank among masterpieces from its delivery, and was never vilipended in any succeeding age, Milton's very shortly fell into disesteem, and is even now valued below its desert. This Mr. St. John explains by the wickedness and malice of priests, loyalists, and the supporters of ancient abuses in general, whose efforts, on the contrary, as will be evident to most persons, were much more likely to have resulted in exalting Milton than in abasing him. The simple explanation is that the comparison of Milton to Demosthenes and Cicero in this point of view is a complete fallacy. Their diction had attained the utmost perfection of which their respective languages were capable, and represented a point beyond which no further progress was possible. Posterity could not displace them, for it could not replace them. Milton, on the other hand, represented a particular stage in the evolution of English, which the next development must necessarily superannuate. He could no more pass for a Demosthenes or a Cicero with the succeeding generation than Lucretius could pass for a Virgil. His fame as a prose-writer must submit to a temporary eclipse, and could only await the inevitable reaction which has replaced him among great prosaists as it has replaced Lucretius among great poets.

The chief lesson to be drawn from Milton's prose works in illustration of his genius and his life is the recognition of his position as the great idealist, the Rousseau or the Ruskin of his generation. The current view of his character does him great injustice, while in itself natural and almost inevitable. A man of strict and austere life, living in a Puritan age and siding with Puritanism in almost all questions at issue between it and contending tendencies, can hardly be taken for anything but a Puritan, and the illusion is augmented by the Scriptural derivation of three out of his five chief poetical works. "Paradise Lost," in particular, has become almost deutero-canonical; and it seems impossible to conceive the author as other than a kind of modern Hebrew. It requires study to discover that this modern representative of Biblical poetry is also the most classical of all our great poets; that, like the great Protestant cathedral, the great Protestant epic descends from the Renaissance. Even as his poetry reveals Milton in the character of a humanist, so the more important of his prose works display him as a revolutionist, eager to sweep away everything obstructive of an ideal existing solely in his own mind. Hence, as the assailant of prelacy, he is utterly indifferent to the majesty, the antiquity, the sacred associations, the hallowed pomp and æsthetic splendour of the institution he assails, so seductive to a poetic mind, and especially to his own votary who, a hundred and fifty years afterwards, would fain have recalled him to life.[1] Writing on family sanctions, he would abolish what had until then been esteemed their chief security; planning schemes of education, he begins by demolishing the universities; defending the execution of Charles, he shows himself entirely insensible of "the divinity that doth hedge a king." In all this there is no coarse rancour or destructiveness; he has seen with the inner eye ideals which dull these venerable realities, and render them mere encumbrance. This establishes a deep distinction between him and Puritanism, whose ideals lie not in the future but the past. It suggests that he took Puritanism up partly, no doubt, because it embodied his favourite virtues of fortitude and temperance, but also because it was the only organised force in that age which, by overthrowing the old order, could offer a chance for the realisation of his ideals. The same instinct would in the following century and in ours have enlisted him under other banners: the French Revolution would have claimed him a hundred years ago, and Socialism now. More splendid and generous visions, not without a ground in reality, were never conceived by any; instead of the staid Genevan whose semblance he wears in the popular mind, he should rather be conceived as the impersonation of Ideal Hope, accidentally vested in the garb of the

---

[1] "Milton, thou should'st be living at this hour,
England hath need of thee."—*Wordsworth.*

INTRODUCTION.   xiii

seventeenth century, but ready for any vesture not wholly worn out. So he would appear if his prose writings were better known, for in them alone he is brought into connection with politics and practical human interests. Yet these in turn reflect light upon his character as a poet. Among the moderns, he is commonly compared with Wordsworth, though Landor thought fit to parallel him with Southey, such is the courage of friendship. The resemblance with Wordsworth is indeed very close in many respects — dignity of aim, gravity of life, early and deliberate dedication to poetry, high self-appreciation, haughty self-reliance, majesty of sentiment, preference for blank verse, especial mastery of the sonnet. But the spiritual kinship with Shelley is really much closer, and would be more evident if the younger poet's exuberant fancy had not veiled his figure in a radiant mist, which conceals the real Shelley as the Genevan habit conceals the real Milton.

It remains to furnish a brief account of the circumstances attending the production of those of Milton's prose pieces from which extracts are given in this selection. Two, the "Areopagitica" and the "Treatise on Education," being reprinted entire, are therefore placed first. This course, though involving a departure from strict chronological order, is further recommended by the fact that Milton's prose writings, being without exception called into being by temporary and occasional incitements, are no index to the development of his mind, and, after the composition of "Areopagitica," register no change but the abating splendour of his style. It is therefore indifferent in what order they are read, so long as they are sorted into their distinctive subjects. "Areopagitica" and the "Treatise on Education" having on the whole a closer relation to politics than to theology, it has been thought advisable that they should be succeeded by the political writings. These followed each other in chronological order, and the same principle has been observed in the arrangement of the theological section. It has of course been a question whether Milton's Latin writings ought to be represented, since the English translations do not proceed from himself. They occupy, nevertheless, so important a portion of his literary life, and his celebrity among his contemporaries was in so great a degree derived from the chief of them, that it does not seem that they ought to be omitted, particularly as they are included in every edition of his complete works. By the irony of fate, indeed, the one especially alluded to as the source and mainstay of his reputation in his own day, has in ours become all but unreadable: nothing can be found in the "Defence of the English People" which could claim admission into an English anthology on the ground either of matter or of style. In the much less famous and much less important reply to Dumoulin and Morus he has happily deviated into biography; and his manly if somewhat over-self-conscious vindication of himself, and his portraits of Cromwell and those around Cromwell, possess the charm alike of biography and of diction. There remains the "Treatise of Christian Doctrine." The very circumstance which bestows a special value on this work renders quotation from it impossible. It is so intimately knit up with the Bible as to be in the main little else than a body of references, only to be read profitably with the Bible at hand, and entirely out of place in a selection of prose passages. The only portion available for such a purpose is the Dedication, not clothed with the grandeur which Milton would have imparted to it in his youth, but an exquisite and touching memorial of his age, showing him at the end of his long struggles, humbly rejoicing in what he deemed the

INTRODUCTION.

assured possession of truth; if abated in strength, purged also of vehemence and arrogance; content with the evening shadow, and wishing to close his days in peace and charity with all men.

"Areopagitica," the first number of our selection, was published in November 1644, and was called forth by a petition to Parliament from the Stationers' Company, presented in the preceding August, complaining of Milton's infringement of the Ordinance of June 14, 1643, by the publication of his tracts on Divorce without authority from the appointed Licensers. Milton had no doubt deliberately taken the consequences upon himself, aware that it would have been in vain to seek such authority from the worthy persons, mostly divines, chosen by Parliament to keep British authorship in order. It was obvious that, if this ordinance were to be enforced, neither pleas for divorce nor aught else distasteful to Puritan orthodoxy would have a chance of being published; and although the prosecution, as it affected him personally, soon went to sleep, he felt it his duty to protest, and the measure of his emotion may be estimated by the magnificence of his language. He does not indeed go the full length of claiming, with necessary exceptions, absolute freedom for the press; he is content that published matter should be suppressed, if it seems to deserve it, and only protests against an institution designed to prevent its coming into the world at all. But, as in the case of Luther and many another, his premises involved larger conclusions than he himself suspected or was prepared for. As the Licensers could not be expected to approve a tract aiming at their own abolition, "Areopagitica" made its appearance without a licence, and this new transgression excited another little storm, shortly allayed as the first had been.

The "Tract on Education" was also published in 1644 (June 5). It undoubtedly grew out of Milton's acquaintance with Samuel Hartlib, to whom it is addressed, the friend of the great Bohemian educator, Comenius. Milton himself had also had much practical experience of education, and his house was full of pupils at the time. This experience, however, had not taught him a just view of the capacities of average persons, nor did it deter him from propounding, in the guise of a benefit to the multitude, a scheme for the education of Miltons. This sublime exaggeration is nevertheless the salt of his tract, whose spirit is as profitable as its letter is frequently unpractical. "The noble moral glow," says Professor Masson, "that pervades the 'Tract on Education,' the mood of magnanimity in which it is conceived and written, and the faith it inculcates in the powers of the young human spirit, if rightly nurtured and directed, are merits everlasting."

"The Tenure of Kings and Magistrates" was written during the trial of Charles the First, and published on February 13, 1649, fourteen days after his execution, and four days after the publication of the *Eikon Basilike*. "Not equal in richness of literary interest," says Professor Masson, "to the best of Milton's previous pamphlets, it is a strong, thoroughly Miltonic performance, falling with hammer-like force on the question discussed." Milton's contention is, first, that a nation is justified in changing its government at its will, and, *a fortiori*, that it has a right to throw off the yoke of a tyrant, and bring him to justice. It is remarkable for its attacks upon the Presbyterians, who are regarded as practically Royalists.

Within a month after the publication of the "Tenure" Milton received his appointment as Latin Secretary to the Commonwealth, and literary tasks were speedily imposed upon him. The most important of these was the composition of the answer to the *Eikon Basilike*, which appeared in October under the title of *Eikonoklastes*, the exordium of which is inserted in this collection. It is an exhaustive answer, following the original paragraph by paragraph, and consequently allowing but little scope for the eloquence and poetry which have made Milton's earlier pamphlets memorable.

"The Ready and Easy Way to Establish a Free Commonwealth" is a more remarkable production; it is in fact among the most remarkable of Milton's prose writings. It was published about the end of February, 1659, and republished with considerable additions and alterations about the beginning of April. It is very interesting for the undaunted courage, notwithstanding an inevitable tincture of despondency, shown by its publication on the very eve of the Restoration; and still more for the originality of the scheme propounded for the establishment of a Commonwealth, which consists in the election of a perpetual Parliament to be renewed only as vacancies should be occasioned by death, and acting through a small executive appointed by itself. By this means Milton fondly hoped to impart that stability to republican institutions which he could not but perceive that they had grievously wanted. Another remarkable proposal, anticipating many modern theories, is the delegation of local business to small local assemblies, where statesmen, it was expected, would be trained to take place in the great council of the nation. The pamphlet produced several replies, but its proposals found no support, and it was entirely inoperative in checking the reaction in favour of royalty. It is very curious that, although the text printed in Milton's works is that of the second and revised edition, not a single original copy of this is known to be in existence.

INTRODUCTION.

Milton's theological pamphlets, the next section of our anthology, bring us back to his very beginnings as a prose author. All were published in 1641 and 1642, under the influence of the fierce reaction against episcopacy which was at last able to manifest itself now that the long tyranny of Laud had come to an end. Partly from the contagious intoxication of this reaction, partly from the flush attending the first display of his literary power, these anti-episcopal manifestoes, from which so little in the way of splendid diction could reasonably have been expected, embody the finest passages of his eloquence, finer even than the "Areopagitica." Notwithstanding that "Satan's Address to the Sun" was written about this time, he was not yet at the summit of his power as a poet; but the strifes and disillusions of the next few years took from him, as a writer of prose, more than Time could ever restore. The titles and approximate dates of publication are as follows:—"Of Reformation touching Church Discipline in England and the causes that hitherto have hindered it," June 1641; "Of Prelatical Episcopacy," July 1641; "Animadversions upon the Remonstrant's Defence against Smectymnuus," July 1641; "The Reason of Church Government urged against Prelacy," February 1642; "An Apology against a Pamphlet called 'A Modest Confutation of the Animadversions of the Remonstrant against Smectymnuus,'" April 1642. "In his first and second tracts," Professor Masson observes, "Milton has adopted mainly the historical method; in the third he is critical and personal; in the fourth he argues against prelacy on grounds of philosophic reason." The fifth was called forth by an attack upon himself, and is chiefly remarkable for a magnificent passage of autobiography.

Milton's tract on Divorce exists in two widely differing

editions, the second greatly enlarged and improved. The first, as Professor Masson has proved to the general astonishment, was published by August 1, 1643, and must consequently have been written, not, as formerly believed on the authority of Phillips, after and on account of his wife's refusal to return to him, but while she was still an inmate of his house. The second edition appeared on February 2, 1644. In conducting his argument, Milton labours under great constraint, being obliged to defend himself by the authority of commentators, canonists, jurists, and other most arid and uninviting writers. Every now and then he gives himself the rein, enough to prove that, could he have approached his subject from the positive side, he might have delivered a discourse on Love in no way inferior to Diotima's. His tract appears to have had a special influence on Emerson, who frequently imitates it. Its appendages, the "Tetrachordon," the "Colasterion," and the compilation from Bucer, are purely controversial, and do not here concern us.

The circumstances which called forth Milton's "Defence of the English People against Salmasius," and its sequel, are too well known to require mention here. None of his writings procured him half the contemporary fame of his reply to Salmasius, still invested with sublimity by his loss of sight during its composition, his deliberate sacrifice to the cause of his country. It would otherwise excite little emotion, while the slighted and less important Second Defence retains much interest from its autobiographic information and portraits of the statesmen and soldiers of the Commonwealth. The first Defence appeared in March 1651; the second in May 1654.

The mere fact that Milton's reply to Salmasius is so profoundly uninstructive for us renders it an invaluable landmark of human progress. It is good to refer to such writings merely to note what a deliverance the human mind has since enjoyed from the yoke of illegitimate authority Milton and his opponent both mainly rely upon quotation. They labour to show not that the antagonist has mistaken reason, but that he has misunderstood his author. They would be seriously disturbed if it could be proved that "Ecphantas, whom you likewise quote," was really of the adversary's way of thinking. To us it seems amazing that monarchy should have been either attacked or defended by such arguments. We incline to observe to both parties, as they observe to each other, "You quote a great many frivolous passages out of the Rabbins." Whether we agree with Salmasius or with Milton, our assent will not be extorted by the logic of either. Yet they were the two most distinguished intellectual gladiators of their time. If the arguments which seemed so formidable then carry no conviction now, it must be because mere authority is no longer regarded, but questions are investigated by the light of reason; because Ecphantas and the Rabbins intimidate nobody now; and because the human mind, whether bound for the desert or the Promised Land, is at all events no longer an inmate of the house of bondage.

The translation of the reply to Salmasius used in this volume was made by Joseph Washington towards the end of the seventeenth century. That of the Second Defence is by Dr. Robert Fellowes. There is another of equal merit by Archdeacon Wrangham.

It only remains to speak of Milton's "Treatise of Christian Doctrine," whose fortune has been more romantic, and less auspicious, than that of any of his other works. It occupied much of his time during his latter years, and was undoubtedly, and not unjustly, regarded by him as not the least worthy among the memorials of himself which he was to bequeath to posterity. It was given by him to his amanuensis, Daniel Skinner, together with copies of the official letters he had written for the Commonwealth, apparently on the understanding that Skinner should cause both to be printed in Holland. He did enter into negotiation with Elzevir for the purpose, but in the meantime a pirated and mutilated edition of the letters was published by a London bookseller, and Skinner, exasperated at being forestalled, applied to Sir Joseph Williamson, Secretary of State, to suppress the spurious edition in favour of the more complete one projected by himself. Sir Joseph, as a Royalist, very naturally thought that if an imperfect edition of Milton was bad, a perfect one would be worse; and the MS. of the letters, as well as that of the disregarded "Treatise of Christian Doctrine," was ultimately given up by the penitent publisher. Williamson, without even looking at them, put them into a book-cupboard, where they remained until their discovery in 1823 by Mr. Robert Lemon, of the State Paper Office. George the Fourth, to his honour, caused the "Treatise" to be translated by Sumner, afterwards Bishop of Winchester, and had both original and translation published at his own expense. It was, however, then too much out of date to be regarded otherwise than as a curiosity. A hundred years earlier, when the Arian controversy was at its height, it might have exercised an important influence on opinion. The impossibility of its wielding any such influence in the present day is sufficient from Professor Masson's accurate description. "Consisting to so large an extent of mere collections of texts from Scripture, all duly cited, it is not even continuously fluent as any ordinary book is, but breaks itself, as it were, into a maze of expository rivulets trickling among banks of Biblical quotations." But it is of extreme importance for the knowledge of Milton himself. "The Miltonic philosophy," says Professor Masson, "presented to us in the other writings only in dispersed poetic gleams or in diffused living glow and fervour, is here exhibited coolly and collectedly in the driest bones of abstract thesis and proposition." Its discovery determined all controversies respecting Milton's theological opinions; exhibited the intense literalness of his mind in some departments, and its daring excursiveness in others; elucidated much that had seemed doubtful in "Paradise Lost"; revealed the tolerant mood to which years of conflict, so often pregnant with the reverse effect, had ultimately brought him; above all, depicted him as to the last day of his life engaged in the unwearied, disinterested, and for him perilous quest after Truth.

R. G.

1894.

PROSE OF MILTON.

PROSE WORKS OF MILTON.

AREOPAGITICA: A SPEECH FOR THE LIBERTY OF UNLICENSED PRINTING.

THEY, who to states and governors of the commonwealth direct their speech, high court of parliament! or wanting such access in a private condition, write that which they foresee may advance the public good; I suppose them, as at the beginning of no mean endeavour, not a little altered and moved inwardly in their minds; some with doubt of what will be the success, others with fear of what will be the censure; some with hope, others with confidence of what they have to speak. And me perhaps each of these dispositions, as the subject was whereon I entered, may have at other times variously affected; and likely might in these foremost expressions now also disclose which of them swayed most, but that the very attempt of this address thus made, and the thought of whom it hath recourse to, hath got the power within me to a passion, far more welcome than incidental to a preface.

Which though I stay not to confess ere any ask, I shall be blameless, if it be no other than the joy and gratulation which it brings to all who wish to promote their country's liberty; whereof this whole discourse proposed will be a certain testimony, if not a trophy. For this is not the liberty which we can hope, that no grievance ever should arise in the commonwealth: that let no man in this world expect; but when complaints are freely heard, deeply considered, and speedily reformed, then is the utmost bound of civil liberty obtained that wise men look for. To which if I now manifest, by the very sound of this which I shall utter, that we are already in good part arrived, and yet from such a steep disadvantage of tyranny and superstition grounded into our principles, as was beyond the manhood of a Roman recovery, it will be attributed first, as is most due, to the strong assistance of God, our deliverer; next, to your faithful guidance and undaunted wisdom, lords and commons of England! Neither is it in God's esteem, the diminution of His glory, when honourable things are spoken of good men, and worthy magistrates; which if I now first should begin to do, after so fair a progress of your laudable deeds, and such a long obligement upon the whole realm to your indefatigable virtues, I might be justly reckoned among the tardiest and the unwillingest of them that praise ye.

Nevertheless there being three principal things, without which all praising is but courtship and flattery: first, when that only is praised which is solidly worth praise; next, when greatest likelihoods are brought, that such things are truly and really in those persons to whom they are ascribed; the other, when he who praises, by showing that such his actual persuasion is of whom he writes, can demonstrate that he flatters not; the former two of these I have heretofore endeavoured, rescuing the employment from him who went about to impair your merits with a trivial and malignant encomium; the latter as belonging chiefly to mine own acquittal, that whom I so extolled I did not flatter, hath been reserved opportunely to this occasion. For he who freely magnifies what hath been nobly done, and fears not to declare as freely what might be done better, gives ye the best covenant of his fidelity; and that his loyalest affection and his hope waits on your proceedings. His highest praising is not flattery, and his plainest advice is a kind of praising; for though I should affirm and hold by argument, that it would fare better with truth, with learning, and the commonwealth, if one of your published orders, which I should name, were called in; yet at the same time it could not but much redound to the lustre of your mild and equal government, whenas private persons are hereby animated to think ye better pleased with public advice than other statists have been delighted heretofore with public flattery. And men will then see what difference there is between the magnanimity of a triennial parliament, and that jealous haughtiness of prelates and cabin counsellors that usurped of late, whenas they shall observe ye in the midst of your victories and successes more gently brooking written exceptions against a voted order, than other courts, which had produced nothing worth memory but the weak ostentation of wealth, would have endured the least signified dislike at any sudden proclamation.

If I should thus far presume upon the meek demeanour of your civil and gentle greatness, lords and commons! as what your published order hath directly said, that to gainsay, I might defend myself with ease, if any should accuse me of being new or insolent, did they but know how much better I find ye esteem it to imitate the old and elegant humanity of Greece, than the barbaric pride of a Hunnish and Norwegian stateliness. And out of those ages, to whose polite wisdom and letters we owe that we are not yet Goths and Jutlanders, I could name him who from his private house wrote that discourse to the parliament of Athens, that persuades them to change the form of democracy which was then established. Such honour was done in those days to men who professed the study of wisdom and eloquence, not only in their own country, but in other lands, that cities and signiories heard them gladly, and with great respect, if they had aught in public to admonish the state. Thus did Dion Prusæus, a stranger and a private orator, counsel the Rhodians against a former edict; and I abound with other like examples, which to set here would be superfluous. But if from the industry of a life wholly dedicated to studious labours, and those natural endowments haply not the worst for two and fifty degrees of northern latitude, so much must be derogated, as to count me not equal to any of those who had this privilege, I would obtain to be thought not so inferior, as yourselves are superior to the most of them who received their counsel; and how far you excel them, be assured, lords and commons! there can no greater testimony appear, than when your prudent spirit acknowledges and obeys the voice of reason, from what quarter soever it be heard speaking; and renders ye as willing to repeal any act of your own setting forth, as any set forth by your predecessors.

If ye be thus resolved, as it were injury to think ye were not, I know not what should withhold me from presenting ye with a fit instance wherein to show both that love of truth which ye eminently profess, and that uprightness of your judgment which is not wont to be partial to yourselves; by judging over again that order which ye have ordained "to regulate printing: that no book, pamphlet, or paper shall be henceforth printed, unless the same be first approved and licensed by such, or at least one of such, as shall be thereto appointed." For that part which preserves justly every man's copy to himself, or provides for the poor, I touch not; only wish they be not made pretences to abuse and persecute honest and painful men, who offend not in either of these particulars. But that other clause of licensing books, which we thought had died with his brother quadragesimal and matrimonial when the prelates expired, I shall now attend with such a homily, as shall lay before ye, first, the inventors of it to be those whom ye will be loath to own; next, what is to be thought in general of reading, whatever sort the books be; and that this order avails nothing to the suppressing of scandalous, seditious, and libellous books, which were mainly intended to be suppressed. Last, that it will be primely to the discouragement of all learning, and the stop of truth, not only by disexercising and blunting our abilities, in what we know already, but by hindering and cropping the discovery that might be yet further made, both in religious and civil wisdom.

I deny not, but that it is of greatest concernment in the church and commonwealth, to have a vigilant eye how books demean themselves, as well as men; and thereafter to confine, imprison, and do sharpest justice on them as malefactors; for books are not absolutely dead things, but do contain a progeny of life in them to be as active as that soul was whose progeny they are; nay, they do preserve as in a vial the purest efficacy and extraction of that living intellect that bred them. I know they are as lively, and as vigorously productive, as those fabulous dragon's teeth: and being sown up and down, may chance to spring up armed men. And yet, on the other hand, unless wariness be used, as good almost kill a man as kill a good book: who kills a man kills a reasonable creature, God's image; but he who destroys a good book, kills reason itself, kills the image of God, as it were, in the eye. Many a man lives a burden to the earth; but a good book is the precious life-blood of a master-spirit, embalmed and treasured up on purpose to a life beyond life. It is true, no age can restore a life, whereof, perhaps, there is no great loss; and revolutions of ages do not oft recover the loss of a rejected truth, for the want of which whole nations fare the worse. We should be wary, therefore, what persecution we raise against the living labours of public men, how we spill that seasoned life of man, preserved and stored up in books; since we see a kind of homicide may be thus committed, sometimes a martyrdom; and if it extend to the whole impression, a kind of massacre, whereof the execution ends not in the slaying of an elemental life, but strikes at the ethereal and fifth essence, the breath of reason itself; slays an immortality rather than a life. But lest I should be condemned of introducing licence, while I oppose licensing, I refuse not the pains to be so much historical, as will serve to show what hath been done by ancient and famous commonwealths, against this disorder, till the very time that this project of licensing crept out of the inquisition, was catched up by our prelates, and hath caught some of our presbyters.

In Athens, where books and wits were ever busier than in any other part of Greece, I find but only two sorts of writings which the magistrate cared to take notice of; those either blasphemous and atheistical, or libellous. Thus the books of Protagoras were by the judges of Areopagus, commanded to be burnt, and himself banished the territory for a discourse, begun with his confessing not to know "whether there were gods, or whether not." And against defaming, it was agreed that none should be traduced by name, as was the manner of Vetus Comœdia, whereby we may guess how they censured libelling; and this course was quick enough, as Cicero writes, to quell both the desperate wits of other atheists, and the open way of defaming, as the event showed. Of other sects and opinions, though tending to voluptuousness, and the denying of divine Providence, they took no heed. Therefore we do not read that either Epicurus, or that libertine school of Cyrene, or what the Cynic impudence uttered, was ever questioned by the laws. Neither is it recorded that the writings of those old comedians were suppressed, though the acting of them were forbid; and that Plato commended the reading of Aristophanes, the loosest of them all, to his royal scholar, Dionysius, is commonly known, and may be excused, if holy Chrysostom, as is reported, nightly studied so much the same author, and had the art to cleanse a scurrilous vehemence into the style of a rousing sermon.

That other leading city of Greece, Lacedæmon, considering that Lycurgus their lawgiver was so addicted to elegant learning, as to have been the first that brought out of Ionia the scattered works of Homer, and sent the poet Thales from Crete, to prepare and mollify the Spartan surliness with his smooth songs and odes, the better to plant among them law and civility; it is to be wondered how museless and unbookish they were, minding nought but the feats of war. There needed no licensing of books among them, for they disliked all but their own laconic apophthegms, and took a slight occasion to chase Archilochus out of their city, perhaps for composing in a higher strain than their own soldiery ballads and roundels could reach to; or if it were for his broad verses, they were not therein so cautious, but they were as dissolute in their promiscuous conversing; whence Euripides affirms, in Andromache, that their women were all unchaste.

This much may give us light after what sort of books were prohibited among the Greeks. The Romans also for many ages trained up only to a military roughness, resembling most the Lacedæmonian guise, knew of learning little but what their twelve tables and the pontific college with their augurs and flamens taught them in religion and law; so unacquainted with other learning, that when Carneades and Critolaus, with the stoic Diogenes, coming ambassadors to Rome, took thereby occasion to give the city a taste of their philosophy, they were suspected for seducers by no less a man than Cato the Censor, who moved it in the senate to dismiss them speedily, and to banish all such Attic babblers out of Italy. But Scipio and others of the noblest senators withstood him and his old Sabine austerity; honoured and admired the men; and the censor himself at last, in his old age, fell to the study of that whereof before he was so scrupulous. And yet, at the same time, Nævius and Plautus, the first Latin comedians, had filled the city with all the borrowed scenes of Menander and Philemon. Then began to be considered there also what was to be done to libellous books and authors; for Nævius was quickly cast into prison for his unbridled pen, and released by the tribunes upon his recantation: we read also that libels were burnt, and the makers punished, by Augustus.

The like severity, no doubt, was used, if aught were impiously written against their esteemed gods. Except in these two points, how the world went in books, the magistrate kept no reckoning. And therefore Lucretius, without impeachment, versifies his Epicurism to Memmius, and had the honour to be set forth the second time by Cicero, so great a father of the commonwealth; although himself disputes against that opinion in his own writings. Nor was the satirical sharpness or naked plainness of Lucilius, or Catullus, or Flaccus, by any order prohibited. And for matters of state, the story of Titus Livius, though it extolled that part which Pompey held, was not therefore suppressed by Octavius Cæsar, of the other faction. But that Naso was by him banished in his old age, for the wanton poems of his youth, was but a mere covert of state over some secret cause; and besides, the books were neither banished nor called in. From hence we shall meet with little else but tyranny in the Roman Empire, that we may not marvel, if not so often bad as good books were silenced. I shall therefore deem to have been large enough, in producing what among the ancients was punishable to write, save only which, all other arguments were free to treat on.

By this time the emperors were become Christians, whose discipline in this point I do not find to have been more severe than what was formerly in practice. The books of those whom they took to be grand heretics were examined, refuted, and condemned in the general councils; and not till then were prohibited, or burnt, by authority of the emperor. As for the writings of heathen authors, unless they were plain invectives against Christianity, as those of Porphyrius and Proclus, they met with no interdict that can be cited, till about the year 400, in a Carthaginian council, wherein bishops themselves were forbid to read the books of Gentiles, but heresies they might read; while others long before them, on the contrary, scrupled more the books of heretics, than of Gentiles. And that the primitive councils and bishops were wont only to declare what books were not commendable, passing no further, but leaving it to each one's conscience to read or to lay by, till after the year 800, is observed already by Padre Paolo, the great unmasker of the Trentine council. After which time the popes of Rome, engrossing what they pleased of political rule into their own hands, extended their dominion over men's eyes, as they had before over their judgments, burning and prohibiting to be read what they fancied not; yet sparing in their censures, and the books not many which they so dealt with; till Martin the Fifth, by his bull, not only prohibited, but was the first that excommunicated the reading of heretical books; for about that time Wickliffe and Husse growing terrible, were they who first drove the papal court to a stricter policy of prohibiting. Which course Leo the Tenth and his successors followed, until the council of Trent and the Spanish inquisition, engendering together, brought forth or perfected those catalogues and expurging indexes, that rake through the entrails of many an old good author, with a violation worse than any could be offered to his tomb.

Nor did they stay in matters heretical, but any subject that was not to their palate, they either condemned in a prohibition, or had it straight into the new purgatory of an index. To fill up the measure of encroachment, their last invention was to ordain that no book, pamphlet, or paper should be printed (as if St. Peter had bequeathed them the keys of the press also as well as of Paradise) unless it were approved and licensed under the hands of two or three gluttonous friars. For example—

> "Let the chancellor Cini be pleased to see if in this present work be contained aught that may withstand the printing.
> "Vincent Rabbata, Vicar of Florence."

> "I have seen this present work, and find nothing athwart the catholic faith and good manners: in witness whereof I have given, etc.
> "Nicolo Cini, Chancellor of Florence."

> "Attending the precedent relation, it is allowed that this present work of Davanzati may be printed.
> "Vincent Rabbata," etc.

> "It may be printed, July 15.
> "Friar Simon Mompei d'Amelia, Chancellor of the Holy Office in Florence."

Sure they have a conceit, if he of the bottomless pit had not long since broke prison, that this quadruple exorcism would bar him down. I fear their next design will be to get into their custody the licensing of that which they say Claudius intended,[*] but went not through with. Vouchsafe to see another of their forms, the Roman stamp—

> "Imprimatur, If it seem good to the reverend master of the Holy Palace.
> "Belcastro, Vicegerent."

> "Imprimatur,
> "Friar Nicholo Rodolphi, Master of the Holy Palace."

---

[*] "Quo veniam daret flatum crepitumque ventris in convivio emittendi."—(*Sueton. in Claudio.*)—MILTON.

Sometimes five imprimaturs are seen together, dialogue wise, in the piazza of one title-page, complimenting and ducking each to other with their shaven reverences, whether the author, who stands by in perplexity at the foot of his epistle, shall to the press or to the spunge. These are the pretty responsories, these are the dear antiphonies, that so bewitched of late our prelates and their chaplains, with the goodly echo they made; and besotted us to the gay imitation of a lordly imprimatur, one from Lambeth House, another from the west end of Paul's; so apishly romanising, that the word of command still was set down in Latin; as if the learned grammatical pen that wrote it would cast no ink without Latin; or perhaps, as they thought, because no vulgar tongue was worthy to express the pure conceit of an imprimatur; but rather, as I hope, for that our English, the language of men ever famous and foremost in the achievements of liberty, will not easily find servile letters enow to spell such a dictatory presumption Englished.

And thus ye have the inventors and the original of book licensing ripped up and drawn as lineally as any pedigree. We have it not, that can be heard of, from any ancient state, or polity, or church, nor by any statute left us by our ancestors elder or later; nor from the modern custom of any reformed city or church abroad; but from the most anti-christian council, and the most tyrannous inquisition that ever inquired. Till then books were ever as freely admitted into the world as any other birth; the issue of the brain was no more stifled than the issue of the womb: no envious Juno sat cross-legged over the nativity of any man's intellectual offspring; but if it proved a monster, who denies but that it was justly burnt, or sunk into the sea? But that a book, in worse condition than a peccant soul, should be to stand before a jury ere it be born to the world, and undergo yet in darkness the judgment of Radamanth and his colleagues, ere it can pass the ferry backward into light, was never heard before, till that mysterious iniquity, provoked and troubled at the first entrance of reformation, sought out new limboes and new hells wherein they might include our books also within the number of their damned.

And this was the rare morsel so officiously snatched up, and so ill-favouredly imitated by our inquisiturient bishops, and the attendant minorites, their chaplains. That ye like not now these most certain authors of this licensing order, and that all sinister intention was far distant from your thoughts, when ye were importuned the passing it, all men who know the integrity of your actions, and how ye honour truth, will clear ye readily.

But some will say, what though the inventors were bad, the thing for all that may be good. It may so; yet if that thing be no such deep invention, but obvious and easy for any man to light on, and yet best and wisest commonwealths through all ages and occasions have forborne to use it, and falsest seducers and oppressors of men were the first who took it up, and to no other purpose but to obstruct and hinder the first approach of reformation; I am of those who believe, it will be a harder alchymy than Lullius ever knew, to sublimate any good use out of such an invention. Yet this only is what I request to gain from this reason, that it may be held a dangerous and suspicious fruit, as certainly it deserves, for the tree that bore it, until I can dissect one by one the properties it has. \ But I have first to finish, as was propounded, what is to be thought in general of reading books, whatever sort they be, and whether be more the benefit or the harm that thence proceeds.

Not to insist upon the examples of Moses, Daniel, and Paul, who were skilful in all the learning of the Egyptians, Chaldeans, and Greeks, which could not probably be without reading their books of all sorts, in Paul especially, who thought it no defilement to insert into holy scripture the sentences of three Greek poets, and one of them a tragedian; the question was notwithstanding sometimes controverted among the primitive doctors, but with great odds on that side which affirmed it both lawful and profitable, as was then evidently perceived, when Julian the Apostate, and subtlest enemy to our faith, made a decree forbidding Christians the study of heathen learning; for, said he, they wound us with our own weapons, and with our own arts and sciences they overcome us. And indeed the Christians were put so to their shifts by this crafty means, and so much in danger to decline into all ignorance, that the two Apollinarii were fain, as a man may say, to coin all the seven liberal sciences out of the Bible, reducing it into divers forms of orations, poems, dialogues, even to the calculating of a new Christian grammar.

But, saith the historian, Socrates, the providence of God provided better than the industry of Apollinarius and his son, by taking away that illiterate law with the life of him who devised it. So great an injury they then held it to be deprived of Hellenic learning; and thought it a persecution more undermining, and secretly decaying the church, than the open cruelty of Decius or Diocletian. And perhaps it was with the same politic drift that the devil whipped St. Jerome in a lenten dream, for reading Cicero; or else it was a phantasm, bred by the fever which had then seized him. For had an angel been his discipliner, unless it were for dwelling too much on Ciceronianisms, and had chastised the reading, not the vanity, it had been plainly partial, first, to correct him for grave Cicero, and not for scurril Plautus, whom he confesses to have been reading not long before; next to correct him only, and let so many more ancient fathers wax old in those pleasant and florid studies, without the lash of such a tutoring apparition; insomuch that Basil teaches how some good use may be made of Margites, a sportful poem, not now extant, writ by Homer; and why not then of Morgante, an Italian romance much to the same purpose?

But if it be agreed we shall be tried by visions, there is a vision recorded by Eusebius, far ancienter than this tale of Jerome, to the nun Eustochium, and besides, has nothing of a fever in it. Dionysius Alexandrinus was, about the year 240, a person of great name in the church, for piety and learning, who had wont to avail himself much against heretics, by being conversant in their books; until a certain presbyter laid it scrupulously to his conscience, how he durst venture himself among those defiling volumes. The worthy man, loath to give offence, fell into a new debate with himself, what was to be thought; when suddenly a vision sent from God (it is his own epistle that so avers it) confirmed him in these words: "Read any books whatever come to thy hands, for thou art sufficient both to judge aright, and to examine each matter." To this revelation he assented the sooner, as he confesses, because it was answerable to that of the apostle to the Thessalonians: "Prove all things, hold fast that which is good."

And he might have added another remarkable saying of the same author: "To the pure, all things are pure;" not only meats and drinks, but all kind of knowledge, whether of good or evil: the knowledge cannot defile, nor consequently the books, if the will and conscience be not defiled. For books are as meats and viands are; some of good, some of evil substance; and yet God in that unapocryphal vision said without exception, "Rise, Peter, kill and eat;" leaving the choice to each man's discretion. Wholesome meats to a vitiated stomach differ little or nothing from unwholesome; and best books to a naughty mind are not unapplicable to occasions of evil. Bad meats will scarce breed good nourishment in the healthiest concoction; but herein the difference is of bad books, that they to a discreet and judicious reader serve in many respects to discover, to confute, to forewarn, and to illustrate. Whereof what better witness can ye expect I should produce, than one of your own now sitting in parliament, the chief of learned men reputed in this land, Mr. Selden; whose volume of natural and national laws proves, not only by great authorities brought together, but by exquisite reasons and theorems almost mathematically demonstrative, that all opinions, yea, errors, known, read, and collated, are of main service and assistance toward the speedy attainment of what is truest.

I conceive, therefore, that when God did enlarge the universal diet of man's body (saving ever the rules of temperance), He then also, as before, left arbitrary the dieting and repasting of our minds; as wherein every mature man might have to exercise his own leading capacity. How great a virtue is temperance, how much of moment through the whole life of man! Yet God commits the managing so great a trust, without particular law or prescription, wholly to the demeanour of every grown man. And therefore when He himself tabled the Jews from heaven, that omer, which was every man's daily portion of manna, is computed to have been more than might have well sufficed the heartiest feeder thrice as many meals. For those actions which enter into a man, rather than issue out of him, and therefore defile not, God uses not to captivate under a perpetual childhood of prescription, but trusts him with the gift of reason to be his own chooser; there were but little work left for preaching, if law and compulsion should grow so fast upon those things which heretofore were governed only by exhortation. Solomon informs us, that much reading is a weariness to the flesh; but neither he, nor other inspired author, tells us that such or such reading is unlawful; yet certainly had God thought good to limit us herein, it had been much more expedient to have told us what was unlawful, than what was wearisome.

As for the burning of those Ephesian books by St. Paul's converts; it is replied, the books were magic, the Syriac so renders them. It was a private act, a voluntary act, and leaves us to a voluntary imitation: the men in remorse burnt those books which were their own; the magistrate by this example is not appointed; these men practised the books, another might perhaps have read them in some sort usefully. Good and evil we know in the field of this world grow up together almost inseparably; and the knowledge of good is so involved and interwoven with the knowledge of evil, and in so many cunning resemblances hardly to be discerned, that those confused seeds which were imposed upon Pysche as an incessant labour to cull out, and sort asunder, were not more intermixed. It was from out the rind of one apple tasted, that the knowledge of good and evil, as two twins cleaving together, leaped forth into the world. And perhaps this is that doom which Adam fell into of knowing good and evil; that is to say, of knowing good by evil.

As therefore the state of man now is; what wisdom can there be to choose, what continence to forbear, without the knowledge of evil? He that can apprehend and consider vice with all her baits and seeming pleasures, and yet abstain, and yet distinguish, and yet prefer that which is truly better, he is the true warfaring Christian. I cannot praise a fugitive and cloistered virtue unexercised and unbreathed, that never sallies out and seeks her adversary, but slinks out of the race, where that immortal garland is to be run for, not without dust and heat. Assuredly we bring not innocence into the world, we bring impurity much rather; that which purifies us is trial, and trial is by what is contrary. That virtue therefore which is but a youngling in the contemplation of evil, and knows not the utmost that vice promises to her followers, and rejects it, is but a blank virtue, not a pure; her whiteness is but an excremental whiteness; which was the reason why our sage and serious poet Spenser (whom I dare be known to think a better teacher than Scotus or Aquinas), describing true temperance under the person of Guion, brings him in with his palmer through the cave of Mammon, and the bower of earthly bliss, that he might see and know, and yet abstain.

Since therefore the knowledge and survey of vice is in this world so necessary to the constituting of human virtue, and the scanning of error to the confirmation of truth, how can we more safely, and with less danger, scout into the regions of sin and falsity, than by reading all manner of tractates, and hearing all manner of reason? And this is the benefit which may be had of books promiscuously read. But of the harm that may result hence, three kinds are usually reckoned. First, is feared the infection that may spread; but then, all human learning and controversy in religious points must remove out of the world, yea, the Bible itself; for that ofttimes relates blasphemy not nicely, it describes the carnal sense of wicked men not unelegantly, it brings in holiest men passionately murmuring against Providence through all the arguments of Epicurus: in other great disputes it answers dubiously and darkly to the common reader; and ask a Talmudist what ails the modesty of his marginal Keri, that Moses and all the prophets cannot persuade him to pronounce the textual Chetiv. For these causes we all know the Bible itself put by the papist into the first rank of prohibited books. The ancientest fathers must be next removed, as Clement of Alexandria, and that Eusebian book of evangelic preparation, transmitting our ears through a hoard of heathenish obscenities to receive the gospel. Who finds not that Irenæus, Epiphanius, Jerome, and others discover more heresies than they well confute, and that oft for heresy which is the truer opinion?

Nor boots it to say for these, and all the heathen writers of greatest infection, if it must be thought so, with whom is bound up the life of human learning, that they wrote in an unknown tongue, so long as we are sure those languages are known as well to the worst of men, who are both most able and most diligent to instil the poison they suck, first into the courts of princes, acquainting them with the choicest delights, and criticisms of sin. As perhaps did that Petronius, whom Nero called his arbiter, the master of his revels; and that notorious ribald of Arezzo, dreaded and yet dear to the Italian courtiers. I name not him, for posterity's sake, whom Henry the Eighth named in merriment his vicar of hell. By which compendious way all the contagion that foreign books can infuse will find a passage to the people far easier and shorter than an Italian voyage, though it could be sailed either by the north of Cataio eastward, or of Canada westward, while our Spanish licensing gags the English press never so severely.

But, on the other side, that infection which is from books of controversy in religion, is more doubtful and dangerous to the learned than to the ignorant; and yet those books must be permitted untouched by the licenser. It will be hard to instance where any ignorant man hath been ever seduced by any papistical book in English, unless it were commended and expounded to him by some of that clergy; and indeed all such tractates, whether false or true, are as the prophecy of Isaiah was to the eunuch, not to be "understood without a guide." But of our priests and doctors how many have been corrupted by studying the comments of Jesuits and Sorbonists, and how fast they could transfuse that corruption into the people, our experience is both late and sad. It is not forgot, since the acute and distinct Arminius was perverted merely by the perusing of a nameless discourse written at Delft, which at first he took in hand to confute.

Seeing therefore that those books, and those in great abundance, which are likeliest to taint both life and doctrine, cannot be suppressed without the fall of learning, and of all ability in disputation, and that these books of either sort are most and soonest catching to the learned (from whom to the common people whatever is heretical or dissolute may quickly be conveyed), and that evil manners are as perfectly learnt without books a thousand other ways which cannot be stopped, and evil doctrine not with books can propagate, except a teacher guide, which he might also do without writing, and so beyond prohibiting; I am not unable to unfold, how this cautelous enterprise of licensing can be exempted from the number of vain and impossible attempts. And he who were pleasantly disposed, could not well avoid to liken it to the exploit of that gallant man, who thought to pound up the crows by shutting his park gate.

Besides another inconvenience, if learned men be the first receivers out of books, and dispreaders both of vice and error, how shall the licensers themselves be confided in, unless we can confer upon them, or they assume to themselves, above all others in the land, the grace of infallibility and uncorruptedness? And again, if it be true, that a wise man, like a good refiner, can gather gold out of the drossiest volume, and that a fool will be a fool with the best book, yea, or without book; there is no reason that we should deprive a wise man of any advantage to his wisdom, while we seek to restrain from a fool that which being restrained will be no hindrance to his folly. For if there should be so much exactness always used to keep that from him which is unfit for his reading, we should in the judgment of Aristotle not only, but of Solomon, and of our Saviour, not vouchsafe him good precepts, and by consequence not willingly admit him to good books; as being certain that a wise man will make better use of an idle pamphlet, than a fool will do of sacred scripture.

It is next alleged, we must not expose ourselves to temptations without necessity, and next to that, not employ our time in vain things. To both these objections one answer will serve, out of the grounds already laid, that to all men such books are not temptations, nor vanities; but useful drugs and materials wherewith to temper and compose effective and strong medicines, which man's life cannot want. The rest, as children and childish men, who have not the art to qualify and prepare these working minerals, well may be exhorted to forbear; but hindered forcibly they cannot be, by all the licensing that sainted inquisition could ever yet contrive; which is what I promised to deliver next: that this order of licensing conduces nothing to the end for which it was framed; and hath almost prevented me by being clear already while thus much hath been explaining. See the ingenuity of truth, who, when she gets a free and willing hand, opens herself faster than the pace of method and discourse can overtake her. It was the task which I began with, to show that no nation, or well instituted state, if they valued books at all, did ever use this way of licensing; and it might be answered, that this is a piece of prudence lately discovered.

To which I return, that as it was a thing slight and obvious to think on, so if it had been difficult to find out, there wanted not among them long since, who suggested such a course; which they not following, leaves us a pattern of their judgment that it was not the not knowing, but the not approving, which was the cause of their not using it. Plato, a man of high authority indeed, but least of all for his Commonwealth, in the book of his laws, which no city ever yet received, fed his fancy with making many edicts to his airy burgomasters, which they who otherwise admire him, wish had been rather buried and excused in the genial cups of an academic night sitting. By which laws he seems to tolerate no kind of learning, but by unalterable decree, consisting most of practical traditions, to the attainment whereof a library of smaller bulk than his own dialogues would be abundant. And there also enacts, that no poet should so much as read to any private man what he had written, until the judges and law-keepers had seen it, and allowed it; but that Plato meant this law peculiarly to that commonwealth which he had imagined, and to no other, is evident. Why was he not else a lawgiver to himself, but a transgressor, and to be expelled by his own magistrates, both for the wanton epigrams and dialogues which he made, and his perpetual reading of Sophron Mimus and Aristophanes, books of grossest infamy; and also for commending the latter of them, though he were the malicious libeller of his chief friends, to be read by the tyrant Dionysius, who had little need of such trash to spend his time on? But that he knew this licensing of poems had reference and dependence to many other provisoes there set down in his fancied republic, which in this world could have no place; and so neither he himself, nor any magistrate or city, ever imitated that course, which, taken apart from those other collateral injunctions, must needs be vain and fruitless.

For if they fell upon one kind of strictness, unless their care were equal to regulate all other things of like aptness to corrupt the mind, that single endeavour they knew would be but a fond labour; to shut and fortify one gate against corruption, and be necessitated to leave others round about wide open. If we think to regulate printing, thereby to rectify manners, we must regulate all recreations and pastimes, all that is delightful to man. No music must be heard, no song be set or sung, but what is grave and doric. There must be licensing dancers, that no gesture, motion, or deportment be taught our youth, but what by their allowance shall be thought honest; for such Plato was provided of. It will ask more than the work of twenty licensers to examine all the lutes, the violins, and the guitars in every house; they must not be suffered to prattle as they do, but must be licensed what they may say. And who shall silence all the airs and madrigals that whisper softness in chambers? The windows also, and the balconies, must be thought on; these are shrewd books, with dangerous frontispieces, set to sale: who shall prohibit them, shall twenty licensers? The villages also must have their visitors to inquire what lectures the bagpipe and the rebec reads, even to the ballatry and the gamut of every municipal fiddler; for these are the countryman's Arcadias, and his Monte Mayors.

Next, what more national corruption, for which England hears ill abroad, than household gluttony? Who shall be the rectors of our daily rioting? And what shall be done to inhibit the multitudes that frequent those houses where drunkenness is sold and harboured? Our garments also should be referred to the licensing of some more sober workmasters, to see them cut into a less wanton garb. Who shall regulate all the mixed conversation of our youth, male and female together, as is the fashion of this country? Who shall still appoint what shall be discoursed, what presumed, and no further? Lastly, who shall forbid and separate all idle resort, all evil company? These things will be, and must be; but how they shall be least hurtful, how least enticing, herein consists the grave and governing wisdom of a state.

To sequester out of the world into Atlantic and Utopian politics, which never can be drawn into use, will not mend our condition; but to ordain wisely as in this world of evil, in the midst whereof God hath placed us unavoidably. Nor is it Plato's licensing of books will do this, which necessarily pulls along with it so many other kinds of licensing, as will make us all both ridiculous and weary, and yet frustrate; but those unwritten, or at least unconstraining laws of virtuous education, religious and civil nurture, which Plato there mentions, as the bonds and ligaments of the commonwealth, the pillars and the sustainers of every written statute; these they be, which will bear chief sway in such matters as these, when all licensing will be easily eluded. Impunity and remissness for certain are the bane of a commonwealth; but here the great art lies, to discern in what the law is to bid restraint and punishment, and in what things persuasion only is to work. If every action which is good or evil in man at ripe years were to be under pittance, prescription, and compulsion, what were virtue but a name, what praise could be then due to well-doing, what gramercy to be sober, just, or continent?

Many there be that complain of divine Providence for suffering Adam to transgress. Foolish tongues! when God gave him reason, he gave him freedom to choose, for reason is but choosing; he had been else a mere artificial Adam, such an Adam as he is in the motions. We ourselves esteem not of that obedience, or love, or gift, which is of force; God therefore left him free, set before him a provoking object ever almost in his eyes; herein consisted his merit, herein the right of his reward, the praise of his abstinence. Wherefore did He create passions within us, pleasures round about us, but that these rightly tempered are the very ingredients of virtue? They are not skilful considerers of human things, who imagine to remove sin, by removing the matter of sin; for, besides that it is a huge heap increasing under the very act of diminishing, though some part of it may for a time be withdrawn from some persons, it cannot from all, in such a universal thing as books are; and when this is done, yet the sin remains entire. Though ye take from a covetous man all his treasure, he has yet one jewel left, ye cannot bereave him of his covetousness. Banish all objects of lust, shut up all youth into the severest discipline that can be exercised in any hermitage, ye cannot make them chaste, that came not thither so: such great care and wisdom is required to the right managing of this point.

Suppose we could expel sin by this means; look how much we thus expel of sin, so much we expel of virtue: for the matter of them both is the same: remove that, and ye remove them both alike. This justifies the high providence of God, who, though he commands us temperance, justice, continence, yet pours out before us even to a profuseness all desirable things, and gives us minds that can wander beyond all limit and satiety. Why should we then affect a rigour contrary to the manner of God and of nature, by abridging or scanting those means, which books freely permitted, are both to the trial of virtue, and the exercise of truth?

It would be better done, to learn that the law must needs be frivolous, which goes to restrain things, uncertainly and yet equally working to good and to evil. And were I the chooser, a dram of well-doing should be preferred before many times as much the forcible hindrance of evil-doing. For God sure esteems the growth and completing of one virtuous person, more than the restraint of ten vicious. And albeit, whatever thing we hear or see, sitting, walking, travelling, or conversing, may be fitly called our book, and is of the same effect that writings are; yet grant the thing to be prohibited were only books, it appears that this order hitherto is far insufficient to the end which it intends. Do we not see, not once or oftener, but weekly, that continued court-libel against the parliament and city, printed, as the wet sheets can witness, and dispersed among us for all that licensing can do? Yet this is the prime service a man would think wherein this order should give proof of itself. If it were executed, you will say. But certain, if execution be remiss or blindfold now, and in this particular, what will it be hereafter, and in other books?

If then the order shall not be vain and frustrate, behold a new labour, lords and commons, ye must repeal and proscribe all scandalous and unlicensed books already printed and divulged; after ye have drawn them up into a list, that all may know which are condemned, and which not; and ordain that no foreign books be delivered out of custody, till they have been read over. This office will require the whole time of not a few overseers, and those no vulgar men. There be also books which are partly useful and excellent, partly culpable and pernicious; this work will ask as many more officials, to make expurgations and expunctions, that the commonwealth of learning be not damnified. In fine, when the multitude of books increase upon their hands, ye must be fain to catalogue all those printers who are found frequently offending, and forbid the importation of their whole suspected typography. In a word, that this your order may be exact, and not deficient, ye must reform it perfectly, according to the model of Trent and Sevil, which I know ye abhor to do.

Yet though ye should condescend to this, which God forbid, the order still would be but fruitless and defective to that end whereto ye meant it. If to prevent sects and schisms, who is so unread or uncatechised in story, that hath not heard of many sects refusing books as a hindrance, and preserving their doctrine unmixed for many ages, only by unwritten traditions? The Christian faith (for that was once a schism!) is not unknown to have spread all over Asia, ere any gospel or epistle was seen in writing. If the amendment of manners be aimed at, look into Italy and Spain, whether those places be one scruple the better, the honester, the wiser, the chaster since all the inquisitional rigour that hath been executed upon books.

Another reason, whereby to make it plain that this order will miss the end it seeks, consider by the quality which ought to be in every licenser. It cannot be denied, but that he who is made judge to sit upon the birth or death of books, whether they may be wafted into this world or not, had need to be a man above the common measure, both studious, learned, and judicious; there may be else no mean mistakes in the censure of what is passable or not; which is also no mean injury. If he be of such worth as behoves him, there cannot be a more tedious and unpleasing journeywork, a greater loss of time levied upon his head, than to be made the perpetual reader of unchosen books and pamphlets, ofttimes huge volumes. There is no book that is acceptable, unless at certain seasons; but to be enjoined the reading of that at all times, and in a hand scarce legible, whereof three pages would not down at any time in the fairest print, is an imposition I cannot believe how he that values time, and his own studies, or is but of a sensible nostril, should be able to endure. In this one thing I crave leave of the present licensers to be pardoned for so thinking: who doubtless took this office up, looking on it through their obedience to the parliament, whose command perhaps made all things seem easy and unlaborious to them; but that this short trial hath wearied them out already, their own expressions and excuses to them who make so many journeys to solicit their licence, are testimony enough. Seeing therefore those, who now possess the employment, by all evident signs wish themselves well rid of it, and that no man of worth, none that is not a plain unthrift of his own hours, is ever likely to succeed them, except he mean to put himself to the salary of a press corrector, we may easily foresee what kind of licensers we are to expect hereafter, either ignorant, imperious, and remiss, or basely pecuniary. This is what I had to show, wherein this order cannot conduce to that end whereof it bears the intention.

I lastly proceed from the no good it can do, to the manifest hurt it causes, in being first the greatest discouragement and affront that can be offered to learning and to learned men. It was the complaint and lamentation of prelates, upon every least of a motion to remove pluralities, and distribute more equally church revenues, that then all learning would be for ever dashed and discouraged. But as for that opinion, I never found cause to think that the tenth part of learning stood or fell with the clergy: nor could I ever but hold it for a sordid and unworthy speech of any churchman, who had a competency left him. If therefore ye be loath to dishearten utterly and discontent, not the mercenary crew of false pretenders to learning, but the free and ingenuous sort of such as evidently were born to study and love learning for itself, not for lucre, or any other end, but the service of God and of truth, and perhaps that lasting fame and perpetuity of praise, which God and good men have consented shall be the reward of those whose published labours advance the good of mankind: then know, that so far to distrust the judgment and the honesty of one who hath but a common repute in learning, and never yet offended, as not to count him fit to print his mind without a tutor and examiner, lest he should drop a schism, or something of corruption, is the greatest displeasure and indignity to a free and knowing spirit that can be put upon him.

What advantage is it to be a man, over it is to be a boy at school, if we have only escaped the ferula, to come under the fescue of an imprimatur? if serious and elaborate writings, as if they were no more than the theme of a grammar-lad under his pedagogue, must not be uttered without the cursory eyes of a temporising and extemporising licenser? He who is not trusted with his own actions, his drift not being known to be evil, and standing to the hazard of law and penalty, has no great argument to think himself reputed in the commonwealth wherein he was born for other than a fool or a foreigner. When a man writes to the world, he summons up all his reason and deliberation to assist him; he searches, meditates, is industrious, and likely consults and confers with his judicious friends; after all which done, he takes himself to be informed in what he writes, as well as any that wrote before him; if in this, the most consummate act of his fidelity and ripeness, no years, no industry, no former proof of his abilities, can bring him to that state of maturity, as not to be still mistrusted and suspected, unless he carry all his considerate diligence, all his midnight watchings, and expense of Palladian oil, to the hasty view of an unleisured licenser, perhaps much his younger, perhaps far his inferior in judgment, perhaps one who never knew the labour of bookwriting; and if he be not repulsed, or slighted, must appear in print like a puny with his guardian, and his censor's hand on the back of his title to be his bail and surety, that he is no idiot or seducer; it cannot be but a dishonour and derogation to the author, to the book, to the privilege and dignity of learning.

And what if the author shall be one so copious of fancy, as to have many things well worth the adding, come into his mind after licensing, while the book is yet under the press, which not seldom happens to the best and diligentest writers; and that perhaps a dozen times in one book. The printer dares not go beyond his licensed copy; so often then must the author trudge to his leave-giver, that those his new insertions may be viewed; and many a jaunt will be made, ere that licenser, for it must be the same man, can either be found, or found at leisure; meanwhile either the press must stand still, which is no small damage, or the author lose his accuratest thoughts, and send the book forth worse than he had made it, which to a diligent writer is the greatest melancholy and vexation that can befall.

And how can a man teach with authority, which is the life of teaching; how can he be a doctor in his book, as he ought to be, or else had better be silent, whenas all he teaches, all he delivers, is but under the tuition, under the correction of his patriarchal licenser, to blot or alter what precisely accords not with the hide-bound humour which he calls his judgment? When every acute reader, upon the first sight of a pedantic licence, will be ready with these like words to ding the book a quoit's distance from him:—"I hate a pupil teacher; I endure not an instructor that comes to me under the wardship of an overseeing fist. I know nothing of the licenser, but that I have his own hand here for his arrogance; who shall warrant me his judgment?" "The state, sir," replies the stationer: but has a quick return:—"The state shall be my governors, but not my critics; they may be mistaken in the choice of a licenser, as easily as this licenser may be mistaken in an author. This is some common stuff:" and he might add from Sir Francis Bacon, that "such authorised books are but the language of the times." For though a licenser should happen to be judicious more than ordinary, which will be a great jeopardy of the next succession, yet his very office and his commission enjoins him to let pass nothing but what is vulgarly received already.

Nay, which is more lamentable, if the work of any deceased author, though never so famous in his lifetime, and even to this day, comes to their hands for licence to be printed, or reprinted, if there be found in his book one sentence of a venturous edge, uttered in the height of zeal (and who knows whether it might not be the dictate of a divine spirit?), yet, not suiting with every low decrepit humour of their own, though it were Knox himself, the reformer of a kingdom, that spake it, they will not pardon him their dash; the sense of that great man shall to all posterity be lost, for the fearfulness, or the presumptuous rashness of a perfunctory licenser. And to what an author this violence hath been lately done, and in what book, of greatest consequence to be faithfully published, I could now instance, but shall forbear till a more convenient season. Yet if these things be not resented seriously and timely by them who have the remedy in their power but that such ironmoulds as these shall have authority to gnaw out the choicest periods of exquisitest books, and to commit such a treacherous fraud against the orphan remainders of worthiest men after death, the more sorrow will belong to that hapless race of men, whose misfortune it is to have understanding. Henceforth let no man care to learn, or care to be more than worldly wise; for certainly in higher matters to be ignorant and slothful, to be a common steadfast dunce, will be the only pleasant life, and only in request.

And as it is a particular disesteem of every knowing person alive, and most injurious to the written labours and monuments of the dead, so to me it seems an undervaluing and vilifying of the whole nation. I cannot set so light by all the invention, the art, the wit, the grave and solid judgment which is in England, as that it can be comprehended in any twenty capacities, how good soever; much less that it should not pass except their superintendence be over it, except it be sifted and strained with their strainers, that it should be uncurrent without their manual stamp. Truth and understanding are not such wares as to be monopolised and traded in by tickets, and statutes, and standards. We must not think to make a staple commodity of all the knowledge in the land, to mark and license it like our broad-cloth and our woolpacks. What is it but a servitude like that imposed by the Philistines, not to be allowed the sharpening of our own axes and coulters, but we must repair from all quarters to twenty licensing forges?

Had any one written and divulged erroneous things and scandalous to honest life, misusing and forfeiting the esteem had of his reason among men, if after conviction this only censure were adjudged him, that he should never henceforth write, but what were first examined by an appointed officer, whose hand should be annexed to pass his credit for him, that now he might be safely read; it could not be apprehended less than a disgraceful punishment. Whence to include the whole nation, and those that never yet thus offended, under such a diffident and suspectful prohibition, may plainly be understood what a disparagement it is. So much the more whenas debtors and delinquents may walk abroad without a keeper, but unoffensive books must not stir forth without a visible jailer in their title. Nor is it to the common people less than a reproach; for if we be so jealous over them, as that we dare not trust them with an English pamphlet, what do we but censure them for a giddy, vicious, and ungrounded people; in such a sick and weak state of faith and discretion, as to be able to take nothing down but through the pipe of a licenser? That this is care or love of them, we cannot pretend, whenas in those popish places, where the laity are most hated and despised, the same strictness is used over them. Wisdom we cannot call it, because it stops but one breach of licence, nor that neither: whenas those corruptions, which it seeks to prevent, break in faster at other doors, which cannot be shut.

And in conclusion it reflects to the disrepute of our ministers also, of whose labours we should hope better, and of their proficiency which their flock reaps by them, than that after all this light of the gospel which is, and is to be, and all this continual preaching, they should be still frequented with such an unprincipled, unedified, and laic rabble, as that the whiff of every new pamphlet should stagger them out of their catechism and Christian walking. This may have much reason to discourage the ministers, when such a low conceit is had of all their exhortations, and the benefiting of their hearers, as that they are not thought fit to be turned loose to three sheets of paper without a licenser; that all the sermons, all the lectures preached, printed, vended in such numbers, and such volumes, as have now well-nigh made all other books unsaleable, should not be armour enough against one single Enchiridion, without the castle of St. Angelo of an imprimatur.

And lest some should persuade ye, lords and commons, that these arguments of learned men's discouragement at this your order are mere flourishes, and not real, I could recount what I have seen and heard in other countries, where this kind of inquisition tyrannises; when I have set among their learned men (for that honour I had), and been counted happy to be born in such a place of philosophic freedom, as they supposed England was, while themselves did nothing but bemoan the servile condition into which learning amongst them was brought; that this was it which had damped the glory of Italian wits; that nothing had been there written now these many years but flattery and fustian. There it was that I found and visited the famous Galileo, grown old, a prisoner to the inquisition, for thinking in astronomy otherwise than the Franciscan and Dominican licensers thought. And though I knew that England then was groaning loudest under the prelatical yoke, nevertheless I took it as a pledge of future happiness, that other nations were so persuaded of her liberty.

Yet was it beyond my hope, that those worthies were then breathing in her air, who should be her leaders to such a deliverance, as shall never be forgotten by any revolution of time that this world hath to finish. When that was once begun, it was as little in my fear, that what words of complaint I heard among learned men of other parts uttered against the inquisition, the same I should hear, by as learned men at home, uttered in time of parliament against an order of licensing; and that so generally, that when I had disclosed myself a companion of their discontent, I might say, if without envy, that he whom an honest quæstorship had endeared to the Sicilians, was not more by them importuned against Verres, than the favourable opinion which I had among many who honour ye, and are known and respected by ye, loaded me with entreaties and persuasions, that I would not despair to lay together that which just reason should bring into my mind, towards the removal of an undeserved thraldom upon learning.

That this is not therefore the disburdening of a particular fancy, but the common grievance of all those who had prepared their minds and studies above the vulgar pitch, to advance truth in others, and from others to entertain it, thus much may satisfy. And in their name I shall for neither friend nor foe conceal what the general murmur is; that if it come to inquisitioning again, and licensing, and that we are so timorous of ourselves, and suspicious of all men, as to fear each book, and the shaking of each leaf, before we know what the contents are; if some who but of late were little better than silenced from preaching, shall come now to silence us from reading, except what they please, it cannot be guessed what is intended by some but a second tyranny over learning: and will soon put it out of controversy, that bishops and presbyters are the same to us, both name and thing.

That those evils of prelaty which before from five or six and twenty sees were distributively charged upon the whole people will now light wholly upon learning, is not obscure to us: whenas now the pastor of a small unlearned parish, on the sudden shall be exalted archbishop over a large diocess of books, and yet not remove, but keep his other cure too, a mystical pluralist. He who but of late cried down the sole ordination of every novice bachelor of art, and denied sole jurisdiction over the simplest parishioner, shall now at home in his private chair, assume both these over worthiest and excellentest books, and ablest authors that write them. This is not the covenants and protestations that we have made! This is not to put down prelacy; this is but to chop an episcopacy; this is but to translate the palace metropolitan from one kind of dominion into another; this is but an old canonical sleight of commuting our penance. To startle thus betimes at a mere unlicensed pamphlet, will, after a while, be afraid of every conventicle, and a while after will make a conventicle of every Christian meeting.

But I am certain, that a state governed by the rules of justice and fortitude, or a church built and founded upon the rock of faith and true knowledge, cannot be so pusillanimous. While things are yet not constituted in religion, that freedom of writing should be restrained by a discipline imitated from the prelates, and learned by them from the inquisition to shut us up all again into the breast of a licenser, must needs give cause of doubt and discouragement to all learned and religious men; who cannot but discern the fineness of this politic drift, and who are the contrivers; that while bishops were to be baited down, then all presses might be open; it was the people's birthright and privilege in time of parliament, it was the breaking forth of light.

But now the bishops abrogated and voided out of the church, as if our reformation sought no more, but to make room for others into their seats under another name; the episcopal arts begin to bud again; the cruse of truth must run no more oil; liberty of printing must be enthralled again, under a prelatical commission of twenty; the privilege of the people nullified; and, which is worse, the freedom of learning must groan again, and to her old fetters: all this the parliament yet sitting. Although their own late arguments and defences against the prelates might remember them, that this obstructing violence meets for the most part with an event utterly opposite to the end which it drives at: instead of suppressing sects and schisms, it raises them and invests them with a reputation: "The punishing of wits enhances their authority," saith the Viscount St. Albans; "and a forbidden writing is thought to be a certain spark of truth, that flies up in the faces of them who seek to tread it out." This order, therefore, may prove a nursing mother to sects, but I shall easily show how it will be stepdame to truth: and first, by disenabling us to the maintenance of what is known already.

Well knows he who uses to consider, that our faith and knowledge thrives by exercise, as well as our limbs and complexion. Truth is compared in scripture to a streaming fountain; if her waters flow not in a perpetual progression, they sicken into a muddy pool of conformity and tradition. A man may be a heretic in the truth; and if he believe things only because his pastor says so, or the assembly so determines, without knowing other reason, though his belief be true, yet the very truth he holds becomes his heresy. There is not any burden that some would gladlier post off to another, than the charge and care of their religion. There be, who knows not that there be? of protestants and professors, who live and die in as errant and implicit faith, as any lay papist of Loretto.

A wealthy man, addicted to his pleasure and to his profits, finds religion to be a traffic so entangled, and of so many piddling accounts, that of all mysteries he cannot skill to keep a stock going upon that trade. What should he do? Fain he would have the name to be religious, fain he would bear up with his neighbours in that. What does he therefore, but resolves to give over toiling, and to find himself out some factor, to whose care and credit he may commit the whole managing of his religious affairs; some divine of note and estimation that must be. To him he adheres, resigns the whole warehouse of his religion, with all the locks and keys, into his custody; and indeed makes the very person of that man his religion; esteems his associating with him a sufficient evidence and commendatory of his own piety. So that a man may say his religion is now no more within himself, but is become a dividual movable, and goes and comes near him, according as that good man frequents the house. He entertains him, gives him gifts, feasts him, lodges him; his religion comes home at night, prays, is liberally supped, and sumptuously laid to sleep; rises, is saluted, and after the malmsey, or some well-spiced bruage, and better breakfasted, than He whose morning appetite would have gladly fed on green figs between Bethany and Jerusalem, his religion walks abroad at eight, and leaves his kind entertainer in the shop trading all day without his religion.

Another sort there be, who when they hear that all things shall be ordered, all things regulated and settled; nothing written but what passes through the custom-house of certain publicans that have the tonnaging and poundaging of all free-spoken truth, will straight give themselves up into your hands, make them and cut them out what religion ye please: there be delights, there be recreations and jolly pastimes, that will fetch the day about from sun to sun, and rock the tedious year as in a delightful dream. What need they torture their heads with that which others have taken so strictly, and so unalterably into their own purveying? These are the fruits which a dull ease and cessation of our knowledge will bring forth among the people. How goodly, and how to be wished were such an obedient unanimity as this! What a fine conformity would it starch us all into! Doubtless a staunch and solid piece of framework, as any January could freeze together.

Nor much better will be the consequence even among the clergy themselves: it is no new thing never heard of before, for a parochial minister, who has his reward, and is at his Hercules' pillars in a warm benefice, to be easily inclinable, if he have nothing else that may rouse up his studies, to finish his circuit in an English Concordance and a topic folio, the gatherings and savings of a sober graduateship, a Harmony and a Catena, treading the constant round of certain common doctrinal heads, attended with their uses, motives, marks, and means; out of which, as out of an alphabet or sol-fa, by forming and transforming, joining and disjoining variously, a little book-craft, and two hours' meditation, might furnish him unspeakably to the performance of more than a weekly charge of sermoning: not to reckon up the infinite helps of interliniaries, breviaries, synopses, and other loitering gear. But as for the multitude of sermons ready printed and piled up, on every text that is not difficult, our London trading St. Thomas in his vestry, and add to boot St. Martin and St. Hugh, have not within their hallowed limits more vendible ware of all sorts ready made: so that penury he never need fear of pulpit provision, having where so plenteously to refresh his magazine. But if his rear and flanks be not impaled, if his back door be not secured by the rigid licenser, but that a bold book may now and then issue forth, and give the assault to some of his old collections in their trenches, it will concern him then to keep waking, to stand in watch, to set good guards and sentinels about his received opinions, to walk the round and counter-round with his fellow-inspectors, fearing lest any of his flock be seduced who also then would be better instructed, better exercised, and disciplined. And God send that the fear of this diligence, which must then be used, do not make us affect the laziness of a licensing church?

For if we be sure we are in the right, and do not hold the truth guiltily, which becomes not, if we ourselves condemn not our own weak and frivolous teaching, and the people for an untaught and irreligious gadding route; what can be more fair, than when a man judicious, learned, and of a conscience, for aught we know, as good as theirs that taught us what we know, shall not privily from house to house, which is more dangerous, but openly by writing, publish to the world what his opinion is, what his reasons, and wherefore that which is now thought cannot be sound? Christ urged it as wherewith to justify himself, that he preached in public; yet writing is more public than preaching; and more easy to refutation if need be, there being so many whose business and profession merely it is to be the champions of truth; which if they neglect, what can be imputed but their sloth or inability?

Thus much we are hindered and disinured by this course of licensing towards the true knowledge of what we seem to know. For how much it hurts and hinders the licensers themselves in the calling of their ministry, more than any secular employment, if they will discharge that office as they ought, so that of necessity they must neglect either the one duty or the other, I insist not, because it is a particular, but leave it to their own conscience, how they will decide it there.

There is yet behind of what I purposed to lay open, the incredible loss and detriment that this plot of licensing puts us to, more than if some enemy at sea should stop up all our havens, and ports, and creeks; it hinders and retards the importation of our richest merchandise,—truth: nay, it was first established and put in practice by anti-christian malice and mystery, or set purpose to extinguish, if it were possible, the light of reformation, and to settle falsehood; little differing from that policy wherewith the Turk upholds his Alcoran, by the prohibiting of printing. It is not denied, but gladly confessed, we are to send our thanks and vows to heaven, louder than most of nations, for that great measure of truth which we enjoy, especially in those main points between us and the pope, with his appurtenances the prelates: but he who thinks we are to pitch our tent here, and have attained the utmost prospect of reformation that the mortal glass wherein we contemplate, can show us, till we come to beatific vision, that man by this very opinion declares that he is yet far short of truth.

Truth indeed came once into the world with her divine Master, and was a perfect shape most glorious to look on; but when He ascended, and his apostles after him were laid asleep, then straight arose a wicked race of deceivers, who, as that story goes of the Egyptian Typhon with his conspirators, how they dealt with the good Osiris, took the virgin Truth, hewed her lovely form into a thousand pieces, and scattered them to the four winds. From that time ever since, the sad friends of Truth, such as durst appear, imitating the careful search that Isis made for the mangled body of Osiris, went up and down gathering up limb by limb still as they could find them. We have not yet found them all, lords and commons, nor ever shall do, till her Master's second coming; He shall bring together every joint and member, and shall mould them into an immortal feature of loveliness and perfection. Suffer not these licensing prohibitions to stand at every place of opportunity forbidding and disturbing them that continue seeking, that continue to do our obsequies to the torn body of our martyred saint.

We boast our light; but if we look not wisely on the sun itself, it smites us into darkness. Who can discern those planets that are oft combust, and those stars of brightest magnitude that rise and set with the sun, until the opposite motion of their orbs bring them to such a place in the firmament, where they may be seen evening or morning? The light which we have gained was given us, not to be ever staring on, but by it to discover onward things more remote from our knowledge. It is not the unfrocking of a priest, the unmitring of a bishop, and the removing him from off the presbyterian shoulders, that will make us a happy nation: no; if other things as great in the church, and in the rule of life both economical and political, be not looked into and reformed, we have looked so long upon the blaze that Zuinglius and Calvin have beaconed up to us, that we are stark blind.

There be who perpetually complain of schisms and sects, and make it such a calamity that any man dissents from their maxims. It is their own pride and ignorance which causes the disturbing, who neither will hear with meekness, nor can convince, yet all must be suppressed which is not found in their Syntagma. They are the troublers, they are the dividers of unity, who neglect and permit not others to unite those dissevered pieces, which are yet wanting to the body of truth. To be still searching what we know not, by what we know, still closing up truth to truth as we find it (for all her body is homogeneal, and proportional), this is the golden rule in theology as well as in arithmetic, and makes up the best harmony in a church; not the forced and outward union of cold, and neutral, and inwardly divided minds.

Lords and commons of England! consider what nation it is whereof ye are, and whereof ye are the governors: a nation not slow and dull, but of a quick, ingenious, and piercing spirit; acute to invent, subtile and sinewy to discourse, not beneath the reach of any point the highest that human capacity can soar to. Therefore the studies of learning in her deepest sciences have been so ancient, and so eminent among us, that writers of good antiquity and able judgment have been persuaded, that even the school of Pythagoras, and the Persian wisdom, took beginning from the old philosophy of this island. And that wise and civil Roman, Julius Agricola, who governed once here for Cæsar, preferred the natural wits of Britain before the laboured studies of the French.

Nor is it for nothing that the grave and frugal Transylvanian sends out yearly from as far as the mountainous borders of Russia, and beyond the Hercynian wilderness, not their youth, but their staid men, to learn our language and our theological arts. Yet that which is above all this, the favour and the love of Heaven, we have great argument to think in a peculiar manner propitious and propending towards us. Why else was this nation chosen before any other, that out of her, as out of Sion, should be proclaimed and sounded forth the first tidings and trumpet of reformation to all Europe? And had it not been the obstinate perverseness of our prelates against the divine and admirable spirit of Wickliffe, to suppress him as a schismatic and innovator, perhaps neither the Bohemian Husse and Jerome, no, nor the name of Luther or of Calvin, had been ever known: the glory of reforming all our neighbours had been completely ours. But now, as our obdurate clergy have with violence demeaned the matter, we are become hitherto the latest and the backwardest scholars, of whom God offered to have made us the teachers.

Now once again by all concurrence of signs, and by the general instinct of holy and devout men, as they daily and solemnly express their thoughts, God is decreeing to begin some new and great period in His church, even to the reforming of reformation itself; what does He then but reveal Himself to His servants, and as His manner is, first to His Englishmen? I say, as His manner is, first to us, though we mark not the method of His counsels, and are unworthy. Behold now this vast city, a city of refuge, the mansion-house of liberty, encompassed and surrounded with His protection; the shop of war hath not there more anvils and hammers working, to fashion out the plates and instruments of armed justice in defence of beleaguered truth, than there be pens and heads there, sitting by their studious lamps, musing, searching, revolving new notions and ideas wherewith to present, as with their homage and their fealty, the approaching reformation. others as fast reading, trying all things, assenting to the force of reason and convincement.

What could a man require more from a nation so pliant and so prone to seek after knowledge? What wants there to such a towardly and pregnant soil, but wise and faithful labourers, to make a knowing people, a nation of prophets, of sages, and of worthies? We reckon more than five months yet to harvest; there need not be five weeks, had we but eyes to lift up, the fields are white already. Where there is much desire to learn, there of necessity will be much arguing, much writing, many opinions; for opinion in good men is but knowledge in the making. Under these fantastic terrors of sect and schism, we wrong the earnest and zealous thirst after knowledge and understanding, which God hath stirred up in this city. What some lament of, we rather should rejoice at, should rather praise this pious forwardness among men, to reassume the ill-deputed care of their religion into their own hands again. A little generous prudence, a little forbearance of one another, and some grain of charity might win all these diligencies to join and unite into one general and brotherly search after truth; could we but forego this prelatical tradition of crowding free consciences and Christian liberties into canons and precepts of men. I doubt not, if some great and worthy stranger should come among us, wise to discern the mould and temper of a people, and how to govern it, observing the high hopes and aims the diligent alacrity of our extended thoughts and reasonings in the pursuance of truth and freedom, but that he would cry out as Pyrrhus did, admiring the Roman docility and courage, "If such were my Epirots, I would not despair the greatest design that could be attempted to make a church or kingdom happy."

Yet these are the men cried out against for schismatics and sectaries, as if, while the temple of the Lord was building, some cutting, some squaring the marble, others hewing the cedars, there should be a sort of irrational men, who could not consider there must be many schisms and many dissections made in the quarry and in the timber ere the house of God can be built. And when every stone is laid artfully together, it cannot be united into a continuity, it can but be contiguous in this world: neither can every piece of the building be of one form; nay, rather the perfection consists in this, that out of many moderate varieties and brotherly dissimilitudes that are not vastly disproportional, arises the goodly and the graceful symmetry that commends the whole pile and structure.

Let us therefore be more considerate builders, more wise in spiritual architecture, when great reformation is expected. For now the time seems come, wherein Moses, the great prophet, may sit in heaven rejoicing to see that memorable and glorious wish of his fulfilled, when not only our seventy elders, but all the Lord's people, are become prophets. No marvel then though some men, and some good men too perhaps, but young in goodness, as Joshua then was, envy them. They fret, and out of their own weakness are in agony, lest these divisions and sub-divisions will undo us. The adversary again applauds, and waits the hour: when they have branched themselves out, saith he, small enough into parties and partitions, then will be our time. Fool! he sees not the firm root, out of which we all grow, though into branches; nor will beware, until he see our small divided maniples cutting through at every angle of his ill-united and unwieldy brigade. And that we are to hope better of all these supposed sects and schisms, and that we shall not need that solicitude, honest perhaps, though over-timorous, of them that vex in this behalf, but shall laugh in the end at those malicious applauders of our differences, I have these reasons to persuade me.

First, when a city shall be as it were besieged and blocked about, her navigable river infested, inroads and incursions round, defiance and battle oft rumoured to be marching up, even to her walls and suburb trenches; that then the people, or the greater part, more than at other times, wholly taken up with the study of highest and most important matters to be reformed, should be disputing, reasoning, reading, inventing, discoursing, even to a rarity and admiration, things not before discoursed or written of, argues first a singular good will, contentedness, and confidence in your prudent foresight, and safe government, lords and commons; and from thence derives itself to a gallant bravery and well-grounded contempt of their enemies, as if there were no small number of as great spirits among us, as his was who, when Rome was nigh besieged by

Hannibal, being in the city, bought that piece of ground at no cheap rate whereon Hannibal himself encamped his own regiment.

Next, it is a lively and cheerful presage of our happy success and victory. For as in a body when the blood is fresh, the spirits pure and vigorous, not only to vital, but to rational faculties, and those in the acutest and the pertest operations of wit and subtlety, it argues in what good plight and constitution the body is; so when the cheerfulness of the people is so sprightly up, as that it has not only wherewith to guard well its own freedom and safety, but to spare, and to bestow upon the solidest and sublimest points of controversy and new invention, it betokens us not degenerated, nor drooping to a fatal decay, by casting off the old and wrinkled skin of corruption to outlive these pangs, and wax young again, entering the glorious ways of truth and prosperous virtue, destined to become great and honourable in these latter ages. Methinks I see in my mind a noble and puissant nation rousing herself like a strong man after sleep, and shaking her invincible locks: methinks I see her as an eagle mewing her mighty youth, and kindling her undazzled eyes at the full midday beam; purging and unscaling her long-abused sight at the fountain itself of heavenly radiance; while the whole noise of timorous and flocking birds, with those also that love the twilight, flutter about, amazed at what she means, and in their envious gabble would prognosticate a year of sects and schisms.

What should ye do then, should ye suppress all this flowery crop of knowledge and new light sprung up and yet springing daily in this city? Should ye set an oligarchy of twenty engrossers over it, to bring a famine upon our minds again, when we shall know nothing but what is measured to us by their bushel? Believe it, lords and commons! they who counsel ye to such a suppressing, do as good as bid ye suppress yourselves; and I will soon show how. If it be desired to know the immediate cause of all this free writing and free speaking, there cannot be assigned a truer than your own mild, and free, and humane government; <u>it is the liberty,</u>

lords and commons, which your own valorous and happy counsels have purchased us; liberty which is the nurse of all great wits: this is that which hath rarefied and enlightened our spirits like the influence of heaven: this is that which hath enfranchised, enlarged, and lifted up our apprehensions degrees above themselves. Ye cannot make us now less capable, less knowing, less eagerly pursuing of the truth, unless ye first make yourselves, that made us so, less the lovers, less the founders of our true liberty. We can grow ignorant again, brutish, formal, and slavish, as ye found us; but you then must first become that which ye cannot be, oppressive, arbitrary, and tyrannous, as they were from whom ye have freed us. That our hearts are now more capacious, our thoughts more erected to the search and expectation of greatest and exactest things, is the issue of your own virtue propagated in us; ye cannot suppress that unless ye reinforce an abrogated and merciless law, that fathers may dispatch at will their own children. And who shall then stick closest to ye and excite others? Not he who takes up arms for coat and conduct, and his four nobles of Danegelt. Although I dispraise not the defence of just immunities, yet love my peace better, if that were all. Give me the liberty to know, to utter, and to argue freely according to conscience, above all liberties.

What would be best advised then, if it be found so hurtful and so unequal to suppress opinions for the newness or the unsuitableness to a customary acceptance, will not be my task to say; I shall only repeat what I have learned from one of your own honourable number, a right noble and pious lord, who had he not sacrificed his life and fortunes to the church and commonwealth, we had not now missed and bewailed a worthy and undoubted patron of this argument. Ye know him, I am sure; yet I for honour's sake, and may it be eternal to him, shall name him, the Lord Brook. He writing of episcopacy, and by the way treating of sects and schisms, left ye his vote, or rather now the last words of his dying charge, which I know will ever be of dear and honoured regard with ye, so full of meekness and breathing charity, that next to His last testament, who bequeathed love and peace to His disciples, I cannot call to mind where I have read or heard words more mild and peaceful. He there exhorts us to hear with patience and humility those, however they be miscalled, that desire to live purely, in such a use of God's ordinances, as the best guidance of their conscience gives them, and to tolerate them, though in some disconformity to ourselves. The book itself will tell us more at large, being published to the world, and dedicated to the parliament by him, who both for his life and for his death deserves, that what advice he left be not laid by without perusal.

And now the time in special is, by privilege to write and speak what may help to the further discussing of matters in agitation. The temple of Janus, with his two controversial faces, might now not unsignificantly be set open. And though all the winds of doctrine were let loose to play upon the earth, so truth be in the field, we do injuriously by licensing and prohibiting to misdoubt her strength. Let her and falsehood grapple; who ever knew truth put to the worse, in a free and open encounter? Her confuting is the best and surest suppressing. He who hears what praying there is for light and clear knowledge to be sent down among us, would think of other matters to be constituted beyond the discipline of Geneva, framed and fabricated already to our hands.

Yet when the new light which we beg for shines in upon us, there be who envy and oppose, if it come not first in at their casements. What a collusion is this, whenas we are exhorted by the wise man to use diligence, "to seek for wisdom as for hidden treasures," early and late, that another order shall enjoin us, to know nothing but by statute? When a man hath been labouring the hardest labour in the deep mines of knowledge, hath furnished out his findings in all their equipage, drawn forth his reasons as it were a battle ranged, scattered and defeated all objections in his way, calls out his adversary into the plain, offers him the advantage of wind and sun, if he please, only that he may try the matter by dint of argument; for his opponents then to skulk, to lay ambushments, to keep a narrow bridge of licensing where the challenger should pass, though it be valour enough in soldiership, is but weakness and cowardice in the wars of truth. For who knows not that truth is strong, next to the Almighty; she needs no policies, nor stratagems, nor licensings to make her victorious; those are the shifts and the defences that error uses against her power: give her but room, and do not bind her when she sleeps, for then she speaks not true, as the old Proteus did, who spake oracles only when he was caught and bound, but then rather she turns herself into all shapes except her own, and perhaps tunes her voice according to the time, as Micaiah did before Ahab, until she be adjured into her own likeness.

Yet is it not impossible that she may have more shapes than one? What else is all that rank of things indifferent, wherein truth may be on this side, or on the other, without being unlike herself? What but a vain shadow else is the abolition of "those ordinances, that hand-writing nailed to the cross?" What great purchase is this Christian liberty which Paul so often boasts of? His doctrine is, that he who eats or eats not, regards a day or regards it not, may do either to the Lord. How many other things might be tolerated in peace, and left to conscience, had we but charity, and were it not the chief stronghold of our hypocrisy to be ever judging one another? I fear yet this iron yoke of outward conformity hath left a slavish print upon our necks; the ghost of a linen decency yet haunts us. We stumble, and are impatient at the least dividing of one visible congregation from another, though it be not in fundamentals; and through our forwardness to suppress, and our backwardness to recover, any enthralled piece of truth out of the gripe of custom, we care not to keep truth separated from truth, which is the fiercest rent and disunion of all. We do not see that while we still affect by all means a rigid external formality, we may as soon fall again into a gross conforming stupidity, a stark and dead congealment of "wood and hay and stubble" forced and frozen together, which is more to the sudden degenerating of a church than many subdichotomies of petty schisms.

Not that I can think well of every light separation; or that all in a church is to be expected "gold and silver, and precious stones:" it is not possible for man to sever the wheat from the tares, the good fish from the other fry; that must be the angels' ministry at the end of mortal things. Yet if all cannot be of one mind, as who looks they should be? this doubtless is more wholesome, more prudent, and more Christian, that many be tolerated rather than all compelled. I mean not tolerated popery, and open superstition, which as it extirpates all religions and civil supremacies, so itself should be extirpate, provided first that all charitable and compassionate means be used to win and regain the weak and the misled: that also which is impious or evil absolutely either against faith or manners, no law can possibly permit, that intends not to unlaw itself: but those neighbouring differences, or rather indifferences, are what I speak of, whether in some point of doctrine or of discipline, which though they may be many, yet need not interrupt the unity of spirit, if we could but find among us the bond of peace.

In the meanwhile, if any one would write, and bring his helpful hand to the slow-moving reformation which we labour under, if truth have spoken to him before others, or but seemed at least to speak, who hath so bejesuited us, that we should trouble that man with asking licence to do so worthy a deed; and not consider this, that if it come to prohibiting, there is not aught more likely to be prohibited than truth itself: whose first appearance to our eyes, bleared and dimmed with prejudice and custom, is more unsightly and unplausible than many errors; even as the person is of many a great man slight and contemptible to see to. And what do they tell us vainly of new opinions, when this very opinion of theirs, that none must be heard but whom they like, is the worst and newest opinion of all others; and is the chief cause why sects and schisms do so much abound, and true knowledge is kept at distance from us; besides yet a greater danger which is in it. For when God shakes a kingdom, with strong and healthful commotions, to a general reforming, it is not untrue that many sectaries and false teachers are then busiest in seducing.

But yet more true it is, that God then raises to His own work men of rare abilities, and more than common industry, not only to look back and revive what hath been taught heretofore, but to gain further, and to go on some new enlightened steps in the discovery of truth. For such is the order of God's enlightening His church, to dispense and deal out by degrees His beam, so as our earthly eyes may best sustain it. Neither is God appointed and confined, where and out of what place these His chosen shall be first heard to speak; for He sees not as man sees, chooses not as man chooses, lest we should devote ourselves again to set places and assemblies, and outward callings of men; planting our faith one while in the old convocation house; and another while in the chapel at Westminster; when all the faith and religion that shall be there canonised, is not sufficient without plain convincement, and the charity of patient instruction, to supple the least bruise of conscience, to edify the meanest Christian, who desires to walk in the spirit, and not in the letter of human trust, for all the number of voices that can be there made; no, though Harry the Seventh himself there, with all his liege tombs about him, should lend them voices from the dead to swell their number.

And if the men be erroneous who appear to be the leading schismatics, what withholds us but our sloth, our self-will, and distrust in the right cause, that we do not give them gentle meetings and gentle dismissions, that we debate not and examine the matter thoroughly with liberal and frequent audience; if not for their sakes yet for our own? Seeing no man who hath tasted learning, but will confess the many ways of profiting by those who, not contented with stale receipts, are able to manage and set forth new positions to the world. And were they but as the dust and cinders of our feet, so long as in that notion they may yet serve to polish and brighten the armoury of truth, even for that respect they were not utterly to be cast away. But if they be of those whom God hath fitted for the special use of these times with eminent and ample gifts, and those perhaps neither among the priests, nor among the pharisees, and we, in the haste of a precipitant zeal, shall make no distinction, but resolve to stop their mouths, because we fear they come with new and dangerous opinions, as we commonly forejudge them ere we understand them; no less than woe to us, while, thinking thus to defend the gospel, we are found the persecutors!

There have been not a few since the beginning of this parliament, both of the presbytery and others, who by their unlicensed books to the contempt of an imprimatur first broke that triple ice clung about our hearts, and taught the people to see day; I hope that none of those were the persuaders to renew upon us this bondage, which they themselves have wrought so much good by contemning. But if neither the check that Moses gave to young Joshua, nor the countermand which our Saviour gave to young John, who was so ready to prohibit those whom he thought unlicensed, be not enough to admonish our elders how unacceptable to God their testy mood of prohibiting is; if neither their own remembrance what evil hath abounded in the church by this lett of licensing, and what good they themselves have begun by transgressing it, be not enough, but that they will persuade and execute the most Dominican part of the inquisition over us, and are already with one foot in the stirrup so active at suppressing, it would be no unequal distribution in the first place to suppress the suppressors themselves; whom the change of their condition hath puffed up, more than their late experience of harder times hath made wise.

And as for regulating the press, let no man think to have the honour of advising ye better than yourselves have done in that order published next before this, "That no book be printed, unless the printer's and the author's name, or at least the printer's be registered." Those which otherwise come forth, if they be found mischievous and libellous, the fire and the executioner will be the timeliest and the most effectual remedy that man's prevention can use. For this authentic Spanish policy of licensing books, if I have said aught, will prove the most unlicensed book itself within a short while; and was the immediate image of a star-chamber decree to that purpose made in those times when that court did the rest of those her pious works, for which she is now fallen from the stars with Lucifer. Whereby ye may guess what kind of state prudence, what love of the people, what care of religion or good manners there was at the contriving, although with singular hypocrisy it pretended to bind books to their good behaviour. And how it got the upper hand of your precedent order so well constituted before, if we may believe those men whose profession gives them cause to inquire most, it may be doubted there was in it the fraud of some old patentees and monopolisers, in the trade of bookselling; who, under pretence of the poor in their company not to be defrauded, and the just retaining of each man his several copy (which God forbid should be gainsaid), brought divers glossing colours to the house, which were indeed but colours, and serving to no end except it be to exercise a superiority over their neighbours; men who do not therefore labour in an honest profession, to which learning is indebted, that they should be made other men's vassals. Another end is thought was aimed at by some of them in procuring by petition this order, that having power in their hands, malignant books might the easier escape abroad, as the event shows. But of these sophisms and elenchs of merchandise I skill not: this I know, that errors in a good government and in a bad are equally almost incident; for what magistrate may not be misinformed, and much the sooner, if liberty of printing be reduced into the power of a few? But to redress willingly and speedily what hath been erred, and in highest authority to esteem a plain advertisement more than others have done a sumptuous bride, is a virtue (honoured lords and commons!) answerable to your highest actions, and whereof none can participate but greatest and wisest men.

ON EDUCATION.

TO MASTER SAMUEL HARTLIB.

I AM long since persuaded, Master Hartlib, that to say or do aught worth memory and imitation, no purpose or respect should sooner move us than simply the love of God, and of mankind. Nevertheless to write now the reforming of education, though it be one of the greatest and noblest designs that can be thought on, and for the want whereof this nation perishes; I had not yet at this time been induced, but by your earnest entreaties and serious conjurements; as having my mind for the present half diverted into the pursuance of some other assertions, the knowledge and the use of which cannot but be a great furtherance both to the enlargement of truth, and honest living with much more peace. Nor should the laws of any private friendship have prevailed with me to divide thus, or transpose my former thoughts, but that I see those aims, those actions, which have won you with me the esteem of a person sent hither by some good providence from a far country to be the occasion and incitement of great good to this island.

And, as I hear, you have obtained the same repute with men of most approved wisdom, and some of the highest authority among us; not to mention the learned correspondence which you hold in foreign parts, and the extraordinary pains and diligence which you have used in this matter, both here and beyond the seas; either by the definite will of God so ruling, or the peculiar sway of nature, which also is God's working. Neither can I think that so reputed and so valued as you are, you would, to the forfeit of your own discerning ability, impose upon me an unfit and over-ponderous argument; but that the satisfaction which you profess to have received, from those incidental discourses which we have wandered into, hath pressed and almost constrained you into a persuasion, that what you require from me in this point, I neither ought nor can in conscience defer beyond this time both of so much need at once, and so much opportunity to try what God hath determined.

I will not resist, therefore, whatever it is, either of divine or human obligement, that you lay upon me; but will forthwith set down in writing, as you request me, that voluntary idea, which hath long, in silence, presented itself to me, of a better education, in extent and comprehension far more large, and yet of time far shorter, and of attainment far more certain, than hath been yet in practice. Brief I shall endeavour to be; for that which I have to say, assuredly this nation hath extreme need should be done sooner than spoken. To tell you, therefore, what I have benefited herein among old renowned authors, I shall spare; and to search what many modern Januas and Didactics, more than ever I shall read, have projected, my inclination leads me not. But if you can accept of these few observations which have flowered off, and are as it were the burnishing of many studious and contemplative years, altogether spent in the search of religious and civil knowledge, and such as pleased you so well in the relating, I here give you them to dispose of.

The end then of learning is to repair the ruins of our first parents by regaining to know God aright, and out of that knowledge to love him, to imitate him, to be like him, as we may the nearest by possessing our souls of true virtue, which being united to the heavenly grace of faith, makes up the highest perfection. But because our understanding cannot in this body found itself but on sensible things, nor arrive so clearly to the knowledge of God and things invisible, as by orderly conning over the visible and inferior creature, the same method is necessarily to be followed in all discreet teaching. And seeing every nation affords not experience and tradition enough for all kinds of learning, therefore we are chiefly taught the languages of those people who have at any time been most industrious after wisdom; so that language is but the instrument conveying to us things useful to be known. And though a linguist should pride himself to have all the tongues that Babel cleft the world into, yet if he have not studied the solid things in them, as well as the words and lexicons, he were nothing so much to be esteemed a learned man, as any yeoman or tradesman competently wise in his mother dialect only.

Hence appear the many mistakes which have made learning generally so unpleasing and so unsuccessful; first, we do amiss to spend seven or eight years merely in scraping together so much miserable Latin and Greek, as might be learned otherwise easily and delightfully in one year. And that which casts our proficiency therein so much behind, is our time lost partly in too oft idle vacancies given both to schools and universities; partly in a preposterous exaction, forcing the empty wits of children to compose themes, verses, and orations, which are the acts of ripest judgment, and the final work of a head filled by long reading and observing, with elegant maxims and copious invention. These are not matters to be wrung from poor striplings, like blood out of the nose, or the plucking of untimely fruit. Besides the ill habit which they get of wretched barbarising against the Latin and Greek idiom, with their untutored Anglicisms, odious to be read, yet not to be avoided without a well-continued and judicious conversing among pure authors digested, which they scarce taste. Whereas, if after some preparatory grounds of speech by their certain forms got into memory, they were led to the praxis thereof in some chosen short book lessoned thoroughly to them, they might then forthwith proceed to learn the substance of good things, and arts in due order, which would bring the whole language quickly into their power. This I take to be the most rational and most profitable way of learning languages, and whereby we may best hope to give account to God of our youth spent herein.

And for the usual method of teaching arts, I deem it to be an old error of universities, not yet well recovered from the scholastic grossness of barbarous ages, that instead of beginning with arts most easy (and those be such as are most obvious to the sense), they present their young unmatriculated novices, at first coming, with the most intellective abstractions of logic and metaphysics; so that they having but newly left those grammatic flats and shallows, where they stuck unreasonably to learn a few words with lamentable construction, and now on the sudden transported under another climate, to be tossed and turmoiled with their unballasted wits in fathomless and unquiet deeps of controversy, do for the most part grow into hatred and contempt of learning, mocked and deluded all this while with ragged notions and babblements, while they expected worthy and delightful knowledge; till poverty or youthful years call them importunately their several ways, and hasten them, with the sway of friends, either to an ambitious and mercenary, or ignorantly zealous divinity: some allured to the trade of law, grounding their purposes not on the prudent and heavenly contemplation of justice and equity, which was never taught them, but on the promising and pleasing thoughts of litigious terms, fat contentions, and flowing fees; others betake them to state affairs, with souls so unprincipled in virtue and true generous breeding, that flattery and court-shifts and tyrannous aphorisms appear to them the highest points of wisdom; instilling their barren hearts with a conscientious slavery; if, as I rather think, it be not feigned. Others, lastly, of a more delicious and airy spirit, retire themselves (knowing no better) to the enjoyments of ease and luxury, living out their days in feast and jollity; which indeed is the wisest and safest course of all these, unless they were with more integrity undertaken. And these are the errors, and these are the fruits of misspending our prime youth at the schools and universities as we do, either in learning mere words, or such things chiefly as were better unlearned.

I shall detain you now no longer in the demonstration of what we should not do, but straight conduct you to a hillside, where I will point you out the right path of a virtuous and noble education; laborious indeed at the first ascent, but else so smooth, so green, so full of goodly prospect, and melodious sounds on every side, that the harp of Orpheus was not more charming. I doubt not but ye shall have more ado to drive our dullest and laziest youth, our stocks and stubs, from the infinite desire of such a happy nurture, than we have now to hale and drag our choicest and hopefullest wits to that asinine feast of sowthistles and brambles, which is commonly set before them as all the food and entertainment of their tenderest and most docible age. I call therefore a complete and generous education, that which fits a man to perform justly, skilfully, and magnanimously all the offices, both private and public, of peace and war. And how all this may be done between twelve and one-and-twenty, less time than is now bestowed in pure trifling at grammar and sophistry, is to be thus ordered.

First, to find out a spacious house and ground about it fit for an academy, and big enough to lodge a hundred and fifty persons, whereof twenty or thereabout may be attendants, all under the government of one, who shall be thought of desert sufficient, and ability either to do all, or wisely to direct and oversee it done. This place should be at once both school and university, not needing a remove to any other house of scholarship, except it be some peculiar college of law, or physic, where they mean to be practitioners; but as for those general studies which take up all our time from Lily to commencing, as they term it, master of art, it should be absolute. After this pattern, as many edifices may be converted to this use as shall be needful in every city throughout this land, which would tend much to the increase of learning and civility everywhere. This number, less or more thus collected, to the convenience of a foot company, or interchangeably two troops of cavalry, should divide their day's work into three parts as it lies orderly: their studies, their exercise, and their diet.

For their studies: first, they should begin with the chief and necessary rules of some good grammar, either that now used, or any better; and while this is doing, their speech is to be fashioned to a distinct and clear pronunciation, as near as may be to the Italian, especially in the vowels. For we Englishmen being far northerly, do not open our mouths in the cold air wide enough to grace a southern tongue; but are observed by all other nations to speak exceeding close and inward, so that to smatter Latin with an English mouth, is as ill a hearing as law French. Next, to make them expert in the usefullest points of grammar, and withal to season them and win them early to the love of virtue and true labour, ere any flattering seducement or vain principle seize them wandering, some easy and delightful book of education would be read to them, whereof the Greeks have store, as Cebes, Plutarch, and other Socratic discourses. But in Latin we have none of classic authority extant, except the two or three first books of Quinctilian, and some select pieces elsewhere.

But here the main skill and groundwork will be, to temper them such lectures and explanations, upon every opportunity, as may lead and draw them in willing obedience, inflamed with the study of learning and the admiration of virtue; stirred up with high hopes of living to be brave men, and worthy patriots, dear to God, and famous to all ages. That they may despise and scorn all their childish and ill-taught qualities, to delight in manly and liberal exercises, which he who hath the art and proper eloquence to catch them with, what with mild and effectual persuasions, and what with the intimation of some fear, if need be, but chiefly by his own example, might in a short space gain them to an incredible diligence and courage, infusing into their young breasts such an ingenuous and noble ardour, as would not fail to make many of them renowned and matchless men. At the same time, some other hour of the day, might be taught them the rules of arithmetic; and soon after the elements of geometry, even playing, as the old manner was. After evening repast, till bedtime, their thoughts would be best taken up in the easy grounds of religion, and the story of scripture.

The next step would be to the authors of agriculture, Cato, Varro, and Columella, for the matter is most easy; and, if the language be difficult, so much the better, it is not a difficulty above their years. And here will be an occasion of inciting, and enabling them hereafter to improve the tillage of their country, to recover the bad soil, and to remedy the waste that is made of good; for this was one of Hercules' praises. Ere half these authors be read (which will soon be with plying hard and daily) they cannot choose but be masters of any ordinary prose. So that it will be then seasonable for them to learn in any modern author the use of the globes, and all the maps, first, with the old names, and then with the new; or they might be then capable to read any compendious method of natural philosophy.

And at the same time might be entering into the Greek tongue, after the same manner as was before prescribed in the Latin; whereby the difficulties of grammar being soon overcome, all the historical physiology of Aristotle and Theophrastus are open before them, and, as I may say, under contribution. The like access will be to Vitruvius, to Seneca's natural questions, to Mela, Celsus, Pliny, or Solinus. And having thus passed the principles of arithmetic, geometry, astronomy, and geography, with a general compact of physics, they may descend in mathematics to the instrumental science of trigonometry, and from thence to fortification, architecture, enginery, or navigation. And in natural philosophy they may proceed leisurely from the history of meteors, minerals, plants, and living creatures, as far as anatomy.

Then also in course might be read to them, out of some not tedious writer, the institution of physic, that they may know the tempers, the humours, the seasons, and how to manage a crudity; which he who can wisely and timely do, is not only a great physician to himself and to his friends, but also may, at some time or other, save an army by this frugal and expenseless means only; and not let the healthy and stout bodies of young men rot away under him for want of this discipline; which is a great pity, and no less a shame to the commander. To set forward all these proceedings in nature and mathematics, what hinders but that they may procure, as oft as shall be needful, the helpful experience of hunters, fowlers, fishermen, shepherds, gardeners, apothecaries; and in the other sciences, architects, engineers, mariners, anatomists; who doubtless would be ready, some for reward, and some to favour such a hopeful seminary. And this will give them such a real tincture of natural knowledge, as they shall never forget, but daily augment with delight. Then also those poets which are now counted most hard, will be both facile and pleasant, Orpheus, Hesiod, Theocritus, Aratus, Nicander, Oppian, Dionysius; and in Latin, Lucretius, Manilius, and the rural part of Virgil.

By this time, years and good general precepts will have furnished them more distinctly with that act of reason which in ethics is called Proairesis; that they may with some judgment contemplate upon moral good and evil. Then will be required a special reinforcement of constant and sound indoctrinating, to set them right and firm, instructing them more amply in the knowledge of virtue and the hatred of vice; while their young and pliant affections are led through all the moral works of Plato, Xenophon, Cicero, Plutarch, Laertius, and those Locrian remnants; but still to be reduced in their nightward studies wherewith they close the day's work, under the determinate sentence of David or Solomon, or the evangelists and apostolic scriptures. Being perfect in the knowledge of personal duty, they may then begin the study of economics. And either now or before this, they may have easily learned, at any odd hour, the Italian tongue. And soon after, but with wariness and good antidote, it would be wholesome enough to let them taste some choice comedies, Greek, Latin, or Italian; those tragedies also, that treat of household matters, as Trachiniæ, Alcestis, and the like.

The next removal must be to the study of politics; to know the beginning, end, and reasons of political societies; that they may not, in a dangerous fit of the commonwealth, be such poor, shaken, uncertain reeds, of such a tottering conscience, as many of our great counsellors have lately shown themselves, but steadfast pillars of the state. After this, they are to dive into the grounds of law, and legal justice; delivered first and with best warrant by Moses; and as far as human prudence can be trusted, in those extolled remains of Grecian lawgivers,

Lycurgus, Solon, Zaleucus, Charondas, and thence to all the Roman edicts and tables with their Justinian; and so down to the Saxon and common laws of England, and the statutes.

Sundays also and every evening may be now understandingly spent in the highest matters of theology, and church history, ancient and modern; and ere this time the Hebrew tongue at a set hour might have been gained, that the scriptures may be now read in their own original; whereto it would be no impossibility to add the Chaldee and the Syrian dialect. When all these employments are well conquered, then will the choice histories, heroic poems, and Attic tragedies of stateliest and most regal argument, with all the famous political orations, offer themselves; which if they were not only read, but some of them got by memory, and solemnly pronounced with right accent and grace, as might be taught, would endue them even with the spirit and vigour of Demosthenes or Cicero, Euripides or Sophocles.

And now, lastly, will be the time to read with them those organic arts, which enable men to discourse and write perspicuously, elegantly, and according to the fittest style, of lofty, mean, or lowly. Logic, therefore, so much as is useful, is to be referred to this due place with all her well-couched heads and topics, until it be time to open her contracted palm into a graceful and ornate rhetoric, taught out of the rule of Plato, Aristotle, Phalereus, Cicero, Hermogenes, Longinus. To which poetry would be made subsequent, or indeed rather precedent, as being less subtile and fine, but more simple, sensuous, and passionate. I mean not here the prosody of a verse, which they could not but have hit on before among the rudiments of grammar; but that sublime art which in Aristotle's poetics, in Horace, and the Italian commentaries of Castelvetro, Tasso, Mazzoni, and others, teaches what the laws are of a true epic poem, what of a dramatic, what of a lyric, what decorum is, which is the grand masterpiece to observe. This would make them soon perceive what despicable creatures our common rhymers and play-writers be; and show them what religious,

ON EDUCATION. 57

what glorious and magnificent use might be made of poetry, both in divine and human things.

From hence, and not till now, will be the right season of forming them to be able writers and composers in every excellent matter, when they shall be thus fraught with an universal insight into things. Or whether they be to speak in parliament or council, honour and attention would be waiting on their lips. There would then also appear in pulpits other visage, other gestures, and stuff otherwise wrought than what we now sit under, ofttimes to as great a trial of our patience as any other that they preach to us. These are the studies wherein our noble and our gentle youth ought to bestow their time, in a disciplinary way, from twelve to one-and-twenty: unless they rely more upon their ancestors dead, than upon themselves living. In which methodical course it is so supposed they must proceed by the steady pace of learning onward, as at convenient times, for memory's sake, to retire back into the middle ward, and sometimes into the rear of what they have been taught, until they have confirmed and solidly united the whole body of their perfected knowledge, like the embattling of a Roman legion. Now will be worth the seeing, what exercises and recreations may best agree, and become these studies.

The course of study hitherto briefly described is, what I can guess by reading, likest to those ancient and famous schools of Pythagoras, Plato, Isocrates, Aristotle, and such others, out of which were bred such a number of renowned philosophers, orators, historians, poets, and princes all over Greece, Italy, and Asia, besides the flourishing studies of Cyrene and Alexandria. But herein it shall exceed them, and supply a defect as great as that which Plato noted in the commonwealth of Sparta; whereas that city trained up their youth most for war, and these in their academies and Lycæum all for the gown, this institution of breeding which I here delineate shall be equally good both for peace and war. Therefore about an hour and a half ere they eat at noon should be allowed them for exercise, and due rest afterwards; but the time for this may be enlarged at pleasure, according as their rising in the morning shall be early.

The exercise which I commend first, is the exact use of their weapon, to guard, and to strike safely with edge or point; this will keep them healthy, nimble, strong, and well in breath; is also the likeliest means to make them grow large and tall, and to inspire them with a gallant and fearless courage, which being tempered with seasonable lectures and precepts to them of true fortitude and patience, will turn into a native and heroic valour, and make them hate the cowardice of doing wrong. They must be also practised in all the locks and gripes of wrestling, wherein Englishmen were wont to excel, as need may often be in fight to tug, to grapple, and to close. And this perhaps will be enough, wherein to prove and heat their single strength.

The interim of unsweating themselves regularly, and convenient rest before meat, may, both with profit and delight, be taken up in recreating and composing their travailed spirits with the solemn and divine harmonies of music, heard or learned; either whilst the skilful organist plies his grave and fancied descant in lofty fugues, or the whole symphony with artful and unimaginable touches adorn and grace the well-studied chords of some choice composer; sometimes the lute or soft organ-stop waiting on elegant voices, either to religious, martial, or civil ditties; which, if wise men and prophets be not extremely out, have a great power over dispositions and manners, to smooth and make them gentle from rustic harshness and distempered passions. The like also would not be inexpedient after meat, to assist and cherish nature in her first concoction, and send their minds back to study in good tune and satisfaction. Where having followed it close under vigilant eyes, till about two hours before supper, they are, by a sudden alarum or watchword, to be called out to their military motions, under sky or covert, according to the season, as was the Roman wont; first on foot, then, as their age permits, on horseback, to all the art of cavalry; that having in sport, but with much exactness and daily muster, served out the rudiments of their soldiership, in all the skill of embattling, marching, encamping, fortifying, besieging, and battering, with all the helps of ancient and modern stratagems, tactics, and warlike maxims, they may as it were out of a long war come forth renowned and perfect commanders in the service of their country. They would not then, if they were trusted with fair and hopeful armies, suffer them, for want of just and wise discipline, to shed away from about them like sick feathers, though they be never so oft supplied; they would not suffer their empty and unrecruitable colonels of twenty men in a company, to quaff out or convey into secret hoards, the wages of a delusive list, and a miserable remnant; yet in the meanwhile to be overmastered with a score or two of drunkards, the only soldiery left about them, or else to comply with all rapines and violences. No, certainly, if they knew aught of that knowledge that belongs to good men or good governors, they would not suffer these things.

But to return to our own institute: besides these constant exercises at home, there is another opportunity of gaining experience to be won from pleasure itself abroad; in those vernal seasons of the year when the air is calm and pleasant, it were an injury and sullenness against nature, not to go out and see her riches, and partake in her rejoicing with heaven and earth. I should not therefore be a persuader to them of studying much then, after two or three years that they have well laid their grounds, but to ride out in companies, with prudent and staid guides, to all the quarters of the land: learning and observing all places of strength, all commodities of building and of soil, for towns and tillage, harbours and ports for trade. Sometimes taking sea as far as to our navy, to learn there also what they can in the practical knowledge of sailing and of sea-fight.

These ways would try all their peculiar gifts of nature; and if there were any secret excellence among them would fetch it out, and give it fair opportunities to advance itself by, which could not but mightily redound to the good of this nation, and bring into fashion again those old admired virtues and excellencies, with far more advantage now in this purity of Christian knowledge. Nor shall we then need the monsieurs of Paris to take our hopeful youth into their slight and prodigal custodies, and send them over, back again, transformed into mimics, apes, and kickshaws. But if they desire to see other countries at three or four and twenty years of age, not to learn principles, but to enlarge experience, and make wise observation, they will by that time be such as shall deserve the regard and honour of all men where they pass, and the society and friendship of those in all places who are best and most eminent. And, perhaps, then other nations will be glad to visit us for their breeding, or else to imitate us in their own country.

Now, lastly, for their diet there cannot be much to say, save only that it would be best in the same house; for much time else would be lost abroad, and many ill habits got; and that it should be plain, healthful, and moderate, I suppose is out of controversy. Thus, Mr. Hartlib, you have a general view in writing, as your desire was, of that which at several times I had discoursed with you concerning the best and noblest way of education; not beginning, as some have done, from the cradle, which yet might be worth many considerations, if brevity had not been my scope; many other circumstances also I could have mentioned, but this, to such as have the worth in them to make trial, for light and direction may be enough. Only I believe that this is not a bow for every man to shoot in, that counts himself a teacher; but will require sinews almost equal to those which Homer gave Ulysses; yet I am withal persuaded that it may prove much more easy in the assay, than it now seems at distance, and much more illustrious; howbeit, not more difficult than I imagine, and that imagination presents me with nothing but very happy, and very possible according to best wishes; if God have so decreed, and this age have spirit and capacity enough to apprehend.

FROM "THE TENURE OF KINGS AND MAGISTRATES."

IF men within themselves would be governed by reason, and not generally give up their understanding to a double tyranny of custom from without, and blind affections within, they would discern better what it is to favour and uphold the tyrant of a nation. But, being slaves within doors, no wonder that they strive so much to have the public state conformably governed to the inward vicious rule by which they govern themselves. For, indeed, none can love freedom heartily but good men; the rest love not freedom but licence, which never hath more scope or more indulgence than under tyrants. Hence is it that tyrants are not oft offended, nor stand much in doubt of bad men, as being all naturally servile; but in whom virtue and true worth most is eminent, them they fear in earnest, as by right their masters; against them lies all their hatred and suspicion. Consequently, neither do bad men hate tyrants, but have been always readiest, with the falsified names of loyalty and obedience, to colour over their base compliances.

And although sometimes for shame, and when it comes to their own grievances, of purse especially, they would seem good patriots and side with the better cause, yet when others for the deliverance of their country endued with fortitude and heroic virtue to fear nothing but the curse written against those "that do the work of the Lord negligently," would go on to remove, not only the calamities and thraldoms of a people, but the roots and causes whence they spring; straight these men, and sure helpers at need, as if they hated only the miseries, but not the mischiefs, after they have juggled and paltered with the world, bandied and borne arms against their king, divested him, disanointed him, nay, cursed him all over in their pulpits, and their pamphlets, to the engaging of sincere and real men beyond what is possible or honest to retreat from, not only turn revolters from those principles, which only could at first move them, but lay the strain of disloyalty, and worse, on those proceedings which are the necessary consequences of their own former actions; nor disliked by themselves, were they managed to the entire advantages of their own faction; not considering the while that he toward whom they boasted their new fidelity, counted them accessory; and by those statutes and laws, which they so impotently brandish against others, would have doomed them to a traitor's death for what they have done already.

It is true, that most men are apt enough to civil wars and commotions as a novelty, and for a flash hot and active; but through sloth or inconstancy, and weakness of spirit, either fainting ere their own pretences, though never so just, be half attained, or through an inbred falsehood and wickedness, betray, ofttimes to destruction with themselves, men of noblest temper joined with them for causes whereof they in their rash undertakings were not capable. If God and a good cause give them victory, the prosecution whereof for the most part inevitably draws after it the alteration of laws, change of government, downfall of princes with their families; then comes the task to those worthies which are the soul of that enterprise, to be sweat and laboured out amidst the throng and noses of vulgar and irrational men. Some contesting for privileges, customs, forms, and that old entanglement of iniquity, their gibberish laws, though the badge of their ancient slavery. Others, who have been fiercest against their prince, under the notion of a tyrant, and no mean incendiaries of the war against them, when God, out of His providence and high disposal, hath delivered him into the hand of their brethren, on a sudden and in a new garb of allegiance, which their doings have long since cancelled, they plead for him, pity him, extol him, protest against those that talk of bringing him to the trial of justice, which is the sword of

God, superior to all mortal things, in whose hand soever by apparent signs his testified will is to put it.

But certainly, if we consider who and what they are, on a sudden grown so pitiful, we may conclude their pity can be no true and Christian commiseration, but either levity and shallowness of mind or else a carnal admiring of that worldly pomp and greatness from whence they see him fallen; or rather, lastly, a dissembled and seditious pity, feigned of industry to beget new discord. As for mercy, if it be to a tyrant, under which name they themselves have cited him so oft in the hearing of God, of angels, and the holy church assembled, and there charged him with the spilling of more innocent blood by far than ever Nero did, undoubtedly the mercy which they pretend is the mercy of wicked men; and "their mercies," we read, "are cruelties;" hazarding the welfare of a whole nation, to have saved one whom they so oft have termed Ageg, and vilifying the blood of many Jonathans who have saved Israel; insisting with much niceness on the unnecessariest clause of their covenant wrested, wherein the fear of change and the absurd contradiction of a flattering hostility had hampered them, but not scrupling to give away for compliments, to an implacable revenge, the heads of many thousand Christians more.

Another sort there is, who coming in the course of these affairs to have their share in great actions above the form of law or custom, at least to give their voice and approbation, begin to swerve and almost shiver at the majesty and grandeur of some noble deed, as if they were newly entered into a great sin; disputing precedents, forms, and circumstances, when the commonwealth nigh perishes for want of deeds in substance, done with just and faithful expedition. To these I wish better instruction, and virtue equal to their calling; the former of which, that is to say, instruction, I shall endeavour, as my duty is, to bestow on them; and exhort them not to startle from the just and pious resolution of adhering, with all their strength and assistance, to the present parliament and army, in the glorious way wherein justice and victory hath set them — the only warrants through all ages, next under immediate revelation, to exercise supreme power—in those proceedings, which hitherto appear equal to what hath been done in any age or nation heretofore justly or magnanimously.

Nor let them be discouraged or deterred by any new apostate scarecrows, who, under show of giving counsel, send out their barking monitories and mementoes, empty of aught else but the spleen of a frustrated faction. For how can that pretended counsel be either sound or faithful, when they that give it see not, for madness and vexation of their ends lost, that those statutes and scriptures which both falsely and scandalously they wrest against their friends and associates, would, by sentence of the common adversary, fall first and heaviest upon their own heads? Neither by mild and tender dispositions be foolishly softened from their duty and perseverance with the unmasculine rhetoric of any puling priest or chaplain, sent as a friendly letter of advice, for fashion's sake in private, and forthwith published by the sender himself, that we may know how much of friend there was in it, to cast an odious envy upon them to whom it was pretended to be sent in charity. Nor let any man be deluded by either the ignorance or the notorious hypocrisy and self-repugnance of our dancing divines, who have the conscience and the boldness to come with scripture in their mouths, glossed and fitted for their turns with a double contradictory sense, transforming the sacred verity of God to an idol with two faces, looking at once two several ways; and with the same quotations to charge others, which in the same case they made serve to justify themselves. For while the hope to be made classic and provincial lords led them on, while pluralities greased them thick and deep, to the shame and scandal of religion, more than all the sects and heresies they exclaim against; then to fight against the king's person, and no less a party of his lords and commons, or to put force upon both the houses, was good, was lawful, was no resisting of superior powers; they only were powers not to be resisted, who countenanced the good, and punished the evil.

But now that their censorious domineering is not suffered

to be universal, truth and conscience to be freed, tithes and pluralities to be no more, though competent allowance provided, and the warm experience of large gifts, and they so good at taking them; yet now to exclude and seize upon impeached members, to bring delinquents without exemption to a fair tribunal by the common national law against murder, is now to be no less than Korah, Dathan, and Abiram. He who but erewhile in the pulpits was a cursed tyrant, an enemy to God and saints, laden with all the innocent blood spilt in three kingdoms, and so to be fought against, is now, though nothing penitent or altered from his first principles, a lawful magistrate, a sovereign lord, the Lord's anointed, not to be touched, though by themselves imprisoned. As if this only were obedience, to preserve the mere useless bulk of his person, and that only in prison, not in the field, not to disobey his commands, deny him his dignity and office, everywhere to resist his power, but where they think it only surviving in their own faction.

But who in particular is a tyrant, cannot be determined in a general discourse, otherwise than by supposition; his particular charge, and the sufficient proof of it, must determine that: which I leave to magistrates, at least to the uprighter sort of them, and of the people, though in number less by many, in whom faction least hath prevailed above the law of nature and right reason, to judge as they find cause. But this I dare own as part of my faith, that if such a one there be, by whose commission whole massacres have been committed on his faithful subjects, his provinces offered to pawn or alienation, as the hire of those whom he had solicited to come in and destroy whole cities and countries; be he king, or tyrant, or emperor, the sword of justice is above him; in whose hand soever is found sufficient power to avenge the effusion, and so great a deluge of innocent blood. For if all human power to execute, not accidentally but intendedly, the wrath of God upon evil-doers without exception, be of God; then that power, whether ordinary, or if that fail, extraordinary, so executing that intent of God, is lawful, and not to be resisted. But to unfold more at large this whole question, though with all expedient brevity, I shall here set down, from first beginning, the original, of kings; how and wherefore exalted to that dignity above their brethren; and from thence shall prove, that turning to tyranny they may be as lawfully deposed and punished, as they were at first elected: this I shall do by authorities and reasons, not learnt in corners among schisms and heresies, as our doubling divines are ready to calumniate, but fetched out of the midst of choicest and most authentic learning, and no prohibited authors; nor many heathen, but Mosaical, Christian, orthodoxal, and, which must needs be more convincing to our adversaries, presbyterial.

No man, who knows aught, can be so stupid to deny, that all men naturally were born free, being the image and resemblance of God himself, and were, by privilege above all the creatures, born to command, and not to obey: and that they lived so, till from the root of Adam's transgression falling among themselves to do wrong and violence, and foreseeing that such courses must needs tend to the destruction of them all, they agreed by common league to bind each other from mutual injury, and jointly to defend themselves against any that gave disturbance or opposition to such agreement. Hence came cities, towns, and commonwealths. And because no faith in all was found sufficiently binding, they saw it needful to ordain some authority that might restrain by force and punishment what was violated against peace and common right.

This authority and power of self-defence and preservation being originally and naturally in every one of them, and unitedly in them all; for ease, for order, and lest each man should be his own partial judge, they communicated and derived either to one, whom for the eminence of his wisdom and integrity they chose above the rest, or to more than one, whom they thought of equal deserving: the first was called a king; the other, magistrates: not to be their lords and masters (though afterward those names in some places were given voluntarily to such as have been authors of inestimable good to the people), but to be their deputies and commissioners, to execute, by virtue of their intrusted power, that justice, which else every man by the bond of nature and of covenant must have executed for himself, and for one another. And to him that shall consider well, why among free persons one man by civil right should bear authority and jurisdiction over another, no other end or reason can be imaginable.

These for a while governed well, and with much equity decided all things at their own arbitrement; till the temptation of such a power, left absolute in their hands, perverted them at length to injustice and partiality. Then did they, who now by trial had found the danger and inconveniencies of committing arbitrary power to any, invent laws, either framed or consented to by all, that should confine and limit the authority of whom they chose to govern them: that so man, of whose failing they had proof, might no more rule over them, but law and reason, abstracted as much as might be from personal errors and frailties. "While, as the magistrate was set above the people, so the law was set above the magistrate." When this would not serve, but that the law was either not executed, or misapplied, they were constrained from that time, the only remedy left them, to put conditions and take oaths from all kings and magistrates at their first instalment, to do impartial justice by law: who, upon those terms and no other, received allegiance from the people, that is to say, bond or covenant to obey them in execution of those laws, which they, the people, had themselves made or assented to. And this ofttimes with express warning, that if the king or magistrate proved unfaithful to his trust, the people would be disengaged. They added also counsellors and parliaments, not to be only at his beck, but, with him or without him, at set times, or at all times, when any danger threatened, to have care of the public safety. Therefore saith Claudius Sesell, a French statesman, "The parliament was set as a bridle to the king;" which I instance rather, not because our English lawyers have not said the same long before, but because that French monarchy is granted by all to be a far more absolute one than ours. That this and the rest of what hath hitherto been spoken is most true, might be copiously made appear through all stories, heathen and

Christian; even of those nations where kings and emperors have sought means to abolish all ancient memory of the people's right by their encroachments and usurpations. But I spare long insertions, appealing to the German, French, Italian, Arragonian, English, and not least the Scottish histories: not forgetting this only by the way, that William the Norman, though a conqueror, and not unsworn at his coronation, was compelled a second time to take oath at St. Albans ere the people would be brought to yield obedience.

It being thus manifest, that the power of kings and magistrates is nothing else but what is only derivative, transferred, and committed to them in trust from the people to the common good of them all, in whom the power yet remains fundamentally, and cannot be taken from them, without a violation of their natural birthright; and seeing that from hence Aristotle, and the best of political writers, have defined a king, "him who governs to the good and profit of his people, and not for his own ends;" it follows from necessary causes, that the titles of sovereign lord, natural lord, and the like, are either arrogancies or flatteries, not admitted by emperors and kings of best note, and disliked by the church both of Jews (Isa. xxvi. 13) and ancient Christians, as appears by Tertullian and others. Although generally the people of Asia, and with them the Jews also, especially since the time they chose a king against the advice and counsel of God, are noted by wise authors much inclinable to slavery.

Secondly, that to say, as is usual, the king hath as good right to his crown and dignity as any man to his inheritance, is to make the subject no better than the king's slave, his chattel, or his possession that may be bought and sold: and doubtless, if hereditary title were sufficiently inquired, the best foundation of it would be found but either in courtesy or convenience. But suppose it to be of right hereditary, what can be more just and legal, if a subject for certain crimes be to forfeit by law from himself and posterity all his inheritance to the king, than that a king, for crimes proportional, should forfeit all his title and inheritance to the people? Unless the people must be thought created all for him, he not for them, and they all in one body inferior to him single; which were a kind of treason against the dignity of mankind to affirm.

Thirdly, it follows, that to say kings are accountable to none but God, is the overturning of all law and government. For if they may refuse to give account, then all covenants made with them at coronation, all oaths are in vain, and mere mockeries; all laws which they swear to keep, made to no purpose: for if the king fear not God (as how many of them do not), we hold then our lives and estates by the tenure of his mere grace and mercy, as from a god, not a mortal magistrate; a position that none but court-parasites or men besotted would maintain! Aristotle, therefore, whom we commonly allow for one of the best interpreters of nature and morality, writes in the fourth of his *Politics*, chap. x., that "monarchy unaccountable is the worst sort of tyranny, and least of all to be endured by free-born men."

And surely no Christian prince, not drunk with high mind, and prouder than those pagan Cæsars that deified themselves, would arrogate so unreasonably above human condition, or derogate so basely from a whole nation of men, his brethren, as if for him only subsisting, and to serve his glory, valuing them in comparison of his own brute will and pleasure no more than so many beasts, or vermin under his feet, not to be reasoned with, but to be trod on; among whom there might be found so many thousand men for wisdom, virtue, nobleness of mind, and all other respects but the fortune of his dignity, far above him. Yet some would persuade us that this absurd opinion was King David's, because in the 51st Psalm he cries out to God, "Against thee only have I sinned;" as if David had imagined, that to murder Uriah and adulterate his wife had been no sin against his neighbour, whenas that law of Moses was to the king expressly (Deut. xvii.), not to think so highly of himself above his brethren. David, therefore, by those words, could mean no other, than either that the depth of his guiltiness was known to God only, or to so few as had not the will or power to question him, or that the sin against God was greater beyond compare than against Uriah. Whatever his meaning were, any wise man will see, that the pathetical words of a psalm can be no certain decision to a point that hath abundantly more certain rules to go by.

How much more rationally spake the heathen king Demophoön, in a tragedy of Euripides, than these interpreters would put upon King David! "I rule not my people by tyranny, as if they were barbarians; but am myself liable, if I do unjustly, to suffer justly." Not unlike was the speech of Trajan, the worthy emperor, to one whom he made general of his prætorian forces: "Take this drawn sword," saith he, "to use for me if I reign well; if not, to use against me." Thus Dion relates. And not Trajan only, but Theodosius, the younger, a Christian emperor, and one of the best, caused it to be enacted as a rule undeniable and fit to be acknowledged by all kings and emperors, that a prince is bound to the laws; that on the authority of law the authority of a prince depends, and to the laws ought to submit. Which edict of his remains yet unrepealed in the Code of Justinian (l. i. tit. 24), as a sacred constitution to all the succeeding emperors. How can any king in Europe maintain and write himself accountable to none but God, when emperors in their own imperial statutes have written and decreed themselves accountable to law? And indeed where such account is not feared, he that bids a man reign over him above law, may bid as well a savage beast.

It follows, lastly, that since the king or magistrate holds his authority of the people, both originally and naturally for their good, in the first place, and not his own, then may the people, as oft as they shall judge it for the best, either choose him or reject him, retain him or depose him, though no tyrant, merely by the liberty and right of freeborn men to be governed as seems to them best. This, though it cannot but stand with plain reason, shall be made good also by Scripture (Deut. xvii. 14): "When thou art come into the land which the Lord thy God giveth thee, and shalt say, I will set a king over me, like as all the nations about me." These words confirm us that the right of choosing, yea of changing their own government, is by the grant of God himself in the people. And therefore when they desired a king, though then under another form of government, and though their changing displeased him, yet he that was himself their king, and rejected by them, would not be a hindrance to what they intended, further than by persuasion, but that they might do therein as they saw good (1 Sam. viii.), only he reserved to himself the nomination of who should reign over them. Neither did that exempt the king, as if he were to God only accountable, though by His especial command anointed. Therefore "David first made a covenant with the elders of Israel, and so was by them anointed king" (2 Sam. v. 3; 1 Chron. xi.). And Jehoiada the priest, making Jehoash king, made a covenant between him and the people (2 Kings xi. 17). Therefore when Roboam, at his coming to the crown, rejected those conditions which the Israelites brought him, hear what they answer him: "What portion have we in David, or inheritance in the son of Jesse? See to thine own house, David." And for the like conditions not performed, all Israel before that time deposed Samuel; not for his own default, but for the misgovernment of his sons.

But some will say to both these examples, it was evilly done. I answer, that not the latter, because it was expressly allowed them in the law, to set up a king if they pleased; and God himself joined with them in the work; though in some sort it was at that time displeasing to Him, in respect of old Samuel, who had governed them uprightly. As Livy praises the Romans, who took occasion from Tarquinius, a wicked prince, to gain their liberty, which to have extorted, saith he, from Numa, or any of the good kings before, had not been seasonable. Nor was it in the former example done unlawfully; for when Roboam had prepared a huge army to reduce the Israelites, he was forbidden by the prophet (1 Kings xii. 24): "Thus saith the Lord, ye shall not go up, nor fight against your brethren, for this thing is from me." He calls them their brethren, not rebels, and forbids to be proceeded against them, owning the thing himself, not by single providence, but by approbation, and that not only of the act, as in the former example, but of the fit season also; he had not otherwise forbid to molest them. And those grave and wise counsellors, whom Rehoboam first advised with, spake no such things as our old grey-headed flatterers now are wont—stand upon your birthright, scorn to capitulate; you hold of God, not of them; —for they knew no such matter, unless conditionally, but gave him politic counsel, as in a civil transaction.

Therefore kingdom and magistracy, whether supreme or subordinate, is called "a human ordinance" (1 Pet. ii. 13, etc.), which we are there taught is the will of God we should submit to, so far as for the punishment of evil-doers, and the encouragement of them that do well. "Submit," saith he, "as free men." "But to any civil power, unaccountable, unquestionable, and not to be resisted, no, not in wickedness, and violent actions, how can we submit as free men?" "There is no power but of God," saith Paul (Rom. xiii.); as much as to say, God put it into man's heart to find out that way at first for common peace and preservation, approving the exercise thereof; else it contradicts Peter, who calls the same authority an ordinance of man. It must be also understood of lawful and just power, else we read of great power in the affairs and kingdoms of the world permitted to the devil: for saith he to Christ (Luke iv. 6), "All this power will I give thee, and the glory of them, for it is delivered to me, and to whomsoever I will, I give it:" neither did he lie, or Christ gainsay what he affirmed; for in the thirteenth of the Revelation, we read how the dragon gave to the beast his power, his seat, and great authority: which beast so authorised most expound to be the tyrannical powers and kingdoms of the earth. Therefore Saint Paul in the forecited chapter tells us, that such magistrates he means, as are not a terror to the good, but to the evil; such as bear not the sword in vain, but to punish offenders, and to encourage the good.

If such only be mentioned here as powers to be obeyed, and our submission to them only required, then doubtless those powers that do the contrary are no powers ordained of God;

and by consequence no obligation laid upon us to obey or not to resist them. And it may be well observed, that both these apostles, whenever they give this precept, express it in terms not concrete, but abstract, as logicians are wont to speak; that is, they mention the ordinance, the power, the authority, before the persons that execute it; and what that power is, lest we should be deceived, they describe exactly. So that if the power be not such, or the person execute not such power, neither the one nor the other is of God, but of the devil, and by consequence to be resisted. From this exposition Chrysostom also, on the same place, dissents not; explaining that these words were not written in behalf of a tyrant. And this is verified by David, himself a king, and likeliest to be author of the Psalm (xciv. 20) which saith, "Shall the throne of iniquity have fellowship with thee?" And it were worth the knowing, since kings in these days, and that by Scripture, boast the justness of their title, by holding it immediately of God, yet cannot show the time when God ever set on the throne them or their forefathers, but only when the people chose them; why by the same reason, since God ascribes as oft to himself the casting down of princes from the throne, it should not be thought as lawful, and as much from God, when none are seen to do it but the people, and that for just causes. For if it needs must be a sin in them to depose, it may as likely be a sin to have elected. And contrary, if the people's act in election be pleaded by a king, as the act of God, and the most just title to enthrone him, why may not the people's act of rejection be as well pleaded by the people as the act of God, and the most just reason to depose him? So that we see the title and just right of reigning or deposing, in reference to God, is found in Scripture to be all one; visible only in the people, and depending merely upon justice and demerit. Thus far hath been considered chiefly the power of kings and magistrates; how it was and is originally the people's, and by them conferred in trust only to be employed to the common peace and benefit; with liberty therefore and right remaining in them, to reassume it to themselves, if by kings or magistrates it be abused; or to dispose of it by any alteration, as they shall judge most conducing to the public good.

We may from hence with more ease and force of argument determine what a tyrant is, and what the people may do against him. A tyrant, whether by wrong or by right coming to the crown, is he who, regarding neither law nor the common good, reigns only for himself and his faction: thus St. Basil, among others, defines him. And because his power is great, his will boundless and exorbitant, the fulfilling whereof is for the most part accompanied with innumerable wrongs and oppressions of the people, murders, massacres, rapes, adulteries, desolation, and subversion of cities and whole provinces; look how great a good and happiness a just king is, so great a mischief is a tyrant; as he the public father of his country, so this the common enemy. Against whom what the people lawfully may do, as against a common pest and destroyer of mankind, I suppose no man of clear judgment need go further to be guided than by the very principles of nature in him.

But because it is the vulgar folly of men to desert their own reason, and shutting their eyes, to think they see best with other men's, I shall show, by such examples as ought to have most weight with us, what hath been done in this case heretofore. The Greeks and Romans, as their prime authors witness, held it not only lawful, but a glorious and heroic deed, rewarded publicly with statues and garlands, to kill an infamous tyrant at any time without trial; and but reason, that he, who trod down all law, should not be vouchsafed the benefit of law. Insomuch that Seneca, the tragedian, brings in Hercules, the grand suppressor of tyrants, thus speaking—

> ". . . Victima haud ulla amplior
> Potest, magisque opima mactari Jovi
> Quam rex iniquus . . ."

> ". . . There can be slain
> No sacrifice to God more acceptable
> Than an unjust and wicked king . . ."

But of these I name no more, lest it be objected they were

heathen; and come to produce another sort of men, that had the knowledge of true religion. Among the Jews this custom of tyrant-killing was not unusual. First, Ehud, a man whom God had raised to deliver Israel from Eglon, king of Moab, who had conquered and ruled over them eighteen years, being sent to him as an ambassador with a present, slew him in his own house. But he was a foreign prince, an enemy, and Ehud besides had special warrant from God. To the first I answer, it imports not whether foreign or native: for no prince so native but professes to hold by law; which when he himself overturns, breaking all the covenants and oaths that gave title to his dignity, and were the bond and alliance between him and his people, what differs he from an outlandish king, or from an enemy?

For look how much right the king of Spain hath to govern us at all, so much right hath the king of England to govern us tyrannically. If he, though not bound to us by any league, coming from Spain in person to subdue us, or to destroy us, might lawfully by the people of England either be slain in fight, or put to death in captivity, what hath a native king to plead, bound by so many covenants, benefits, and honours, to the welfare of his people; why he through the contempt of all laws and parliaments, the only tie of our obedience to him, for his own will's sake, and a boasted prerogative unaccountable, after seven years' warring and destroying of his best subjects, overcome, and yielded prisoner, should think to scape unquestionable, as a thing divine, in respect of whom so many thousand Christians destroyed should lie unaccounted for, polluting with their slaughtered carcasses all the land over, and crying for vengeance against the living that should have righted them? Who knows not that there is a mutual bond of amity and brotherhood between man and man over all the world, neither is it the English sea that can sever us from that duty and relation: a straiter bond yet there is between fellow-subjects, neighbours, and friends. But when any of these do one to another so as hostility could do no worse, what doth the law decree less against them, than open enemies and invaders? or if the law be not present or too weak, what doth it warrant us to less than single defence or civil war? and from that time forward the law of civil defensive war differs nothing from the law of foreign hostility. Nor is it distance of place that makes enmity, but enmity that makes distance. He, therefore, that keeps peace with me, near or remote, of whatsoever nation, is to me, as far as all civil and human offices, an Englishman and a neighbour: but if an Englishman, forgetting all laws, human, civil, and religious, offend against life and liberty, to him offended, and to the law in his behalf, though born in the same womb, he is no better than a Turk, a Saracen, a heathen.

This is gospel, and this was ever law among equals; how much rather then in force against any king whatever, who in respect of the people is confessed inferior and not equal: to distinguish, therefore, of a tyrant by outlandish, or domestic, is a weak evasion. To the second, that he was an enemy, I answer, what tyrant is not? yet Eglon by the Jews had been acknowledged as their sovereign, they had served him eighteen years, as long almost as we our William the Conqueror, in all which he could not be so unwise a statesman, but to have taken of them oaths of fealty and allegiance; by which they made themselves his proper subjects, as their homage and present sent by Ehud testified. To the third, that he had special warrant to kill Eglon in that manner, it cannot be granted, because not expressed; it is plain that he was raised by God to be a deliverer, and went on just principles, such as were then and ever held allowable to deal so by a tyrant, that could no otherwise be dealt with.

Neither did Samuel, though a prophet, with his own hand abstain from Agag; a foreign enemy, no doubt; but mark the reason: "As thy sword has made women childless;" a cause that by the sentence of law itself nullifies all relations. And as the law is between brother and brother, father and son, master and servant, wherefore not between king, or rather tyrant, and people? And whereas Jehu had special command to slay Jehoram, a successive and hereditary tyrant, it seems not the less imitable for that; for where a thing grounded so much on natural reason hath the addition of a command from God, what does it but establish the lawfulness of such an act? Nor is it likely that God, who had so many ways of punishing the house of Ahab, would have sent a subject against his prince, if the fact in itself, as done to a tyrant, had been of bad example. And if David refused to lift his hand against the Lord's anointed, the matter between them was not tyranny, but private enmity; and David, as a private person, had been his own revenger, not so much the people's: but when any tyrant at this day can show himself to be the Lord's anointed, the only mentioned reason why David withheld his hand, he may then, but not till then, presume on the same privilege.

We may pass, therefore, hence to Christian times. And first, our Saviour himself, how much he favoured tyrants, and how much intended they should be found or honoured among Christians, declared his mind not obscurely; accounting their absolute authority no better than Gentilism, yea, though they flourished it over with the splendid name of benefactors; charging those that would be His disciples to usurp no such dominion; but that they, who were to be of most authority among them, should esteem themselves ministers and servants to the public—Matt. xx. 25: "The princes of the Gentiles exercise lordship over them;" and Mark x. 42: "They that seem to rule," saith he, either slighting or accounting them no lawful rulers; "but ye shall not be so, but the greatest among you shall be your servant." And although He himself were the meekest, and came on earth to be so, yet to a tyrant we hear Him not vouchsafe an humble word. but, "Tell that fox," Luke xiii. "So far we ought to be from thinking that Christ and His gospel should be made a sanctuary for tyrants from justice, to whom His law before never gave such protection." And wherefore did His mother, the Virgin Mary, give such praise to God in her prophetic song, that he had now, by the coming of Christ, cut down dynastas, or proud monarchs, from the throne, if the church, when God manifests his power in them to do so, should rather choose all misery and vassalage to serve them, and let them still sit on their potent seats to be adored for doing mischief?

Surely it is not for nothing that tyrants, by a kind of natural instinct, both hate and fear none more than the true church and saints of God, as the most dangerous enemies and subverters of monarchy, though indeed of tyranny; hath not this been the perpetual cry of courtiers and court-prelates? whereof no likelier cause can be alleged, but that they well discerned the mind and principles of most devout and zealous men, and indeed the very discipline of church, tending to the dissolution of all tyranny. No marvel then if since the faith of Christ received, in purer or impurer times, to depose a king and put him to death for tyranny, hath been accounted so just and requisite, that neighbour kings have both upheld and taken part with subjects in the action. And Ludovicus Pius, himself an emperor, and son of Charles the Great, being made judge (Du Haillan is my author) between Milegast, king of the Vultzes, and his subjects, who had deposed him, gave his verdict for the subjects, and for him whom they had chosen in his room. Note here, that the right of electing whom they please is, by the impartial testimony of an emperor, in the people: for, said he, "A just prince ought to be preferred before an unjust, and the end of government before the prerogative."

And Constantinus Leo, another emperor, in the Byzantine laws, saith, "That the end of a king is for the general good, which he not performing, is but the counterfeit of a king." And to prove, that some of our own monarchs have acknowledged that their high office exempted them not from punishment, they had the sword of St. Edward borne before them by an officer, who was called earl of the palace, even at the times of their highest pomp and solemnities; to mind them, saith Matthew Paris, the best of our historians, "that if they erred, the sword had power to restrain them." And what restraint the sword comes to at length, having both edge and point, if any sceptic will doubt, let him feel. It is also affirmed from diligent search made in our ancient books of law, that the peers and barons of England had a legal right to judge the king: which was the cause most likely (for it could be no slight cause) that they were called his peers, or equals. This, however, may stand immovable, so long as man hath to deal with no better than man; that if our law judge all men to the lowest by their peers, it should, in all equity, ascend also, and judge the highest.

And so much I find both in our own and foreign story, that dukes, earls, and marquisses were at first not hereditary, not empty and vain titles, but names of trust and office, and with the office ceasing; as induces me to be of opinion, that every worthy man in parliament (for the word baron imports no more) might for the public good be thought a fit peer and judge of the king, without regard had to petty caveats and circumstances, the chief impediment in high affairs, and ever stood upon most by circumstantial men. Whence doubtless our ancestors who were not ignorant with what rights either nature or ancient constitution had endowed them, when oaths both at coronation and renewed in parliament would not serve, thought it no way illegal, to depose and put to death their tyrannous kings. Insomuch that the parliament drew up a charge against Richard the Second, and the commons requested to have judgment decreed against him, that the realm might not be endangered. And Peter Martyr, a divine of foremost rank, on the third of Judges approves their doings. Sir Thomas Smith also, a protestant, and a statesman, in his *Commonwealth of England*, putting the question, "whether it be lawful to rise against a tyrant;" answers, "that the vulgar judge of it according to the event, and the learned according to the purpose of them that do it."

But far before those days, Gildas, the most ancient of all our historians, speaking of those times wherein the Roman empire decaying, quitted and relinquished what right they had by conquest to this island, and resigned it all into the people's hands, testifies that the people thus reinvested with their own original right, about the year 446, both elected them kings, whom they thought best (the first Christian British kings that ever reigned here since the Romans), and by the same right, when they apprehended cause, usually deposed and put them to death. This is the most fundamental and ancient tenure that any king of England can produce or pretend to; in comparison of which, all other titles and pleas are but of yesterday. If any object, that Gildas condemns the Britons for so doing, the answer is as ready; that he condemns them no more for so doing than he did before for choosing such; for, saith he "They anointed them kings not of God, but such as were more bloody than the rest." Next, he condemns them not at all for deposing or putting them to death, but for doing it over hastily, without trial or well examining the cause, and for electing others worse in their room.

Thus we have here both domestic and most ancient examples, that the people of Britain have deposed and put to death their kings in those primitive Christian times. And to couple reason with example, if the church in all ages, primitive, Romish, or protestant, held it ever no less their duty than the power of their keys, though without express warrant of Scripture, to bring indifferently both king and peasant under the utmost rigour of their canons and censures ecclesiastical, even to the smiting him with a final excommunion, if he persist impenitent; what hinders but that the temporal law both may and ought, though without a special text or precedent, extend with like indifference the civil sword, to the cutting off, without exemption, him that capitally offends, seeing that justice and religion are from the same God, and works of justice ofttimes more acceptable? Yet because that some lately, with the tongues and arguments of malignant backsliders, have written that the proceedings now in parliament against the king are without precedent from any protestant state or kingdom, the examples which follow shall be all protestant, and chiefly presbyterian.

In the year 1546, the Duke of Saxony, Landgrave of Hesse, and the whole protestant league, raised open war against Charles the Fifth, their emperor, sent him a defiance, renounced all faith and allegiance toward him, and debated long in council whether they should give him so much as the title of

Cæsar. Let all men judge what this wanted of deposing or of killing, but the power to do it.

In the year 1559, the Scots protestants claiming promise of their queen-regent for liberty of conscience, she answering that promises were not to be claimed of princes beyond what was commodious for them to grant, told her to her face in the parliament then at Stirling, that if it were so, they renounced their obedience; and soon after betook them to arms. Certainly, when allegiance is renounced, that very hour the king or queen is in effect deposed.

In the year 1564, John Knox, a most famous divine, and the reformer of Scotland to the presbyterian discipline, at a general assembly maintained openly, in a dispute against Lethington, the secretary of state, that subjects might and ought to execute God's judgments upon their king; that the fact of Jehu and others against their king, having the ground of God's ordinary command to put such and such offenders to death, was not extraordinary, but to be imitated of all that preferred the honour of God to the affection of flesh and wicked princes; that kings, if they offend, have no privilege to be exempted from the punishments of law more than any other subject: so that if the king be a murderer, adulterer, or idolater, he should suffer, not as a king, but as an offender; and this position he repeats again and again before them. Answerable was the opinion of John Craig, another learned divine, and that laws made by the tyranny of princes, or the negligence of people, their posterity might abrogate, and reform all things according to the original institution of commonwealths. And Knox being commanded by the nobility to write to Calvin and other learned men for their judgments in that question, refused, alleging that both himself was fully resolved in conscience, and had heard their judgments, and had the same opinion under handwriting of many the most godly and most learned that he knew in Europe; that if he should move the question to them again, what should he do but show his own forgetfulness or inconstancy? All this is far more largely in the ecclesiastical history of Scotland (l. iv.), with many other passages to this effect all the book over, set out with diligence by Scotsmen of best repute among them at the beginning of these troubles; as if they laboured to inform us what we were to do, and what they intended upon the like occasion.

And to let the world know, that the whole church and protestant state of Scotland in those purest times of reformation were of the same belief, three years after, they met in the field Mary their lawful and hereditary queen, took her prisoner, yielding before fight, kept her in prison, and the same year deposed her.

And four years after that, the Scots, in justification of their deposing Queen Mary, sent ambassadors to Queen Elizabeth, and in a written declaration alleged, that they had used towards her more lenity than she deserved; that their ancestors had heretofore punished their kings by death or banishment; that the Scots were a free nation, made king whom they freely chose, and with the same freedom unkinged him if they saw cause, by right of ancient laws and ceremonies yet remaining, and old customs yet among the highlanders in choosing the head of their clans or families; all which, with many other arguments, bore witness, that regal power was nothing else but a mutual covenant or stipulation between king and people. These were Scotchmen and Presbyterians: but what measure then have they lately offered, to think such liberty less beseeming us than themselves, presuming to put him upon us for a master, whom their law scarce allows to be their own equal? If now then we hear them in another strain than heretofore in the purest times of their church, we may be confident it is the voice of faction speaking in them, not of truth and reformation. Which no less in England than in Scotland, by the mouths of those faithful witnesses commonly called puritans and nonconformists, spake as clearly for the putting down, yea, the utmost punishing of kings, as in their several treatises may be read; even from the first reign of Elizabeth to these times. Insomuch that one of them, whose name was Gibson, foretold King James he should be rooted out, and conclude his race, if he persisted to uphold bishops. And that very inscription, stamped upon the first coins at his coronation, a naked sword in a hand with these words, "*Si mereor, in me,*"—"Against me, if I deserve,"—not only manifested the judgment of that state, but seemed also to presage the sentence of divine justice in this event upon his son.

In the year 1581, the states of Holland, in a general assembly at the Hague, abjured all obedience and subjection to Philip, king of Spain; and in a declaration justify their so doing; for that by his tyrannous government, against faith so many times given and broken, he had lost his right to all the Belgic provinces; that therefore they deposed him, and declared it lawful to choose another in his stead. From that time to this, no state or kingdom in the world hath equally prospered: but let them remember not to look with an evil and prejudicial eye upon their neighbours, walking by the same rule.

But what need these examples to presbyterians, I mean to those who now of late would seem so much to abhor deposing, whenas they to all Christendom have given the latest and the liveliest example of doing it themselves? I question not the lawfulness of raising war against a tyrant in defence of religion, or civil liberty; for no protestant church, from the first Waldenses of Lyons and Languedoc to this day, but done it round, and maintained it lawful. But this I doubt not to affirm, that the presbyterians, who now so much condemn deposing, were the men themselves that deposed the king, and cannot, with all their shifting and relapsing, wash off the guiltiness from their own hands. For they themselves, by these their late doings, have made it guiltiness, and turned their own warrantable actions into rebellion.

There is nothing that so actually makes a king of England, as rightful possession and supremacy in all causes both civil and ecclesiastical: and nothing that so actually makes a subject of England as those two oaths of allegiance and supremacy observed without equivocating, or any mental reservation. Out of doubt then, when the king shall command things already constituted in church or state, obedience is the true essence of a subject, either to do, if it be lawful, or if he hold the thing unlawful, to submit to that penalty which the law imposes, so long as he intends to remain a subject. Therefore when the people, or any part of them, shall rise against the king and his authority, executing the law in anything established, civil or ecclesiastical, I do not say it is rebellion, if the thing commanded though established be unlawful, and that they sought first all due means of redress (and no man is further bound to law); but I say it is an absolute renouncing both of supremacy and allegiance, which, in one word, is an actual and total deposing of the king, and the setting up of another supreme authority over them.

And whether the presbyterians have not done all this and much more, they will not put me, I suppose, to reckon up a seven years' story, fresh in the memory of all men. Have they not utterly broke the oath of allegiance, rejecting the king's command and authority sent them from any part of the kingdom, whether in things lawful or unlawful? Have they not abjured the oath of supremacy, by setting up the parliament without the king, supreme to all their obedience; and though their vow and covenant bound them in general to the parliament, yet sometimes adhering to the lesser part of lords and commons that remained faithful, as they term it, and even of them, one while to the commons without the lords, another while to the lords without the commons? Have they not still declared their meaning, whatever their oath were, to hold them only for supreme, whom they found at any time most yielding to what they petitioned? Both these oaths, which were the straitest bond of an English subject in reference to the king, being thus broke and made void; it follows undeniably, that the king from that time was by them in fact absolutely deposed, and they no longer in reality to be thought his subjects, notwithstanding their fine clause in the covenant to preserve his person, crown, and dignity, set there by some dodging casuist with more craft than sincerity, to mitigate the matter, in case of ill success, and not taken, I suppose, by any honest man, but as a condition subordinate to every the least particle, that might more concern religion, liberty, or the public peace.

To prove it yet more plainly, that they are the men who have deposed the king, I thus argue. We know that king and subject are relatives, and relatives have no longer being than in the relation; the relation between king and subject can be no other than regal authority and subjection. Hence I infer, past their defending, that if the subject, who is one relative, take away the relation, of force he takes away also the other relative; but the presbyterians, who were one relative, that is to say, subjects, have for this seven years taken away the relation, that is to say, the king's authority, and their subjection to it; therefore the presbyterians for these seven years have removed and extinguished the other relative, that is to say, the king; or, to speak more in brief, have deposed him; not only by depriving him the execution of his authority, but by conferring it upon others.

If then their oaths of subjection broken, new supremacy obeyed, new oaths and covenant taken, notwithstanding frivolous evasions, have in plain terms unkinged the king, much more than hath their seven years' war, not deposed him only, but outlawed him, and defied him as an alien, a rebel to law, and enemy to the state, it must needs be clear to any man not averse from reason, that hostility and subjection are two direct and positive contraries, and can no more in one subject stand together in respect of the same king, than one person at the same time can be in two remote places. Against whom therefore the subject is in act of hostility, we may be confident, that to him he is in no subjection: and in whom hostility takes place of subjection, for they can by no means consist together, to him the king can be not only no king, but an enemy.

So that from hence we shall not need dispute, whether they have deposed him, or what they have defaulted towards him as no king, but show manifestly how much they have done towards the killing him. Have they not levied all these wars against him, whether offensive or defensive (for defence in war equally offends, and most prudently beforehand), and given commission to slay, where they knew his person could not be exempt from danger? And if chance or flight had not saved him, how often had they killed him, directing their artillery, without blame or prohibition, to the very place where they saw him stand? Have they not sequestered him, judged or unjudged, and converted his revenue to other uses, detaining from him, as a grand delinquent, all means of livelihood, so that for them long since he might have perished, or have starved? Have they not hunted and pursued him round about the kingdom with sword and fire? Have they not formerly denied to treat with him, and their now recanting ministers preached against him, as a reprobate incurable, an enemy to God and his Church, marked for destruction, and therefore not to be treated with? Have they not besieged him, and to their power forbid him water and fire, save what they shot against him to the hazard of his life? Yet while they thus assaulted and endangered it with hostile deeds, they swore in words to defend it, with his crown and dignity; not in order, as it seems now, to a firm and lasting peace, or to his repentance after all this blood; but simply, without regard, without remorse, or any comparable value of all the miseries and calamities suffered by the poor people, or to suffer hereafter, through his obstinacy or impenitence.

No understanding man can be ignorant, that covenants are ever made according to the present state of persons and of things; and have ever the more general laws of nature and of reason included in them, though not expressed. If I make a voluntary covenant, as with a man to do him good, and he prove afterward a monster to me, I should conceive a disobligement. If I covenant, not to hurt an enemy, in favour of him and forbearance, and hope of his amendment, and he, after that, shall do me tenfold injury and mischief to what he had done when I so covenanted, and still be plotting what may tend to my destruction, I question not but that his after-actions release me; nor know I covenant so sacred that withholds me from demanding justice on him.

Howbeit, had not their distrust in a good cause, and the fast and loose of our prevaricating divines, overswayed, it had been doubtless better not to have inserted in a covenant unnecessary obligations, and words, not works of supererogating allegiance to their enemy; no way advantageous to themselves, had the king prevailed, as to their cost many would have felt; but full of snare and distraction to our friends, useful only, as we now find, to our adversaries, who under such a latitude and shelter of ambiguous interpretation have ever since been plotting and contriving new opportunities to trouble all again. How much better had it been, and more becoming an undaunted virtue, to have declared openly and boldly whom and what power the people were to hold supreme, as on the like occasion protestants have done before, and many conscientious men now in these times have more than once besought the parliament to do, that they might go on upon a sure foundation, and not with a riddling covenant in their mouths, seeming to swear counter, almost in the same breath, allegiance and no allegiance; which doubtless had drawn off all the minds of sincere men from siding with them, had they not discerned their actions far more deposing him than their words upholding him; which words, made now the subject of cavillous interpretations, stood ever in the covenant, by judgment of the more discerning sort, an evidence of their fear, not of their fidelity.

What I should return to speak on, of those attempts for which the king himself hath often charged the presbyterians of seeking his life, whenas, in the due estimation of things, they might without a fallacy be said to have done the deed outright? Who knows not, that the king is a name of dignity and office, not of person? Who therefore kills a king, must kill him while he is a king. Then they certainly, who by deposing him have long since taken from him the life of a king, his office and his dignity, they in the truest sense may be said to have killed the king: not only by their deposing and waging war against him, which besides the danger to his personal life, set him in the furthest opposite point from any vital function of a king, but by their holding him in prison, vanquished and yielded into their absolute and despotic power, which brought him to the lowest degradement and incapacity of the regal name. I say not by whose matchless valour, next under God, lest the story of their ingratitude thereupon carry me from the purpose in hand, which is to convince them that they, which I repeat again, were the men who in the truest sense killed the king, not only as is proved before, but by depressing him, their king, far below the rank of a subject to the condition of a captive, without intention to restore him, as the chancellor of Scotland in a speech told him plainly at Newcastle, unless he granted fully all their demands, which they knew he never meant.

Nor did they treat, or think of treating, with him, till their hatred to the army that delivered them, not their love or duty to the king, joined them secretly with men sentenced so oft for reprobates in their own mouths, by whose subtle inspiring they grew mad upon a most tardy and improper treaty. Whereas if the whole bent of their actions had not been against the king himself, but only against his evil counsellors, as they feigned, and published, wherefore did they not restore him all that while to the true life of a king, his office, crown, and dignity, when he was in their power, and they themselves his nearest counsellors? The truth, therefore, is, both that they would not, and that indeed they could not without their own certain destruction, having reduced him to such a final pass, as was the very death and burial of all that in him was regal, and from whence never king of England yet revived, but by the new reinforcement of his own party, which was a kind of resurrection to him.

Thus having quite extinguished all that could be in him of a king, and from a total privation clad him over, like another specifical thing, with forms and habitudes destructive to the former, they left in his person, dead as to law and all the civil right either of king or subject, the life only of a prisoner, a captive, and a malefactor: whom the equal and impartial hand of justice finding, was no more to spare than another ordinary man: not only made obnoxious to the doom of law, by a charge more than once drawn up against him, and his own confession to the first article at Newport, but summoned and arraigned in the sight of God and his people, cursed and devoted to perdition worse than any Ahab, or Antiochus, with exhortation to curse all those in the name of God that made not war against him, as bitterly as Meroz was to be cursed, that went not out against a Canaanitish king, almost in all the sermons, prayers, and fulminations, that have been uttered this seven years, by those cloven tongues of falsehood and dissension, who now, to the stirring up of new discord, acquit him; and against their own discipline, which they boast to be the throne and sceptre of Christ, absolve him, unconfound him, though unconverted, unrepentant, insensible of all their precious saints and martyrs, whose blood they have so often laid upon his head. And now again, with a new sovereign anointment, can wash it all off, as if it were as vile, and no more to be reckoned for than the blood of so many dogs in a time of pestilence: giving the most opprobrious lie to all the acted zeal that for these many years hath filled their bellies, and fed them fat upon the foolish people. Ministers of sedition, not of the gospel, who, while they saw it manifestly tend to civil war and bloodshed, never ceased exasperating the people against him; and now that they see it likely to breed new commotion, cease not to incite others against the people, that have saved them from him, as if sedition were their only aim, whether against him or for him.

But God, as we have cause to trust, will put other thoughts into the people, and turn them from giving ear or heed to these mercenary noisemakers, of whose fury and false prophecies we have enough experience; and from the murmurs of new discord will incline them to hearken rather with erected minds to the voice of our supreme magistracy, calling us to liberty, and the flourishing deeds of a reformed commonwealth; with this hope, that as God was heretofore angry with the Jews who rejected him and his form of government to choose a king, so that He will bless us, and be propitious to us, who reject a king to make Him only our leader, and supreme governor, in the conformity, as near as may be, of His own ancient government; if we have at least but so much worth in us to entertain the sense of our future happiness, and the courage to receive what God vouchsafes us; wherein we have the honour to precede other nations, who are now labouring to be our followers.

For as to this question in hand, what the people by their just right may do in change of government, or of governor, we see it cleared sufficiently besides other ample authority, even from the mouths of princes themselves. And surely they that shall boast, as we do, to be a free nation, and not have in themselves the power to remove or to abolish any governor supreme, or subordinate, with the government itself upon urgent causes, may please their fancy with a ridiculous and painted freedom, fit to cozen babies; but we are indeed under tyranny and servitude, as wanting that power, which is the root and source of all liberty, to dispose and economise in the land which God hath given them, as masters of family in their own house and free inheritance. Without which natural and essential power of a free nation, though bearing high their heads, they can in due esteem be thought no better than slaves and vassals born, in the tenure and occupation of another inheriting lord; whose government, though not illegal, or intolerable, hangs over them as a lordly scourge, not as a free government; and therefore to be abrogated.

How much more justly then may they fling off tyranny, or tyrants; who being once deposed can be no more than private men, as subject to the reach of justice and arraignment as any other transgressors? And certainly if men, not to speak of heathen, both wise and religious, have done justice upon tyrants what way they could soonest, how much more mild and humane then is it to give them fair and open trial; to teach lawless kings, and all who so much adore them, that not mortal man, or his imperious will, but justice, is the only true sovereign and supreme majesty upon earth? Let men cease, therefore, out of faction and hypocrisy, to make outcries and horrid things of things so just and honourable. Though perhaps till now, no protestant state or kingdom can be alleged to have openly put to death their king, which lately some have written, and imputed to their great glory; much mistaking the matter. It is not, neither ought to be, the glory of a protestant state never to have put their king to death; it is the glory of a protestant king never to have deserved death. And if the parliament and military council do what they do without precedent, if it appear their duty, it argues the more wisdom, virtue, and magnanimity, that they know themselves able to be a precedent to others; who perhaps in future ages, if they prove not too degenerate, will look up with honour, and aspire towards these exemplary and matchless deeds of their ancestors, as to the highest top of their civil glory and emulation; which heretofore, in the pursuance of fame and foreign dominion, spent itself vaingloriously abroad; but henceforth may learn a better fortitude, to dare execute highest justice on them that shall by force of arms endeavour the oppressing and bereaving of religion and their liberty at home. That no unbridled potentate or tyrant, but to his sorrow, for the future may presume such high and irresponsible licence over mankind, to havoc and turn upside down whole kingdoms of men, as though they were no more in respect of his perverse will than a nation of pismires.

PREFACE TO "EIKONOKLASTES."

To descant on the misfortunes of a person fallen from so high a dignity, who hath also paid his final debt both to nature and his faults, is neither of itself a thing commendable, nor the intention of this discourse. Neither was it fond ambition, nor the vanity to get a name, present or with posterity, by writing against a king. I never was so thirsty after fame, nor so destitute of other hopes and means, better and more certain to attain it; for kings have gained glorious titles from their favourers by writing against private men, as Henry VIII. did against Luther; but no man ever gained much honour by writing against a king, as not usually meeting with that force of argument in such courtly antagonists, which to convince might add to his reputation. Kings most commonly, though strong in legions, are but weak at argument; as they who ever have accustomed from their cradle to use their will only as their right hand, their reason always as their left. Whence unexpectedly constrained to that kind of combat, they prove but weak and puny adversaries: nevertheless, for their sakes, who through custom, simplicity, or want of better teaching, have not more seriously considered kings, than in the gaudy name of majesty, and admire them and their doings, as if they breathed not the same breath with other mortal men, I shall make no scruple to take up (for it seems to be the challenge both of him and all his party) to take up this gauntlet, though a king's, in the behalf of liberty and the commonwealth.

And further, since it appears manifestly the cunning drift of a factious and defeated party, to make the same advantage

PREFACE TO "EIKONOKLASTES." 93

of his book which they did before of his regal name and authority, and intend it not so much the defence of his former actions, as the promoting of their own future designs (making thereby the book their own rather than the king's, as the benefit now must be their own more than his); now the third time to corrupt and disorder the minds of weaker men, by new suggestions and narrations, either falsely or fallaciously representing the state of things to the dishonour of this present government, and the retarding of a general peace, so needful to this afflicted nation, and so nigh obtained; I suppose it no injury to the dead, but a good deed rather to the living, if by better information given them, or, which is enough, by only remembering them the truth of what they themselves know to be here misaffirmed, they may be kept from entering the third time unadvisedly into war and bloodshed. For as to any moment of solidity in the book itself (save only that a king is said to be the author, a name than which there needs no more among the blockish vulgar, to make it wise, and excellent, and admired, nay to set it next the Bible, though otherwise containing little else but the common grounds of tyranny and popery, dressed up the better to deceive, in a new protestant guise, trimly garnished over), or as to any need of answering, in respect of staid and well-principled men, I take it on me as a work assigned rather, than by me chosen or affected: which was the cause both of beginning it so late, and finishing it so leisurely in the midst of other employments and diversions.

And though well it might have seemed in vain to write at all, considering the envy and almost infinite prejudice likely to be stirred up among the common sort, against whatever can be written or gainsaid to the king's book, so advantageous to a book it is only to be a king's; and though it be an irksome labour, to write with industry and judicious pains, that which, neither weighed nor well read, shall be judged without industry or the pains of well-judging, by faction and the easy literature of custom and opinion; it shall be ventured yet, and the truth not smothered, but sent abroad, in the native confidence of her single self, to earn, how she can, her entertainment in the world, and to find out her own readers: few perhaps, but those few, of such value and substantial worth, as truth and wisdom, not respecting numbers and big names, have been ever wont in all ages to be contented with.

And if the late king had thought sufficient those answers and defences made for him in his lifetime, they who on the other side accused his evil government, judging that on their behalf enough also hath been replied, the heat of this controversy was in all likelihood drawing to an end; and the further mention of his deeds, not so much unfortunate as faulty, had in tenderness to his late sufferings been willingly forborne; and perhaps for the present age might have slept with him unrepeated, while his adversaries, calmed and assuaged with the success of their cause, had been the less unfavourable to his memory. But since he himself, making new appeal to truth and the world, hath left behind him this book, as the best advocate and interpreter of his own actions, and that his friends, by publishing, dispersing, commending, and almost adoring it, seem to place therein the chief strength and nerves of their cause; it would argue doubtless in the other party great deficience and distrust of themselves, not to meet the force of his reason in any field whatsoever, the force and equipage of whose arms they have so often met victoriously. And he who at the bar stood excepting against the form and manner of his judicature, and complained that he was not heard; neither he nor his friends shall have that cause now to find fault, being met and debated with in this open and monumental court of his erecting; and not only heard uttering his whole mind at large, but answered: which to do effectually, if it be necessary, that to his book nothing the more respect be had for being his, they of his own party can have no just reason to exclaim.

For it were too unreasonable that he, because dead, should have the liberty in his book to speak all evil of the parliament; and they, because living, should be expected to have less freedom, or any for them, to speak home the plain truth of a full and pertinent reply. As he, to acquit himself, hath not spared his adversaries to load them with all sorts of blame and accusation, so to him as in his book alive, there will be used no more courtship than he uses; but what is properly his own guilt, not imputed any more to his evil counsellors (a ceremony used longer by the parliament than he himself desired), shall be laid here without circumlocutions at his own door. That they who from the first beginning, or but now of late, by what unhappiness I know not, are so much affatuated, not with his person only, but with his palpable faults, and dote upon his deformities, may have none to blame but their own folly, if they live and die in such a stricken blindness, as next to that of Sodom hath not happened to any sort of men more gross, or more misleading. Yet neither let his enemies expect to find recorded here all that hath been whispered in the court, or alleged openly, of the king's bad actions; it being the proper scope of this work in hand, not to rip up and relate the misdoings of his whole life, but to answer only and refute the missayings of his book.

First, then, that some men (whether this were by him intended, or by his friends) have by policy accomplished after death that revenge upon their enemies, which in life they were not able, hath been oft related. And among other examples we find, that the last will of Cæsar being read to the people, and what bounteous legacies he had bequeathed them, wrought more in that vulgar audience to the avenging of his death, than all the art he could ever use to win their favour in his lifetime. And how much their intent, who published these over-late apologies and meditations of the dead king, drives to the same end of stirring up the people to bring him that honour, that affection, and by consequence that revenge to his dead corpse, which he himself living could never gain to his person, it appears both by the conceited portraiture before his book, drawn out of the full measure of a masking scene, and set there to catch fools and silly gazers; and by those Latin words after the end, *Vota dabunt quæ bella negarunt;* intimating, that what he could not compass by war, he should achieve by his meditations: for in words which admit of various sense, the liberty is ours, to choose that interpretation, which may best mind us of what our restless enemies endeavour, and what we are timely to prevent.

And here may be well observed the loose and negligent curiosity of those, who took upon them to adorn the setting out of this book; for though the picture set in front would martyr him and saint him to befool the people, yet the Latin motto in the end, which they understand not, leaves him, as it were, a politic contriver to bring about that interest, by fair and plausible words, which the force of arms denied him. But quaint emblems and devices, begged from the old pageantry of some twelfthnight's entertainment at Whitehall, will do but ill to make a saint or martyr: and if the people resolve to take him sainted at the canonising, I shall suspect their calendar more than the Gregorian. In one thing I must commend his openness, who gave the title to this book, Εἰκὼν Βασιλικὴ, that is to say, The King's Image; and by the shrine he dresses out for him, certainly would have the people come and worship him. For which reason this answer also is entitled, Eikonoklastes, the famous surname of many Greek emperors, who, in their zeal to the command of God, after long tradition of idolatry in the church, took courage and broke all superstitious images to pieces.

But the people, exorbitant and excessive in all their motions, are prone ofttimes not to a religious only, but to a civil kind of idolatry, in idolising their kings: though never more mistaken in the object of their worship; heretofore being wont to repute for saints those faithful and courageous barons, who lost their lives in the field, making glorious war against tyrants for the common liberty; as Simon de Montfort, Earl of Leicester, against Henry III.; Thomas Plantagenet, Earl of Lancaster, against Edward II. But now, with a besotted and degenerate baseness of spirit, except some few who yet retain in them the old English fortitude and love of freedom, and have testified it by their matchless deeds, the rest, imbastardised from the ancient nobleness of their ancestors, are ready to fall flat, and give adoration to the image and memory of this man, who hath offered at more cunning fetches to undermine our liberties, and put tyranny into an art, than any British king before him. Which low dejection and debasement of mind in the people, I must confess, I cannot willingly ascribe to the natural disposition of an Englishman, but rather to two other causes; first, to the prelates and their fellow-teachers, though of another name and sect, whose pulpit-stuff, both first and last, hath been the doctrine and perpetual infusion of servility and wretchedness to all their hearers, and whose lives the type of worldliness and hypocrisy, without the least true pattern of virtue, righteousness, or self-denial in their whole practice. I attribute it, next to the factious inclination of most men divided from the public by several ends and humours of their own.

At first no man less beloved, no man more generally condemned, than was the king; from the time that it became his custom to break parliaments at home, and either wilfully or weakly to betray protestants abroad, to the beginning of these combustions. All men inveighed against him; all men, except court-vassals, opposed him and his tyrannical proceedings; the cry was universal; and this full parliament was at first unanimous in their dislike and protestation against his evil government. But when they, who sought themselves and not the public, began to doubt, that all of them could not by one and the same way attain to their ambitious purposes, then was the king, or his name at least, as a fit property, first made use of, his doings made the best of, and by degrees justified; which begot him such a party, as, after many wiles and strugglings with his inward fears, emboldened him at length to set up his standard against the parliament: whenas before that time, all his adherents, consisting most of dissolute swordsmen and suburb-roysterers, hardly amounted to the making up of one ragged regiment strong enough to assault the unarmed house of commons. After which attempt seconded by a tedious and bloody war on his subjects, wherein he hath so far exceeded those his arbitrary violences in time of peace, they who before hated him for his high misgovernment, nay, fought against him with displayed banners in the field, now applaud him and extol him for the wisest and most religious prince that lived.

By so strange a method amongst the mad multitude is a sudden reputation won, of wisdom by wilfulness and subtle shifts, of goodness by multiplying evil, of piety by endeavouring to root out true religion.

But it is evident that the chief of his adherents never loved him, never honoured either him or his cause, but as they took him to set a face upon their own malignant designs, nor bemoan his loss at all, but the loss of their own aspiring hopes: like those captive women, whom the poet notes in Iliad, to have bewailed the death of Patroclus in outward show, but indeed their own condition.

Πάτροκλον πρόφασιν, σφῶν δ' αὐτῶν κήδε' ἑκάστη.
Hom. Iliad, τ. 302.

And it needs must be ridiculous to any judgment unenthralled, that they, who in other matters express so little fear either of God or man, should in this one particular outstrip all precisianism with their scruples and cases, and fill men's ears continually with the noise of their conscientious loyalty and allegiance to the king, rebels in the meanwhile to God in all their actions besides: much less that they, whose professed loyalty and allegiance led them to direct arms against the king's person, and thought him nothing violated by the sword of hostility drawn by them against him, should now in earnest think him violated by the unsparing sword of justice, which undoubtedly so much the less in vain she bears among men, by how much greater and in highest place the offender. Else justice, whether moral or political, were not justice, but a false counterfeit of that impartial and godlike virtue. The only grief is, that the head was not struck off to the best advantage and commodity of them that held it by the hair; an ingrateful and perverse generation, who having first cried to God to be delivered from their king, now murmur against God that heard their prayers, and cry as loud for their king against those that delivered them.

But as to the author of these soliloquies, whether it were undoubtedly the late king, as is vulgarly believed, or any secret coadjutor, and some stick not to name him; it can add nothing, nor shall take from the weight, if any be, of reason which he brings. But allegations, not reasons, are the main contents of this book, and need no more than other contrary allegations to lay the question before all men in an even balance; though it were supposed, that the testimony of one man, in his own cause affirming, could be of any moment to bring in doubt the authority of a parliament denying. But if these his fair-spoken words shall be here fairly confronted, and laid parallel to his own far differing deeds, manifest and visible to the whole nation, then surely we may look on them who, notwithstanding, shall persist to give to bare words more credit than to open deeds, as men whose judgment was not rationally evinced and persuaded, but fatally stupefied and bewitched into such a blind and obstinate belief: for whose cure it may be doubted, not whether any charm, though never so wisely murmured, but whether any prayer can be available.

This however would be remembered and well noted, that while the king, instead of that repentance which was in reason and in conscience to be expected from him, without which we could not lawfully readmit him, persists here to maintain and justify the most apparent of his evil doings, and washes over with a court-fucus the worst and foulest of his actions, disables and uncreates the parliament itself, with all our laws and native liberties that ask not his leave, dishonours and attaints all protestant churches not prelatical and what they piously reformed, with the slander of rebellion, sacrilege, and hypocrisy; they, who seemed of late to stand up hottest for the covenant, can now sit mute and much pleased to hear all these opprobrious things uttered against their faith, their freedom, and themselves in their own doings made traitors to boot. The divines, also, their wizards, can be so brazen as to cry Hosanna to this his book, which cries louder against them for no disciples of Christ, but of Iscariot; and to seem now convinced with these withered arguments and reasons here, the same which in some other writings of that party, and in his own former declarations and expresses, they have so often heretofore endeavoured to confute and to explode; none appearing all this while to vindicate church or state from these calumnies and reproaches but a small handful of men, whom they defame and spit at with all the odious names of schism and sectarism. I never knew that time in England, when men of truest religion were not counted sectaries: but wisdom now, valour, justice, constancy, prudence united and embodied to defend religion and our liberties, both by word and deed, against tyranny, is counted schism and faction.

Thus in a graceless age things of highest praise and imitation under a right name, to make them infamous and hateful to the people, are miscalled. Certainly, if ignorance and perverseness will needs be national and universal, then they who adhere to wisdom and to truth, are not therefore to be blamed, for being so few as to seem a sect or faction. But in my opinion it goes not ill with that people where these virtues grow so numerous and well joined together, as to resist and make head against the rage and torrent of that boisterous folly and superstition, that possesses and hurries on the vulgar sort. This therefore we may conclude to be a high honour done us from God, and a special mark of his favour, whom He hath selected as the sole remainder, after all these changes and commotions, to stand upright and steadfast in his cause; dignified with the defence of truth and public liberty; while others, who aspired to be the top of zealots, and had almost brought religion to a kind of trading monopoly, have not only by their late silence and neutrality belied their profession, but foundered themselves and their consciences, to comply with enemies in that wicked cause and interest, which they have too often cursed in others, to prosper now in the same themselves.

FROM "THE SECOND DEFENCE OF THE PEOPLE OF ENGLAND."

LET us now come to the charges which were brought against myself. Is there anything reprehensible in my manners or my conduct? Surely nothing. What no one, not totally divested of all generous sensibility, would have done, he reproaches me with want of beauty and loss of sight.

> "A monster huge and hideous, void of sight."

I certainly never supposed that I should have been obliged to enter into a competition for beauty with the Cyclops; but he immediately corrects himself, and says, "though not indeed huge, for there cannot be a more spare, shrivelled, and bloodless form." It is of no moment to say anything of personal appearance, yet lest (as the Spanish vulgar, implicitly confiding in the relations of their priests, believe of heretics) any one, from the representations of my enemies, should be led to imagine that I have either the head of a dog, or the horn of a rhinoceros, I will say something on the subject, that I may have an opportunity of paying my grateful acknowledgments to the Deity, and of refuting the most shameless lies. I do not believe that I was ever once noted for deformity, by any one who ever saw me; but the praise of beauty I am not anxious to obtain. My stature certainly is not tall; but it rather approaches the middle than the diminutive. Yet what if it were diminutive, when so many men, illustrious both in peace and war, have been the same? And how can that be called diminutive, which is great enough for every virtuous achievement? Nor, though very thin, was I ever deficient in courage or in strength; and I was wont constantly to exercise myself in the use of the broadsword, as long as it comported with my habit and my years. Armed with this weapon, as I usually was, I should have thought myself quite a match for any one, though much stronger than myself; and I felt perfectly secure against the assault of any open enemy. At this moment I have the same courage, the same strength, though not the same eyes; yet so little do they betray any external appearance of injury, that they are as unclouded and bright as the eyes of those who most distinctly see. In this instance alone I am a dissembler against my will. My face, which is said to indicate a total privation of blood, is of a complexion entirely opposite to the pale and the cadaverous; so that, though I am more than forty years old, there is scarcely any one to whom I do not appear ten years younger than I am; and the smoothness of my skin is not, in the least, affected by the wrinkles of age. If there be one particle of falsehood in this relation, I should deservedly incur the ridicule of many thousands of my countrymen, and even many foreigners to whom I am personally known. But if he, in a matter so foreign to his purpose, shall be found to have asserted so many shameless and gratuitous falsehoods, you may the more readily estimate the quantity of his veracity on other topics. Thus much necessity compelled me to assert concerning my personal appearance. Respecting yours, though I have been informed that it is most insignificant and contemptible, a perfect mirror of the worthlessness of your character and the malevolence of your heart, I say nothing, and no one will be anxious that anything should be said. I wish that I could with equal facility refute what this barbarous opponent has said of my blindness; but I cannot do it; and I must submit to the affliction. It is not so wretched to be blind, as it is not to be capable of enduring blindness. But why should I not endure a misfortune, which it behoves every one to be prepared to endure if it should happen; which may, in the common course of things, happen to any man; and which has been known to happen to the most distinguished and virtuous persons in history. Shall I mention those wise and ancient bards, whose misfortunes the gods are said to have compensated by superior endowments, and whom men so much revered, that they chose rather to impute their want of sight to the injustice of heaven than to their own want of innocence or virtue? What is reported of the Augur Tiresias is well known; of whom Apollonius sung thus in his Argonauts:

> " To men he dar'd the will divine disclose,
> Nor fear'd what Jove might in his wrath impose.
> The gods assigned him age, without decay,
> But snatched the blessing of his sight away."

But God himself is truth; in propagating which, as men display a greater integrity and zeal, they approach nearer to the similitude of God, and possess a greater portion of his love. We cannot suppose the Deity envious of truth, or unwilling that it should be freely communicated to mankind. The loss of sight, therefore, which this inspired sage, who was so eager in promoting knowledge among men, sustained, cannot be considered as a judicial punishment. Or shall I mention those worthies who were as distinguished for wisdom in the cabinet, as for valour in the field? And first Timoleon of Corinth, who delivered his city and all Sicily from the yoke of slavery; than whom there never lived in any age, a more virtuous man, or a more incorrupt statesman: next Appius Claudius, whose discreet counsels in the senate, though they could not restore sight to his own eyes, saved Italy from the formidable inroads of Pyrrhus: then Cæcilius Metellus the high-priest, who lost his sight, while he saved, not only the city, but the palladium, the protection of the city, and the most sacred relics, from the destruction of the flames. On other occasions Providence has indeed given conspicuous proofs of its regard for such singular exertions of patriotism and virtue; what, therefore, happened to so great and so good a man, I can hardly place in the catalogue of misfortunes. Why should I mention others of later times, as Dandolo of Venice, the incomparable Doge; or Boemar Zisca, the bravest of generals, and the champion of the cross; or Jerome Zanchius, and some other theologians of the highest reputation? For it is evident that the patriarch Isaac, than whom no man ever enjoyed more of the divine regard, lived blind for many years; and perhaps also his son Jacob, who was equally an object of the divine benevolence. And in short, did not our Saviour himself clearly declare that that poor man whom he restored to sight had not been born blind, either on account of his own sins or those of his progenitors? And with respect to myself, though I have accurately examined my conduct, and scrutinised my soul, I call thee, O God, the searcher of hearts, to witness, that I am not conscious, either in the more early or in the later periods of my life, of having committed any enormity, which might deservedly have marked me out as a fit object for such a calamitous visitation. But since my enemies boast that this affliction is only a retribution for the transgressions of my pen, I again invoke the Almighty to witness, that I never, at any time, wrote anything which I did not think agreeable to truth, to justice, and to piety. This was my persuasion then, and I feel the same persuasion now. Nor was I ever prompted to such exertions by the influence of ambition, by the lust of lucre or of praise; it was only by the conviction of duty and the feeling of patriotism, a disinterested passion for the extension of civil and religious liberty. Thus, therefore, when I was publicly solicited to write a reply to the Defence of the royal cause, when I had to contend with the pressure of sickness, and with the apprehension of soon losing the sight of my remaining eye, and when my medical attendants clearly announced, that if I did engage in the work, it would be irreparably lost, their premonitions caused no hesitation and inspired no dismay. I would not have listened to the voice even of Esculapius himself from the shrine of Epidauris, in preference to the suggestions of the heavenly monitor within my breast; my resolution was unshaken, though the alternative was either the loss of my sight, or the desertion of my duty: and I called to mind those two destinies, which the oracle of Delphi announced to the son of Thetis—

> "Two fates may lead me to the realms of night;
> If staying here, around Troy's wall I fight,
> To my dear home no more must I return;
> But lasting glory will adorn my urn.
> But, if I withdraw from the martial strife,
> Short is my fame, but long will be my life."—*Il.* ix.

I considered that many had purchased a less good by a greater evil, the meed of glory by the loss of life; but that I might procure great good by little suffering; that though I am blind, I might still discharge the most honourable duties, the performance of which, as it is something more durable than glory, ought to be an object of superior admiration and esteem; I resolved, therefore, to make the short interval of sight, which was left me to enjoy, as beneficial as possible to the public interest. Thus it is clear by what motives I was governed in the measures which I took, and the losses which I sustained. Let then the calumniators of the divine goodness cease to revile, or to make me the object of their superstitious imaginations. Let them consider, that my situation, such as it is, is neither an object of my shame or my regret, that my resolutions are too firm to be shaken, that I am not depressed by any sense of the divine displeasure; that, on the other hand, in the most momentous periods, I have had full experience of the divine favour and protection; and that, in the solace and the strength which have been infused into me from above, I have been enabled to do the will of God; that I may oftener think on what He has bestowed, than on what He has withheld; that, in short, I am unwilling to exchange my consciousness of rectitude with that of any other person; and that I feel the recollection a treasured store of tranquillity and delight. But, if the choice were necessary, I would, sir, prefer my blindness to yours : yours is a cloud spread over the mind, which darkens both the light of reason and of conscience; mine keeps from my view only the coloured surfaces of things, while it leaves me at liberty to contemplate the beauty and stability of virtue and of truth. How many things are there besides which I would not willingly see; how many which I must see against my will; and how few which I feel any anxiety to see! There is, as the apostle has remarked, a way to strength through weakness. Let me then be the most feeble creature alive, as long as that feebleness serves to invigorate the energies of my rational and immortal spirit; as long as in that obscurity, in which I am enveloped, the light of the divine presence more clearly shines, then, in proportion as I am weak, I shall be invincibly strong; and in proportion as I am blind, I shall more clearly see. Oh, that I may thus be perfected by feebleness, and irradiated by obscurity! And, indeed, in my blindness, I enjoy in no inconsiderable degree the favour of the Deity, who regards me with more tenderness and compassion in proportion as I am able to behold nothing but Himself. Alas! for him who insults me, who maligns and merits public execration! For the divine law not only shields me from injury, but almost renders me too sacred to attack; not indeed so much from the privation of my sight, as from the overshadowing of those heavenly wings which seem to have occasioned this obscurity; and which, when occasioned, he is wont to illuminate with an interior light, more precious and more pure. To this I ascribe the more tender assiduities of my friends, their soothing attentions, their kind visits, their reverential observances; among whom there are some with whom I may interchange the Pyladean and Thesean dialogue of inseparable friends—

"OREST. Proceed, and be rudder of my feet, by showing me the most endearing love."

Eurip. in Orest.

And in another place,

" Lend your hand to your devoted friend,
Throw your arm round my neck, and I will conduct
you on the way."

This extraordinary kindness, which I experience, cannot be any

THE SECOND DEFENCE.

fortuitous combination; and friends, such as mine, do not suppose that all the virtues of a man are contained in his eyes. Nor do the persons of principal distinction in the commonwealth suffer me to be bereaved of comfort, when they see me bereaved of sight, amid the exertions which I made, the zeal which I showed, and the dangers which I run for the liberty which I love. But, soberly reflecting on the casualties of human life, they show me favour and indulgence, as to a soldier who has served his time, and kindly concede to me an exemption from care and toil. They do not strip me of the badges of honour which I have once worn; they do not deprive me of the places of public trust to which I have been appointed; they do not abridge my salary or emoluments; which, though I may not do so much to deserve as I did formerly, they are too considerate and too kind to take away; and, in short, they honour me as much as the Athenians did those whom they determined to support at the public expense in the Prytaneum. Thus, while both God and man unite in solacing me under the weight of my affliction, let no one lament my loss of sight in so honourable a cause. And let me not indulge in unavailing grief, or want the courage either to despise the revilers of my blindness, or the forbearance easily to pardon the offence.

. . . .

I will now mention who and whence I am. I was born at London, of an honest family; my father was distinguished by the undeviating integrity of his life; my mother, by the esteem in which she was held, and the alms which she bestowed. My father destined me from a child to the pursuits of literature; and my appetite for knowledge was so voracious, that, from twelve years of age, I hardly ever left my studies, or went to bed before midnight. This primarily led to my loss of sight. My eyes were naturally weak, and I was subject to frequent headaches; which, however, could not chill the ardour of my curiosity, or retard the progress of my improvement. My father had me daily instructed in the grammar-school, and by other masters at home. He then, after I had acquired a proficiency in various languages, and had made a considerable progress in philosophy, sent me to the University of Cambridge. Here I passed seven years in the usual course of instruction and study, with the approbation of the good, and without any stain upon my character, till I took the degree of Master of Arts. After this I did not, as this miscreant feigns, run away into Italy, but of my own accord retired to my father's house, whither I was accompanied by the regrets of most of the fellows of the college, who showed me no common marks of friendship and esteem. On my father's estate, where he had determined to pass the remainder of his days, I enjoyed an interval of uninterrupted leisure, which I entirely devoted to the perusal of the Greek and Latin classics; though I occasionally visited the metropolis, either for the sake of purchasing books, or of learning something new in mathematics or in music, in which I, at that time, found a source of pleasure and amusement. In this manner I spent five years till my mother's death. I then became anxious to visit foreign parts, and particularly Italy. My father gave me his permission, and I left home with one servant. On my departure, the celebrated Henry Wootton, who had long been King James's ambassador at Venice, gave me a signal proof of his regard, in an elegant letter which he wrote, breathing not only the warmest friendship, but containing some maxims of conduct which I found very useful in my travels. The noble Thomas Scudamore, King Charles's ambassador, to whom I carried letters of recommendation, received me most courteously at Paris. His lordship gave me a card of introduction to the learned Hugo Grotius, at that time ambassador from the Queen of Sweden to the French court; whose acquaintance I anxiously desired, and to whose house I was accompanied by some of his lordship's friends. A few days after, when I set out for Italy, he gave me letters to the English merchants on my route, that they might show me any civilities in their power. Taking ship at Nice, I arrived at Genoa, and afterwards visited Leghorn, Pisa, and Florence. In the latter city, which I have always more particularly esteemed for the elegance of its dialect, its genius, and its taste, I stopped about two months; when I contracted an intimacy with many persons of rank and learning; and was a constant attendant at their literary parties; a practice which prevails there, and tends so much to the diffusion of knowledge, and the preservation of friendship. No time will ever abolish the agreeable recollections which I cherish of Jacob Gaddi, Carolo Dati, Frescobaldo, Cultellero, Bonomatthai, Clementillo, Francisco, and many others. From Florence I went to Siena, thence to Rome, where, after I had spent about two months in viewing the antiquities of that renowned city, where I experienced the most friendly attentions from Lucas Holstein, and other learned and ingenious men, I continued my route to Naples. There I was introduced by a certain recluse, with whom I had travelled from Rome, to John Baptista Manso, marquis of Villa, a nobleman of distinguished rank and authority, to whom Torquato Tasso, the illustrious poet, inscribed his book on friendship. During my stay, he gave me singular proofs of his regard: he himself conducted me round the city, and to the palace of the viceroy; and more than once paid me a visit at my lodgings. On my departure he gravely apologised for not having shown me more civility, which he said he had been restrained from doing, because I had spoken with so little reserve on matters of religion. When I was preparing to pass over into Sicily and Greece, the melancholy intelligence which I received of the civil commotions in England made me alter my purpose; for I thought it base to be travelling for amusement abroad, while my fellow-citizens were fighting for liberty at home. While I was on my way back to Rome, some merchants informed me that the English Jesuits had formed a plot against me if I returned to Rome, because I had spoken too freely on religion; for it was a rule which I laid down to myself in those places, never to be the first to begin any conversation on religion; but if any questions were put to me concerning my faith, to declare it without any reserve or fear. I, nevertheless, returned to Rome. I took no steps to conceal either my person or my character; and for about the space of two months I again openly defended, as I had done before, the reformed religion in the very metropolis of popery. By the favour of God, I got safe back to Florence, where I was received with as much affection as if I had returned to my native country. There I stopped as many months as I had done before, except that I made an excursion for a few days to Lucca; and, crossing the Apennines, passed through Bologna and Ferrara to Venice. After I had spent a month in surveying the curiosities of this city, and had put on board a ship the books which I had collected in Italy, I proceeded through Verona and Milan, and along the Leman lake to Geneva. The mention of this city brings to my recollection the slandering More, and makes me again call the Deity to witness, that in all those places in which vice meets with so little discouragement, and is practised with so little shame, I never once deviated from the paths of integrity and virtue, and perpetually reflected that, though my conduct might escape the notice of men, it could not elude the inspection of God. At Geneva I held daily conferences with John Deodati, the learned professor of Theology. Then pursuing my former route through France, I returned to my native country, after an absence of one year and about three months; at the time when Charles, having broken the peace, was renewing what is called the episcopal war with the Scots, in which the royalists being routed in the first encounter, and the English being universally and justly disaffected, the necessity of his affairs at last obliged him to convene a parliament. As soon as I was able, I hired a spacious house in the city for myself and my books; where I again with rapture renewed my literary pursuits, and where I calmly awaited the issue of the contest, which I trusted to the wise conduct of Providence, and to the courage of the people. The vigour of the parliament had begun to humble the pride of the bishops. As long as the liberty of speech was no longer subject to control, all mouths began to be opened against the bishops; some complained of the vices of the individuals, others of those of the order. They said that it was unjust that they alone should differ from the model of other reformed churches; that the government of the church should be according to the pattern of other churches, and particularly the Word of God. This awakened all my attention and my zeal. I saw that a way was opening for the establishment of real liberty; that the foundation was laying for the deliverance of man from the yoke of slavery and superstition; that the principles of religion, which were the first objects of our care, would exert a salutary influence on the manners and constitution of the republic; and as I had from my youth studied the distinctions between religious and civil rights, I perceived that if I ever wished to be of use, I ought at least not to be wanting to my country, to the church, and to so many of my fellow-Christians, in a crisis of so much danger; I therefore determined to relinquish the other pursuits in which I was engaged, and to transfer the whole force of my talents and my industry to this one important object. I accordingly wrote two books to a friend concerning the reformation of the Church of England. Afterwards, when two bishops of superior distinction vindicated their privileges against some principal ministers, I thought that on those topics, to the consideration of which I was led solely by my love of truth, and my reverence for Christianity, I should not probably write worse than those who were contending only for their own emoluments and usurpations. I therefore answered the one in two books, of which the first is inscribed, "Concerning Prelatical Episcopacy," and the other "Concerning the Mode of Ecclesiastical Government"; and I replied to the other in some "Animadversions," and soon after in an "Apology." On this occasion it was supposed that I brought a timely succour to the ministers, who were hardly a match for the eloquence of their opponents; and from that time I was actively employed in refuting any answers that appeared. When the bishops could no longer resist the multitude of their assailants, I had leisure to turn my thoughts to other subjects; to the promotion of real and substantial liberty; which is rather to be sought from within than from without; and whose existence depends, not so much on the terror of the sword, as on sobriety of conduct and integrity of life.

When, therefore, I perceived that there were three species of liberty which are essential to the happiness of social life—religious, domestic, and civil; and as I had already written concerning the first, and the magistrates were strenuously active in obtaining the third, I determined to turn my attention to the second, or the domestic species. As this seemed to involve three material questions, the conditions of the conjugal tie, the education of the children, and the free publication of the thoughts, I made them objects of distinct consideration. I explained my sentiments, not only concerning the solemnisation of the marriage, but the dissolution, if circumstances rendered it necessary; and I drew my arguments from the divine law, which Christ did not abolish, or publish another more grievous than that of Moses. I stated my own opinions, and those of others, concerning the exclusive exception of fornication, which our illustrious Selden has since, in his *Hebrew Wife*, more copiously discussed; for he in vain makes a vaunt of liberty in the senate or in the forum, who languishes under the vilest servitude, to an inferior at home. On this subject, therefore, I published some books which were more particularly necessary at that time, when man and wife were often the most inveterate foes, when the man often stayed to take care of his children at home, while the mother of the family was seen in the camp of the enemy, threatening death and destruction to her husband. I then discussed the principles of education in a summary manner, but sufficiently copious for those who attend seriously to the subject; than which nothing can be more necessary to principle the minds of men in virtue, the only genuine source of political and individual liberty, the only true safeguard of states, the bulwark of their prosperity and renown. Lastly, I wrote my "Areopagitica," in order to deliver the press from the restraints with which it was encumbered; that the power of determining what was true and what was false, what ought to be published and what to be suppressed, might no longer be entrusted to a few illiterate and illiberal individuals, who refused their sanction to any work which contained views or sentiments at all above the level of the vulgar superstition.

On the last species of civil liberty, I said nothing, because I saw that sufficient attention was paid to it by the magistrates; nor did I write anything on the prerogative of the crown, till the king, voted an enemy by the parliament, and vanquished in the field, was summoned before the tribunal which condemned him to lose his head. But when, at length, some presbyterian ministers, who had formerly been the most bitter enemies to Charles, became jealous of the growth of the independents, and of their ascendency in the parliament, most tumultuously clamoured against the sentence, and did all in their power to prevent the execution, though they were not angry, so much on account of the act itself, as because it was not the act of their party; and when they dared to affirm, that the doctrine of the protestants, and of all the reformed churches, was abhorrent to such an atrocious proceeding against kings; I thought that it became me to oppose such a glaring falsehood; and accordingly, without any immediate or personal application to Charles, I showed, in an abstract consideration of the question, what might lawfully be done against tyrants; and in support of what I advanced, produced the opinions of the most celebrated divines; while I vehemently inveighed against the egregious ignorance or effrontery of men, who professed better things, and from whom better things might have been expected. That book did not make its appearance till after the death of Charles; and was written rather to reconcile the minds of the people to the event, than to discuss the legitimacy of that particular sentence which concerned the magistrates, and which was already executed. Such were the fruits of my private studies, which I gratuitously presented to the church and to the state; and for which I was recompensed by nothing but impunity; though the actions themselves procured me peace of conscience, and the approbation of the good; while I exercised that freedom of discussion which I loved. Others, without labour or desert, got possession of honours and emoluments; but no one ever knew me either soliciting anything myself or through the medium of my friends, ever beheld me in a supplicating posture at the doors of the senate, or the levees of the great. I usually kept myself secluded at home, where my own property, part of which had been withheld during the civil commotions, and part of which had been absorbed in the oppressive contributions which I had to sustain, afforded me a scanty subsistence. When I was released from these engagements, and thought that I was about to enjoy an interval of uninterrupted ease, I turned my thoughts to a continued history of my country, from the earliest times to the present period. I had already finished four books, when, after the subversion of the monarchy, and the establishment of a republic, I was surprised by an invitation from the council of state, who desired my services in the office for foreign affairs. A book appeared soon after, which was ascribed to the king, and contained the most invidious charges against the parliament. I was ordered to answer it; and opposed the Iconoclast to his Icon. I did not insult over fallen majesty, as is pretended; I only preferred queen Truth to king Charles. The charge of insult, which I saw that the malevolent would urge, I was at some pains to remove in the beginning of the work; and as often as possible in other places. Salmasius then appeared, to whom they were not, as More says, long in looking about for an opponent, but immediately appointed me, who happened at the time to be present in the council.

. . . .

In speaking of such a man, who has merited so well of his country, I should do nothing if I only exculpated him from crimes; particularly since it not only so nearly concerns the country, but even myself, who am so closely implicated in the same disgrace, to evince to all nations, and, as far as I can, to all ages, the excellence of his character, and the splendour of his renown. Oliver Cromwell was sprung from a line of illustrious ancestors, who were distinguished for the civil functions which they sustained under the monarchy, and still more for the part which they took in restoring and establishing true religion in this country. In the vigour and maturity of his life, which he passed in retirement, he was conspicuous for nothing more than for the strictness of his religious habits, and the innocence of his life; and he had tacitly cherished in his breast that flame of piety which was afterwards to stand him in so much stead on the greatest occasions, and in the most critical exigencies. In the last parliament which was called by the king, he was elected to represent his native town, when he soon became distinguished by the justness of his opinions, and the vigour and decision of his councils. When the sword was drawn, he offered his services, and was appointed to a troop of horse, whose numbers were soon increased by the pious and the good, who flocked from all quarters to his standard; and in a short time he almost surpassed the greatest generals in the magnitude and the rapidity of his achievements. Nor is this surprising; for he was a soldier disciplined to perfection in the knowledge of himself. He had either extinguished, or by habit had learned to subdue, the whole host of vain hopes, fears, and passions, which infest the soul. He first acquired the government of himself, and over himself acquired the most signal victories; so that on the first day he took the field against the external enemy, he was a veteran in arms, consummately practised in the toils and exigencies of war. It is not possible for me in the narrow limits in which I circumscribe myself on this occasion, to enumerate the many towns which he has taken, the many battles which he has won. The whole surface of the British empire has been the scene of his exploits, and the theatre of his triumphs; which alone would furnish ample materials for a history, and want a copiousness of narration not inferior to the magnitude and diversity of the transactions. This alone seems to be a sufficient proof of his extraordinary and almost supernatural virtue, that by the vigour of his genius, or the excellence of his discipline, adapted, not more to the necessities of war than to the precepts of Christianity, the good and the brave were from all quarters attracted to his camp, not only as to the best school of military talents, but of piety and virtue; and that during the whole war, and the occasional intervals of peace, amid so many vicissitudes of faction and of events, he retained and still retains the obedience of his troops, not by largesses or indulgence, but by his sole authority and the regularity of his pay. In this instance his fame may rival that of Cyrus, of Epaminondas, or any of the great generals of antiquity. Hence he collected an army as numerous and as well equipped as any one ever did in so short a time; which was uniformly obedient to his orders, and dear to the affections of the citizens; which was formidable to the enemy in the field, but never cruel to those who laid down their arms; which committed no lawless ravages on the persons or the property of the inhabitants; who, when they compared their conduct with the turbulence, the intemperance, the impiety, and the debauchery of the royalists, were wont to salute them as friends, and to consider them as guests. They were a stay to the good, a terror to the evil, and the warmest advocates for every exertion of piety and virtue. Nor would it be right to pass over the name of Fairfax, who united the utmost fortitude with the utmost courage; and the spotless innocence of whose life seemed to point him out as the peculiar favourite of Heaven. Justly, indeed, may you be excited to receive this wreath of praise; though you have retired as much as possible from the world, and seek those shades of privacy which were the delight of Scipio. Nor was it only the enemy whom you subdued, but you have triumphed over that flame of ambition and that lust of glory which are wont to make the best and the greatest of men their slaves. The purity of your virtues and the splendour of your actions consecrate those sweets of ease which you enjoy, and which constitute the wished-for haven of the toils of man. Such was the ease which, when the heroes of antiquity possessed, after a life of exertion and glory not greater than yours, the poets, in despair of finding ideas or expressions better suited to the subject, feigned that they were received into heaven, and invited to recline at the tables of the gods. But whether it were your health, which I principally believe, or any other motive which caused you to retire, of this I am convinced, that nothing could have induced you to relinquish the service of your country; if you had not known that in your successor liberty would meet with a protector, and England with a stay to its safety, and a pillar to its glory. For, while you, O Cromwell, are left among us, he hardly shows a proper confidence in the Supreme, who distrusts the security of England; when he sees that you are in so special a manner the favoured object of the divine regard. But there was another department of the war, which was destined for your exclusive exertions.

Without entering into any length of detail, I will, if possible, describe some of the most memorable actions, with as much brevity as you performed them with celerity. After the loss of all Ireland, with the exception of one city, you in one battle immediately discomfited the forces of the rebels: and were busily employed in settling the country, when you were suddenly recalled to the war in Scotland. Hence you proceeded with unwearied diligence against the Scots, who were on the point of making an irruption into England with the king in their train: and in about the space of one year you entirely subdued, and added to the English dominion, that kingdom which all our monarchs, during a period of 800 years, had in vain struggled to subject. In one battle you almost annihilated the remainder of their forces, who, in a fit of desperation had made a sudden incursion into England, then almost destitute of garrisons, and got as far as Worcester; where you came up with them by forced marches, and captured almost the whole of their nobility. A profound peace ensued; when we found, though indeed not then for the first time, that you was as wise in the cabinet as valiant in the field. It was your constant endeavour in the senate either to induce them to adhere to those treaties which they had entered into with the enemy, or speedily to adjust others which promised to be beneficial to the country. But when you saw that the business was artfully procrastinated, that every one was more intent on his own selfish interest than on the public good, that the people complained of the disappointments which they had experienced, and the fallacious promises by which they had been gulled, that they were the dupes of a few overbearing individuals, you put an end to their domination. A new parliament is summoned; and the right of election given to those to whom it was expedient. They meet; but do nothing; and, after having wearied themselves by their mutual dissensions, and fully exposed their incapacity to the observation of the country, they consent to a voluntary dissolution. In this state of desolation, to which we were reduced, you, O Cromwell! alone remained to conduct the government, and to save the country. We all willingly yield the palm of sovereignty to your unrivalled ability and virtue, except the few among us, who, either ambitious of honours which they have not the capacity to sustain, or who envy those which are conferred on one more worthy than themselves, or else who do not know that nothing in the world is more pleasing to God, more agreeable to reason, more politically just, or more generally useful, than that the supreme power should be vested in the best and the wisest of men. Such, O Cromwell, all acknowledge you to be; such are the services which you have rendered, as the leader of our councils, the general of our armies, and the father of your country. For this is the tender appellation by which all the good among us salute you from the very soul. Other names you neither have nor could endure; and you deservedly reject that pomp of title which attracts the gaze and admiration of the multitude. For what is a title but a certain definite mode of dignity; but actions such as yours surpass, not only the bounds of our admiration, but our titles; and, like the points of pyramids, which are lost in the clouds, they soar above the possibilities of titular commendation. But since, though it be not fit, it may be expedient, that the highest pitch of virtue should be circumscribed within the bounds of some human appellation, you endured to receive, for the public good, a title most like to that of the father of your country; not to exalt, but rather to bring you nearer to the level of ordinary men; the title of king was unworthy the transcendent majesty of your character. For if you had been captivated by a name over which, as a private man, you had so completely triumphed and crumbled into dust, you would have been doing the same thing as if, after having subdued some idolatrous nation by the help of the true God, you should afterwards fall down and worship the gods which you had vanquished. Do you then, sir, continue your course with the same unrivalled magnanimity; it sits well upon you;—to you our country owes its liberties; nor can you sustain a character at once more momentous and more august than that of the author, the guardian, and the preserver of our liberties; and hence you have not only eclipsed the achievements of all our kings, but even those which have been fabled of our heroes. Often reflect what a dear pledge the beloved land of your nativity has entrusted to your care; and that liberty which she once expected only from the chosen flower of her talents and her virtues, she now expects from you only, and by you only hopes to obtain. Revere the fond expectations which we cherish, the solicitudes of your anxious country; revere the looks and the wounds of your brave companions in arms, who, under your banners, have so strenuously fought for liberty; revere the shades of those who perished in the contest; revere also the opinions and the hopes which foreign states entertain concerning us, who promise to themselves so many advantages from that liberty which we have so bravely acquired, from the establishment of that new government which has begun to shed its splendour on the world, which, if it be suffered to vanish like a dream, would involve us in the deepest abyss of shame; and lastly, revere yourself; and, after having endured so many sufferings and encountered so many perils for the sake of liberty, do not suffer it, now it is obtained, either to be violated by yourself, or in any one instance impaired by others. You cannot be truly free unless we are free too; for such is the nature of things, that he who entrenches on the liberty of others, is the first to lose his own and become a slave. But if you, who have hitherto been the patron and tutelary genius of liberty, if you, who are exceeded by no one in justice, in piety, and goodness, should hereafter invade that liberty which you have defended, your conduct must be fatally operative, not only against the cause of liberty, but the general interests of piety and virtue. Your integrity and virtue will appear to have evaporated, your faith in religion to have been small; your character with posterity will dwindle into insignificance, by which a most destructive blow will be levelled against the happiness of mankind. The work which you have undertaken is of incalculable moment, which will thoroughly sift and expose every principle and sensation of your heart, which will fully display the vigour and genius of your character, which will evince whether you really possess those great qualities of piety, fidelity, justice, and self-denial, which made us believe that you were elevated by the special direction of the Deity to the highest pinnacle of power. At once wisely and discreetly to hold the sceptre over three powerful nations, to persuade people to relinquish inveterate and corrupt for new and more beneficial maxims and institutions, to penetrate into the remotest parts of the country, to have the mind present and operative in every quarter, to watch against surprise, to provide against danger, to reject the blandishments of pleasure and pomp of power;—these are exertions compared with which the labour of war is mere pastime; which will require every energy and employ every faculty that you possess; which demand a man supported from above, and almost instructed by immediate inspiration. These and more than these are, no doubt, the objects which occupy your attention and engross your soul; as well as the means by which you may accomplish these important ends, and render our liberty at once more ample and more secure. And this you can, in my opinion, in no other way so readily effect, as by associating in your councils the companions of your dangers and your toils; men of exemplary modesty, integrity, and courage; whose hearts have not been hardened in cruelty and rendered insensible to pity by the sight of so much ravage and so much death, but whom it has rather inspired with the love of justice, with a respect for religion, and with the feeling of compassion, and who are more zealously interested in the preservation of liberty, in proportion as they have encountered more perils in its defence. They are not strangers or foreigners, a hireling rout scraped together from the dregs of the people, but, for the most part, men of the better conditions in life, of families not disgraced if not ennobled, of fortunes either ample or moderate; and what if some among them are recommended by their poverty? for it was not the lust of ravage which brought them into the field; it was the calamitous aspect of the times, which, in the most critical circumstances, and often amid the most disastrous turn of fortune, roused them to attempt the deliverance of their country from the fangs of despotism. They were men prepared, not only to debate, but to fight; not only to argue in the senate, but to engage the enemy in the field. But unless we will continually cherish indefinite and illusory expectations, I see not in whom we can place any confidence, if not in these men and such as these. We have the surest and most indubitable pledge of their fidelity in this, that they have already exposed themselves to death in the service of their country; of their piety in this, that they have been always wont to ascribe the whole glory of their successes to the favour of the Deity, whose help they have so suppliantly implored, and so conspicuously obtained; of their justice in this, that they even brought the king to trial, and when his guilt was proved, refused to save his life; of their moderation in our own uniform experience of its effects, and because, if by any outrage, they should disturb the peace which they have procured, they themselves will be the first to feel the miseries which it will occasion, the first to meet the havoc of the sword, and the first again to risk their lives for all those comforts and distinctions which they have so happily acquired; and lastly, of their fortitude in this, that there is no instance of any people who ever recovered their liberty with so much courage and success; and therefore let us not suppose, that there can be any persons who will be more zealous in preserving it. I now feel myself irresistibly compelled to commemorate the names of some of those who have most conspicuously signalised themselves in these times: and first thine, O Fleetwood! whom I have known from a boy to the present blooming maturity of your military fame, to have been inferior to none in humanity, in gentleness, in benignity of disposition, whose intrepidity in the combat, and whose clemency in victory, have been acknowledged even by the enemy: next thine, O

Lambert! who, with a mere handful of men, checked the progress, and sustained the attack, of the Duke of Hamilton, who was attended by the whole flower and vigour of the Scottish youth: next thine, O Desborough! and thine, O Hawley! who wast always conspicuous in the heat of the combat, and the thickest of the fight: thine, O Overton! who hast been most endeared to me now for so many years by the similitude of our studies, the suavity of your manners, and the more than fraternal sympathy of our hearts; you, who, in the memorable battle of Marston Moor, when our left wing was put to the rout, were beheld with admiration, making head against the enemy with your infantry and repelling his attack, amid the thickest of the carnage; and lastly, you, who, in the Scotch war, when under the auspices of Cromwell, occupied the coast of Fife, opened a passage beyond Stirling, and made the Scotch of the west, and of the north, and even the remotest Orkneys, confess your humanity, and submit to your power. Besides these, I will mention some as celebrated for their political wisdom and their civil virtues, whom you, sir, have admitted into your councils, and who are known to me by friendship or by fame. Whitlocke, Pickering, Strickland, Sydenham, Sydney (a name indissolubly attached to the interests of liberty), Montacute, Laurence, both of highly cultivated minds and polished taste; besides many other citizens of singular merit, some of whom were distinguished by their exertions in the senate, and others in the field. To these men, whose talents are so splendid, and whose worth has been so thoroughly tried, you would without doubt do right to trust the protection of our liberties; nor would it be easy to say to whom they might more safely be entrusted. Then, if you leave the church to its own government, and relieve yourself and the other public functionaries from a charge so onerous, and so incompatible with your functions; and will no longer suffer two powers, so different as the civil and the ecclesiastical, to commit fornication together, and by their mutual and delusive aids in appearance to strengthen, but in reality to weaken and finally to subvert, each other; if you shall remove all power of persecution out of the church (but persecution will never cease, so long as men are bribed to preach the gospel by a mercenary salary, which is forcibly extorted, rather than gratuitously bestowed, which serves only to poison religion and to strangle truth), you will then effectually have cast those money-changers out of the temple, who do not merely truckle with doves but with the Dove itself, with the Spirit of the Most High. Then, since there are often in a republic men who have the same itch for making a multiplicity of laws, as some poetasters have for making many verses, and since laws are usually worse in proportion as they are more numerous, if you shall not enact so many new laws as you abolish old, which do not operate so much as warnings against evil, as impediments in the way of good; and if you shall retain only those which are necessary, which do not confound the distinctions of good and evil, which while they prevent the frauds of the wicked, do not prohibit the innocent freedoms of the good, which punish crimes, without interdicting those things which are lawful only on account of the abuses to which they may occasionally be exposed. For the intention of laws is to check the commission of vice; but liberty is the best school of virtue, and affords the strongest encouragements to the practice. Then, if you make a better provision for the education of our youth than has hitherto been made, if you prevent the promiscuous instruction of the docile and the indocile, of the idle and the diligent, at the public cost, but reserve the rewards of learning for the learned, and of merit for the meritorious. If you permit the free discussion of truth without any hazard to the author, or any subjection to the caprice of an individual, which is the best way to make truth flourish and knowledge abound, the censure of the half-learned, the envy, the pusillanimity, or the prejudice which measures the discoveries of others, and in short every degree of wisdom, by the measure of its own capacity, will be prevented from doling out information to us according to their own arbitrary choice. Lastly, if you shall not dread to hear any truth, or any falsehood, whatever it may be, but if you shall least of all listen to those who think that they can never be free till the liberties of others depend on their caprice, and who attempt nothing with so much zeal and vehemence as to fetter, not only the bodies but the minds of men, who labour to introduce into the state the worst of all tyrannies, the tyranny of their own depraved habits and pernicious opinions; you will always be dear to those who think not merely that their own sect or faction, but that all citizens of all descriptions, should enjoy equal rights and equal laws. If there be any one who thinks that this is not liberty enough, he appears to me to be rather inflamed with the lust of ambition or of anarchy, than with the love of a genuine and well-regulated liberty; and particularly since the circumstances of the country, which has been so convulsed by the storms of faction, which are yet hardly still, do not permit us to adopt a more perfect or desirable form of government.

For it is of no little consequence, O citizens, by what principles you are governed, either in acquiring liberty, or in retaining it when acquired. And unless that liberty which is of such a kind as arms can neither procure nor take away, which alone is the fruit of piety, of justice, of temperance, and unadulterated virtue, shall have taken deep root in your minds and hearts, there will not long be wanting one who will snatch from you by treachery what you have acquired by arms. War has made many great whom peace makes small. If after being released from the toils of war, you neglect the arts of peace, if your peace and your liberty be a state of warfare, if war be your only virtue, the summit of your praise, you will, believe me, soon find peace the most adverse to your interests. Your peace will be only a more distressing war; and that which you imagined liberty will prove the worst of slavery. Unless by the means of piety, not frothy and loquacious, but operative, unadulterated, and sincere, you clear the horizon of the mind from those mists of superstition which arise from the ignorance of true religion, you will always have those who will bend your necks to the yoke as if you were brutes, who, notwithstanding all your triumphs, will put you up to the highest bidder, as if you were mere booty made in war; and will find an exuberant source of wealth in your ignorance and superstition. Unless you will subjugate the propensity to avarice, to ambition, and sensuality, and expel all luxury from yourselves and from your families, you will find that you have cherished a more stubborn and intractable despot at home, than you ever encountered in the field; and even your very bowels will be continually teeming with an intolerable progeny of tyrants. Let these be the first enemies whom you subdue; this constitutes the campaign of peace; these are triumphs, difficult indeed, but bloodless; and far more honourable than those trophies which are purchased only by slaughter and by rapine. Unless you are victors in this service, it is in vain that you have been victorious over the despotic enemy in the field. For if you think that it is a more grand, a more beneficial, or a more wise policy, to invent subtle expedients for increasing the revenue, to multiply our naval and military force, to rival in craft the ambassadors of foreign states, to form skilful treaties and alliances, than to administer unpolluted justice to the people, to redress the injured, and to succour the distressed, and speedily to restore to every one his own, you are involved in a cloud of error; and too late will you perceive, when the illusion of those mighty benefits has vanished, that in neglecting these, which you now think inferior considerations, you have only been precipitating your own ruin and despair. The fidelity of enemies and allies is frail and perishing, unless it be cemented by the principles of justice; that wealth and those honours, which most covet, readily change masters; they forsake the idle, and repair where virtue, where industry, where patience flourish most. Thus nation precipitates the downfall of nation; thus the more sound part of one people subverts the more corrupt; thus you obtained the ascendent over the royalists. If you plunge into the same depravity, if you imitate their excesses, and hanker after the same vanities, you will become royalists as well as they, and liable to be subdued by the same enemies, or by others in your turn; who, placing their reliance on the same religious principles, the same patience, the same integrity and discretion which made you strong, will deservedly triumph over you who are immersed in debauchery, in the luxury and the sloth of kings. Then, as if God was weary of protecting you, you will be seen to have passed through the fire, that you might perish in the smoke; the contempt which you will then experience will be great as the admiration which you now enjoy; and, what may in future profit others, but cannot benefit yourselves, you will leave a salutary proof what great things the solid reality of virtue and of piety might have effected, when the mere counterfeit and varnished resemblance could attempt such mighty achievements, and make such considerable advances towards the execution. For, if either through your want of knowledge, your want of constancy, or your want of virtue, attempts so noble, and actions so glorious, have had an issue so unfortunate, it does not therefore follow that better men should be either less daring in their projects or less sanguine in their hopes. But from such an abyss of corruption into which you so readily fall, no one, not even Cromwell himself, nor a whole nation of Brutuses, if they were alive, could deliver you if they would, or would deliver you if they could. For who would vindicate your right of unrestrained suffrage, or of choosing what representatives you liked best, merely that you might elect the creatures of your own faction, whoever they might be, or him, however small might be his worth, who would give you the most lavish feasts, and enable you to drink to the greatest excess? Thus not wisdom and authority, but turbulence and gluttony, would soon exalt the vilest miscreants from our taverns and our brothels, from our towns and villages, to the rank and dignity of senators. For, should the management of the republic be entrusted to persons to whom no one would willingly entrust the management of his private concerns; and the treasury of the state be left to the care of those who had lavished their own fortunes in an infamous prodigality? Should they have the charge of the public purse, which they would soon convert into a private, by their unprincipled peculations? Are they fit to be the legislators of a whole people who themselves know not what law, what reason, what right and wrong, what crooked and straight, what licit and illicit means? who think that all power consists in outrage, all dignity in the parade of insolence? who neglect every other consideration for the corrupt gratification of their friendships, or the prosecution of their resentments? who disperse their own relations and creatures through the provinces, for the sake of levying taxes and confiscating goods; men, for the greater part, the most profligate and vile, who buy up for themselves what they pretend to expose to sale, who thence collect an exorbitant mass of wealth, which they fraudulently divert from the public service; who thus spread their pillage through the country, and in a moment emerge from penury and rags to a state of splendour and of wealth? Who could endure such thievish servants, such vicegerents of their lords? Who could believe that the masters and the patrons of a banditti could be the proper guardians of liberty? or who would suppose that he should ever be made one hair more free by such a set of public functionaries (though they might amount to five hundred elected in this manner from the counties and boroughs), when among them who are the very guardians of liberty, and to whose custody it is committed, there must be so many, who know not either how to use or to enjoy liberty, who neither understand the principles nor merit the possession? But, what is worthy of remark, those who are the most unworthy of liberty are wont to behave most ungratefully towards their deliverers. Among such persons, who would be willing either to fight for liberty, or to encounter the least peril in its defence? It is not agreeable to the nature of things that such persons ever should be free. However much they may brawl about liberty, they are slaves, both at home and abroad, but without perceiving it; and when they do perceive it, like unruly horses that are impatient of the bit, they will endeavour to throw off the yoke, not from the love of genuine liberty (which a good man only loves and knows how to obtain), but from the impulses of pride and little passions. But though they often attempt it by arms, they will make no advances to the execution; they may change their masters, but will never be able to get rid of their servitude. This often happened to the ancient Romans, wasted by excess, and enervated by luxury: and it has still more so been the fate of the moderns; when, after a long interval of years, they aspired, under the auspices of Crescentius, Nomentanus, and afterwards of Nicolas Rentius, who had assumed the title of Tribune of the People, to restore the splendour and re-establish the government of ancient Rome. For, instead of fretting with vexation, or thinking that you can lay the blame on any one but yourselves, know that to be free is the same thing as to be pious, to be wise, to be temperate and just, to be frugal and abstinent, and lastly, to be magnanimous and brave; so to be the opposite of all these is the same as to be a slave; and it usually happens, by the appointment, and as it were retributive justice, of the Deity, that that people which cannot govern themselves, and moderate their passions, but crouch under the slavery of their lusts, should be delivered up to the sway of those whom they abhor, and made to submit to an involuntary servitude. It is also sanctioned by the dictates of justice and by the constitution of nature, that he who from the imbecility or derangement of his intellect, is incapable of governing himself, should, like a minor, be committed to the government of another; and least of all should he be appointed to superintend the affairs of others or the interest of the state. You, therefore, who wish to remain free, either instantly be wise, or, as soon as possible, cease to be fools; if you think slavery an intolerable evil, learn obedience to reason and the government of yourselves; and finally bid adieu to your dissensions, your jealousies, your superstitions, your outrages, your rapine, and your lusts. Unless you will spare no pains to effect this, you must be judged unfit, both by God and mankind, to be entrusted with the possession of liberty and the administration of the government; but will rather, like a nation in a state of pupilage, want some active and courageous guardian to undertake the management of your affairs. With respect to myself, whatever turn things may take, I thought that my exertions on the present occasion would be serviceable to my country; and as they have been cheerfully bestowed, I hope that they have not been bestowed in vain. And I have not circumscribed my defence of liberty within any petty circle around me, but have made it so general and comprehensive, that the justice and the reasonableness of such uncommon occurrences, explained and defended, both among my countrymen and among foreigners, and which all good men cannot but approve, may serve to exalt the glory of my country, and to excite the imitation of posterity. If the conclusion do not answer to the beginning, that is their concern; I have delivered my testimony, I would almost say, have erected a monument, that will not readily be destroyed, to the reality of those singular and mighty achievements which were above all praise. As the epic poet, who adheres at all to the rules of that species of composition, does not profess to describe the whole life of the hero whom he celebrates, but only some particular action of his life, as the resentment of Achilles at Troy, the return of Ulysses, or the coming of Æneas into Italy; so it will be sufficient, either for my justification or apology, that I have heroically celebrated at least one exploit of my countrymen; I pass by the rest, for who could recite the achievements of a whole people? If after such a display of courage and of vigour, you basely relinquish the path of virtue, if you do anything unworthy of yourselves, posterity will sit in judgment on your conduct. They will see that the foundations were well laid; that the beginning (nay, it was more than a beginning) was glorious; but with deep emotions of concern will they regret, that those were wanting who might have completed the structure. They will lament that perseverance was not conjoined with such exertions and such virtues. They will see that there was a rich harvest of glory, and an opportunity afforded for the greatest achievements, but that men only were wanting for the execution; while they were not wanting who could rightly counsel, exhort, inspire, and bind an unfading wreath of praise round the brows of the illustrious actors in so glorious a scene.

THE READY AND EASY WAY TO ESTABLISH A FREE COMMONWEALTH,

AND THE EXCELLENCE THEREOF, COMPARED WITH THE INCONVENIENCES AND DANGERS OF READMITTING KINGSHIP IN THIS NATION.

ALTHOUGH, since the writing of this treatise, the face of things hath had some change, writs for new elections have been recalled, and the members at first chosen readmitted from exclusion; yet not a little rejoicing to hear declared the resolution of those who are in power, tending to the establishment of a free commonwealth, and to remove, if it be possible, this noxious humour of returning to bondage, instilled of late by some deceivers, and nourished from bad principles and false apprehensions among too many of the people; I thought best not to suppress what I had written, hoping that it may now be of much more use and concernment to be freely published, in the midst of our elections to a free parliament, or their sitting to consider freely of the government; whom it behoves to have all things represented to them that may direct their judgment therein; and I never read of any state, scarce of any tyrant, grown so incurable, as to refuse counsel from any in a time of public deliberation, much less to be offended. If their absolute determination be to enthral us, before so long a Lent of servitude, they may permit us a little shroving-time first, wherein to speak freely, and take our leaves of liberty. And because in the former edition, through haste, many faults escaped, and many books were suddenly dispersed, ere the note to mend them could be sent, I took the opportunity from this occasion to revise and somewhat to enlarge the whole discourse, especially that part which argues for a perpetual senate. The treatise thus revised and enlarged, is as follows :—

The Parliament of England, assisted by a great number of the people who appeared and stuck to them faithfulest in defence of religion and their civil liberties, judging kingship by long experience a government unnecessary, burdensome, and dangerous, justly and magnanimously abolished it, turning regal bondage into a free commonwealth, to the admiration and terror of our emulous neighbours. They took themselves not bound by the light of nature or religion to any former covenant, from which the king himself, by many forfeitures of a latter date or discovery, and our own longer consideration thereon, had more and more unbound us, both to himself and his posterity; as hath been ever the justice and the prudence of all wise nations that have ejected tyranny. They covenanted "to preserve the king's person and authority, in the preservation of the true religion, and our liberties;" not in his endeavouring to bring in upon our consciences a popish religion; upon our liberties, thraldom; upon our lives, destruction, by his occasioning, if not complotting, as was after discovered, the Irish massacre; his fomenting and arming the rebellion; his covert leaguing with the rebels against us; his refusing, more than seven times, propositions most just and necessary to the true religion and our liberties, tendered him by the parliament both of England and Scotland. They made not their covenant concerning him with no difference between a king and a God; or promised him, as Job did to the Almighty, "to trust in him though he slay us:" they understood that the solemn engagement, wherein we all forswore kingship, was no more a breach of the covenant, than the covenant was of the protestation before, but a faithful and prudent going on both in words well weighed, and in the true sense of the covenant "without respect of persons," when we could not serve two contrary masters, God and the king, or the king and that more supreme law, sworn in the first place to maintain our safety and our liberty. They knew the people of England to be a free people, themselves the representers of that freedom; and although many were excluded, and as many fled (so they pretended) from tumults to Oxford, yet they were left a sufficient number to act in parliament, therefore not bound by any statute of preceding parliaments, but by the law of nature only, which is the only law of laws truly and properly to all mankind fundamental; the beginning and the end of all government; to which no parliament or people that will throughly reform, but may and must have recourse, as they had, and must yet have, in church reformation (if they throughly intend it) to evangelic rules; not to ecclesiastical canons, though never so ancient, so ratified and established in the land by statutes which for the most part are mere positive laws, neither natural nor moral: and so by any parliament, for just and serious considerations, without scruple to be at any time repealed.

If others of their number in these things were under force, they were not, but under free conscience; if others were excluded by a power which they could not resist, they were not therefore to leave the helm of government in no hands, to discontinue their care of the public peace and safety, to desert the people in anarchy and confusion, no more than when so many of their members left them, as made up in outward formality a more legal parliament of three estates against them. The best affected also, and best principled of the people, stood not numbering or computing, on which side were most voices in parliament, but on which side appeared to them most reason, most safety, when the house divided upon main matters. What was well mentioned and advised, they examined not whether fear or persuasion carried it in the vote, neither did they measure votes and counsels by the intentions of them that voted; knowing that intentions either are but guessed at, or not soon enough known; and although good, can neither make the deed such, nor prevent the consequence from being bad. Suppose bad intentions in things otherwise well done; what was well done, was by them who so thought, not the less obeyed or followed in the state; since in the church, who had not rather follow Iscariot or Simon, the magician, though to covetous ends, preaching, than Saul, though in the uprightness of his heart persecuting the gospel?

Safer they, therefore, judged what they thought the better counsels, though carried on by some perhaps to bad ends, than the worse by others, though endeavoured with best intentions. And yet they were not to learn that a greater number might be corrupt within the walls of a parliament, as well as of a city; whereof in matters of nearest concernment all men will be judges; nor easily permit that the odds of voices in their greatest council shall more endanger them by corrupt or credulous votes, than the odds of enemies by open assaults; judging that most voices ought not always to prevail, where main matters are in question. If others hence will pretend to disturb all counsels; what is that to them who pretend not, but are in real danger; not they only so judging, but a great, though not the greatest number of their chosen patriots, who might be more in weight than the others in numbers: there being in number little virtue, but by weight and measure wisdom working all things, and the dangers on either side they seriously thus weighed?

From the treaty, short fruits of long labours, and seven years' war; security for twenty years, if we can hold it; reformation in the church for three years: then put to shift again with our vanquished master. His justice, his honour, his conscience declared quite contrary to ours; which would have furnished him with many such evasions, as in a book entitled *An Inquisition for Blood*, soon after were not concealed: bishops not totally removed, but left, as it were, in ambush, a reserve, with ordination in their sole power; their lands already sold, not to be alienated, but rented, and the sale of them called "sacrilege"; delinquents, few of many brought to condign punishment; accessories punished, the chief author, above pardon, though, after utmost resistance, vanquished; not to give, but to receive, laws; yet besought, treated with, and to be thanked for his gracious concessions, to be honoured, worshipped, glorified.

If this we swore to do, with what righteousness in the sight of God, with what assurance that we bring not by such an oath, the whole sea of blood-guiltiness upon our heads? If on the other side we prefer a free government, though for the present not obtained, yet all those suggested fears and difficulties, as the event will prove, easily overcome, we remain finally secure from the exasperated regal power, and out of snares; shall retain the best part of our liberty, which is our religion, and the civil part will be from these who defer us, much more easily recovered, being neither so subtle nor so awful as a king reinthroned. Nor were their actions less both at home and abroad, than might become the hopes of a glorious rising commonwealth: nor were the expressions both of army and people, whether in their public declarations, or several writings, other than such as testified a spirit in this nation, no less noble and well-fitted to the liberty of a commonwealth, than in the ancient Greeks or Romans. Nor was the heroic cause unsuccessfully defended to all Christendom, against the tongue of a famous and thought invincible adversary; nor the constancy and fortitude, that so nobly vindicated our liberty, our victory at once against two the most prevailing usurpers over mankind, superstition and tyranny, unpraised or uncelebrated in a written monument, likely to outlive detraction, as it hath hitherto convinced or silenced not a few of our detractors, especially in parts abroad.

After our liberty and religion thus prosperously fought for, gained, and many years possessed, except in those unhappy interruptions, which God hath removed; now that nothing remains, but in all reason the certain hopes of a speedy and immediate settlement for ever in a firm and free commonwealth, for this extolled and magnified nation, regardless both of honour won, or deliverances vouchsafed from heaven, to fall back, or rather to creep back so poorly, as it seems the multitude would, to their once abjured and detested thraldom of kingship, to be ourselves the slanderers of our own just and religious deeds, though done by some to covetous and ambitious ends, yet not therefore to be stained with their infamy, or they to asperse the integrity of others; and yet these now by revolting from the conscience of deeds well done, both in church and state, to throw away and forsake, or rather to betray a just and noble cause for the mixture of bad men who have ill-managed and abused it (which had our fathers done heretofore, and on the same pretence deserted true religion, what had long ere this become of our gospel, and all protestant reformation so much intermixed with the avarice and ambition of some reformers?), and by thus relapsing, to verify all the bitter predictions of our triumphing enemies, who will now think they wisely discerned and justly censured both us and all our actions as rash, rebellious, hypocritical, and impious; not only argues a strange, degenerate contagion suddenly spread among us, fitted and prepared for new slavery, but will render us a scorn and derision to all our neighbours.

And what will they at best say of us, and of the whole English name, but scoffingly, as of that foolish builder mentioned by our Saviour, who began to build a tower, and was not able to finish it? Where is this goodly tower of a commonwealth, which the English boasted they would build to overshadow kings, and be another Rome in the west? The foundation indeed they lay gallantly, but fell into a worse confusion, not of tongues, but of factions, than those at the tower of Babel; and have left no memorial of their work behind them remaining but in the common laughter of Europe! Which must needs redound the more to our shame, if we but look on our neighbours the United Provinces, to us inferior in all outward advantages; who notwithstanding, in the midst of greater difficulties, courageously, wisely, constantly went through with the same work, and are settled in all the happy enjoyments of a potent and flourishing republic to this day.

Besides this, if we return to kingship, and soon repent (as undoubtedly we shall, when we begin to find the old encroachment coming on by little and little upon our consciences, which must necessarily proceed from king and bishop united inseparably in one interest), we may be forced perhaps to fight over again all that we have fought, and spend over again all that we have spent, but are never like to attain thus far as we are now advanced to the recovery of our freedom, never to have it in possession as we now have it, never to be vouchsafed hereafter the like mercies and signal assistances from Heaven in our cause, if by our ingrateful backsliding we make these fruitless; flying now to regal concessions from his divine condescensions and gracious answers to our once importuning prayers against the tyranny which we then groaned under; making vain and viler than dirt the blood of so many thousand faithful and valiant Englishmen, who left us in this liberty, bought with their lives; losing by a strange after-game of folly all the battles we have won, together with all Scotland as to our conquest, hereby lost, which never any of our kings could conquer, all the treasure we have spent, not that corruptible treasure only, but that far more precious of all our late miraculous deliverances; treading back again with lost labour all our happy steps in the progress of reformation, and most pitifully depriving ourselves the instant fruition of that free government, which we have so dearly purchased, a free commonwealth, not only held by wisest men in all ages the noblest, the manliest, the equallest, the justest government, the most agreeable to all due liberty and proportioned equality, both human, civil, and Christian, most cherishing to virtue and true religion, but also (I may say it with greatest probability) plainly commended, or rather enjoined by our Saviour himself, to all Christians, not without remarkable disallowance, and the brand of Gentilism upon kingship.

God in much displeasure gave a king to the Israelites, and imputed it a sin to them that they sought one; but Christ apparently forbids his disciples to admit of any such heathenish government: "The kings of the Gentiles," saith He, "exercise lordship over them," and they that "exercise authority upon them are called benefactors: but ye shall not be so; but he that is greatest among you, let him be as the younger; and he that is chief, as he that serveth." The occasion of these His words was the ambitious desire of Zebedee's two sons to be exalted above their brethren in His kingdom, which they thought was to be ere long upon earth. That He speaks of civil government, is manifest by the former part of the comparison, which infers the other part to be always in the same kind. And what government comes nearer to this precept of Christ, than a free commonwealth; wherein they who are the greatest, are perpetual servants and drudges to the public at their own cost and charges, neglect their own affairs, yet are not elevated above their brethren; live soberly in their families, walk the street as other men, may be spoken to freely, familiarly, friendly, without adoration? Whereas a king must be adored like a demigod, with a dissolute and haughty court about him, of vast expense and luxury, masks and revels, to the debauching of our prime gentry, both male and female; not in their pastimes only, but in earnest, by the loose employments of court-service, which will be then thought honourable. There will be a queen of no less charge; in most likelihood outlandish and a papist; besides a queen-mother such already; together with both their courts and numerous train: then a royal issue, and ere long severally their sumptuous courts; to the multiplying of a servile crew, not of servants only, but of nobility and gentry, bred up then to the hopes not of public, but of court-offices, to be stewards, chamberlains, ushers, grooms even of the close-stool; and the lower their minds debased with court-opinions, contrary to all virtue and reformation, the haughtier will be their pride and profuseness. We may well remember this not long since at home; nor need but look at present into the French court, where enticements and preferments daily draw away and pervert the protestant nobility.

As to the burden of expense, to our cost we shall soon know it; for any good to us deserving to be termed no better than the vast and lavish price of our subjection, and their debauchery, which we are now so greedily cheapening, and would so fain be paying most inconsiderately to a single person: who, for anything wherein the public really needs him, will have little else to do, but to bestow the eating and drinking of excessive dainties, to set a pompous face upon the superficial actings of state, to pageant himself up and down in progress among the perpetual bowings and cringings of an abject people, on either side deifying and adoring him for nothing done that can deserve it. For what can he more than another man? who, even in the expression of a late court-poet, sits only like a great cipher set to no purpose before a long row of other significant figures. Nay, it is well and happy for the people, if their king be but a cipher, being ofttimes a mischief, a pest, a scourge of the nation, and, which is worse, not to be removed, not to be controlled, much less accused or brought to punishment, without the danger of a common ruin, without the shaking and almost subversion of the whole land; whereas in a free commonwealth, any governor or chief counsellor offending may be removed and punished, without the least commotion.

Certainly then that people must needs be mad or strangely infatuated, that build the chief hope of their common happiness or safety on a single person; who, if he happen to be good, can do no more than another man; if to be bad, hath in his hands to do more evil without check, than millions of other men. The happiness of a nation must needs be firmest and certainest in full and free council of their own electing, where no single person, but reason only, sways. And what madness is it for them who might manage nobly their own affairs themselves, sluggishly and weakly to devolve all on a single person; and, more like boys under age than men, to commit all to his patronage and disposal, who neither can perform what he undertakes; and yet for undertaking it, though royally paid, will not be their servant, but their lord! How unmanly must it needs be, to count such a one the breath of our nostrils, to hang all our felicity on him, all our safety, our well-being, for which if we were aught else but sluggards or babies, we need depend on none but God and our own counsels, our own active virtue and industry! "Go to the ant, thou sluggard," saith Solomon; "consider her ways, and be wise; which having no prince, ruler, or lord, provides her meat in the summer, and gathers her food in the harvest:" which evidently shows us, that they who think the nation undone without a king, though they look grave or haughty, have not so much true spirit and understanding in them as a pismire: neither are these diligent creatures hence concluded to live in lawless anarchy, or that commended; but are set the examples to imprudent and ungoverned men, of a frugal and self-governing democracy or commonwealth: safer and more thriving in the joint providence and counsel of many industrious equals than under the single domination of one imperious lord.

It may be well wondered that any nation, styling themselves free, can suffer any man to pretend hereditary right over them as their lord; whenas, by acknowledging that right, they conclude themselves his servants and his vassals, and so renounce their own freedom. Which how a people and their leaders especially can do, who have fought so gloriously for liberty; how they can change their noble words and actions, heretofore so becoming the majesty of a free people, into the base necessity of court flatteries and prostrations, is not only strange and admirable, but lamentable to think on. That a nation should be so valorous and courageous to win their liberty in the field, and when they have won it, should be so heartless and unwise in their counsels, as not to know how to use it, value it, what to do with it, or with themselves; but after ten or twelve years' prosperous war and contestation with tyranny, basely and besottedly to run their necks again into the yoke which they have broken, and prostrate all the fruits of their victory for nought at the feet of the vanquished, besides our loss of glory, and such an example as kings or tyrants never yet had the like to boast of, will be an ignominy if it befall us, that never yet befell any nation possessed of their liberty; worthy indeed themselves, whatsoever they be, to be for ever slaves, but that part of the nation which consents not with them, as I persuade me of a great number, far worthier than by their means to be brought into the same bondage.

Considering these things so plain, so rational, I cannot but yet further admire on the other side, how any man, who hath the true principles of justice and religion in him, can presume or take upon him to be a king and lord over his brethren, whom he cannot but know, whether as men or Christians, to be for the most part every way equal or superior to himself: how he can display with such vanity and ostentation his regal splendour, so supereminently above other mortal men; or, being a Christian, can assume such extraordinary honour and worship to himself, while the kingdom of Christ, our common king and lord, is hid to this world, and such gentilish imitation forbid in express words by Himself to all His disciples. All protestants hold that Christ in His church hath left no vicegerent of His power; but Himself, without deputy, is the only head thereof governing it from heaven: how then can any Christian man derive his kingship from Christ, but with worse usurpation than the pope his headship over the church, since Christ not only hath not left the least shadow of a command for any such vicegerence from Him in the state, as the pope pretends for his in the church, but hath expressly declared that such regal dominion is from the Gentiles, not from Him, and hath strictly charged us not to imitate them therein?

I doubt not but all ingenuous and knowing men will easily agree with me, that a free commonwealth without single person or house of lords is by far the best government, if it can be had; but we have all this while, say they, been expecting it, and cannot yet attain it. It is true, indeed, when monarchy was dissolved, the form of a commonwealth should have forthwith been framed, and the practice thereof immediately begun; that the people might have soon been satisfied and delighted with the decent order, ease, and benefit thereof; we had been then by this time firmly rooted, past fear of commotions or mutations, and now flourishing; this care of timely settling a new government instead of the old, too much neglected, hath been our mischief. Yet the cause thereof may be ascribed with most reason to the frequent disturbances, interruptions, and dissolutions, which the parliament hath had partly from the impatient or disaffected people, partly from some ambitious leaders in the army; much contrary, I believe, to the mind and approbation of the army itself, and their other commanders, once undeceived, or in their own power.

Now is the opportunity, now the very season, wherein we may obtain a free commonwealth, and establish it for ever in the land, without difficulty or much delay. Writs are sent out for elections, and, which is worth observing, in the name, not of any king, but of the keepers of our liberty, to summon a free parliament; which then only will indeed be free, and deserve the true honour of that supreme title, if they preserve us a free people. Which never parliament was more free to do, being now called not as heretofore, by the summons of a king, but by the voice of liberty. And if the people, laying aside prejudice and impatience, will seriously and calmly now consider their own good, both religious and civil, their own liberty and the only means thereof, as shall be here laid down before them, and will elect their knights and burgesses able men, and according to the just and necessary qualifications (which, for aught I hear, remain yet in force unrepealed, as they were formerly decreed in parliament), men not addicted to a single person or house of lords, the work is done; at least the foundation firmly laid of a free commonwealth, and good part also erected of the main structure. For the ground and basis of every just and free government (since men have smarted so oft for committing all to one person), is a general council of ablest men, chosen by the people to consult of public affairs from time to time for the common good. In this grand council must the sovereignty, not transferred, but delegated only, and as it were deposited, reside; with this caution, they must have the forces by sea and land committed to them for preservation of the common peace and liberty; must raise and manage the public revenue, at least with some inspectors deputed for satisfaction of the people, how it is employed; must make or propose, as more expressly shall be said anon, civil laws, treat of commerce, peace or war with foreign nations; and, for the carrying on some particular affairs with more secrecy and expedition, must elect, as they have already out of their own number and others, a council of state.

And, although it may seem strange at first hearing, by reason that men's minds are prepossessed with the notion of successive parliaments, I affirm, that the grand or general council, being well chosen, should be perpetual: for so their business is or may be, and ofttimes urgent; the opportunity of affairs gained or lost in a moment. The day of council cannot be set as the day of a festival; but must be ready always to prevent or answer all occasions. By this continuance they will become every way skilfulest, best provided of intelligence from abroad, best acquainted with the people at home, and the people with them. The ship of the commonwealth is always under sail; they sit at the stern, and if they steer well, what need is there to change them, it being rather dangerous? Add to this, that the grand council is both foundation and main pillar of the whole state; and to move pillars and foundations, not faulty, cannot be safe for the building.

I see not, therefore, how we can be advantaged by successive and transitory parliaments; but that they are much likelier continually to unsettle rather than to settle a free government, to breed commotions, changes, novelties, and uncertainties, to bring neglect upon present affairs and opportunities, while all minds are in suspense with expectation of a new assembly, and the assembly, for a good space, taken up with the new settling of itself. After which, if they find no great work to do, they will make it, by altering or repealing former acts, or making and multiplying new; that they may seem to see what their predecessors saw not, and not to have assembled for nothing; till all law be lost in the multitude of clashing statutes. But if the ambition of such as think themselves injured, that they also partake not of the government, and are impatient till they be chosen, cannot brook the perpetuity of others chosen before them; or if it be feared, that long continuance of power may corrupt sincerest men, the known expedient is, and by some lately propounded, that annually (or if the space be longer, so much perhaps the better) the third part of senators may go out according to the precedence of their election, and the like number be chosen in their places, to prevent their settling of

A FREE COMMONWEALTH. 143

too absolute a power, if it should be perpetual: and this they call "partial rotation."

But I could wish that this wheel, or partial wheel in state, if it be possible, might be avoided, as having too much affinity with the wheel of Fortune. For it appears not how this can be done, without danger and mischance of putting out a great number of the best and ablest: in whose stead new elections may bring in as many raw, unexperienced, and otherwise affected, to the weakening and much altering for the worse of public transactions. Neither do I think a perpetual senate, especially chosen or entrusted by the people, much in this land to be feared, where the well-affected, either in a standing army, or in a settled militia, have their arms in their own hands. Safest therefore to me it seems, and of least hazard or interruption to affairs, that none of the grand council be moved, unless by death, or just conviction of some crime: for what can be expected firm or steadfast from a floating foundation? However, I forejudge not any probable expedient, any temperament that can be found in things of this nature, so disputable on either side.

Yet lest this which I affirm be thought my single opinion, I shall add sufficient testimony. Kingship itself is therefore counted the more safe and durable because the king, and for the most part his council, is not changed during life. But a commonwealth is held immortal, and therein firmest, safest, and most above fortune; for the death of a king causeth ofttimes many dangerous alterations; but the death now and then of a senator is not felt, the main body of them still continuing permanent in greatest and noblest commonwealths and as it were eternal. Therefore among the Jews, the supreme council of seventy, called the Sanhedrim, founded by Moses, in Athens that of Areopagus, in Sparta that of the ancients, in Rome the senate, consisted of members chosen for term of life; and by that means remained as it were still the same to generations. In Venice they change indeed oftener than every year some particular council of state, as that of six, or such other: but the true senate, which upholds and sustains the government, is the whole aristocracy immovable. So in the United Provinces, the states-general, which are indeed but a council of state deputed by the whole union, are not usually the same persons for above three or six years; but the states of every city, in whom the sovereignty hath been placed time out of mind, are a standing senate, without succession, and accounted chiefly in that regard the main prop of their liberty. And why they should be so in every well-ordered commonwealth, they who write of policy give these reasons: That to make the senate successive, not only impairs the dignity and lustre of the senate, but weakens the whole commonwealth, and brings it into manifest danger; while by this means the secrets of state are frequently divulged, and matters of greatest consequence committed to inexpert and novice counsellors, utterly to seek in the full and intimate knowledge of affairs past.

I know not therefore what should be peculiar in England, to make successive parliaments thought safest, or convenient here more than in other nations, unless it be the fickleness which is attributed to us as we are islanders. But good education and acquisite wisdom ought to correct the fluxible fault, if any such be, of our watery situation. It will be objected, that in those places where they had perpetual senates, they had also popular remedies against their growing too imperious: as in Athens, besides Areopagus, another senate of four or five hundred; in Sparta, the Ephori; in Rome, the tribunes of the people.

But the event tells us, that these remedies either little availed the people, or brought them to such a licentious and unbridled democracy, as in fine ruined themselves with their own excessive power. So that the main reason urged why popular assemblies are to be trusted with the people's liberty, rather than a senate of principal men, because great men will be still endeavouring to enlarge their power, but the common sort will be contented to maintain their own liberty, is by experience found false; none being more immoderate and ambitious to amplify their power, than such popularities, which were seen in the people of Rome; who, at first contented to have their tribunes, at length contended with the senate that one consul, then both; soon after, that the censors and prætors also should be created plebeian, and the whole empire put into their hands; adoring lastly, those who most were adverse to the senate, till Marius, by fulfilling their inordinate desires, quite lost them all the power for which they had so long been striving, and left them under the tyranny of Sylla. The balance therefore must be exactly so set, as to preserve and keep up due authority on either side, as well in the senate as in the people. And this annual rotation of a senate to consist of three hundred, as is lately propounded, requires also another popular assembly upward of a thousand, with an answerable rotation. Which, besides that it will be liable to all those inconveniences found in the aforesaid remedies, cannot but be troublesome and chargeable, both in their motion and their session, to the whole land, unwieldy with their own bulk, unable in so great a number to mature their consultations as they ought, if any be allotted them, and that they meet not from so many parts remote to sit a whole year lieger in one place, only now and then to hold up a forest of fingers, or to convey each man his bean or ballot into the box, without reason shown or common deliberation; incontinent of secrets, if any be imparted to them; emulous and always jarring with the other senate. The much better way doubtless will be, in this wavering condition of our affairs, to defer the changing or circumscribing of our senate, more than may be done with ease, till the commonwealth be thoroughly settled in peace and safety, and they themselves give us the occasion.

Military men hold it dangerous to change the form of battle in view of an enemy: neither did the people of Rome bandy with their senate, while any of the Tarquins lived, the enemies of their liberty; nor sought, by creating tribunes, to defend themselves against the fear of their patricians, till, sixteen years after the expulsion of their kings, and in full security of their state, they had or thought they had just cause given them by the senate. Another way will be, to well qualify and refine elections: not committing all to the noise and shouting of a rude multitude, but permitting only those of them who are rightly qualified, to nominate as many as they will; and out of that number others of a better breeding, to choose a less number more judiciously, till after a third or fourth sifting and refining of exactest choice, they only be left chosen who are the due number, and seem by most voices the worthiest.

To make the people fittest to choose, and the chosen fittest to govern, will be to mend our corrupt and faulty education, to teach the people faith, not without virtue, temperance, modesty, sobriety, parsimony, justice; not to admire wealth or honour; to hate turbulence and ambition; to place every one his private welfare and happiness in the public peace, liberty, and safety. They shall not then need to be much mistrustful of their chosen patriots in the grand council; who will be then rightly called the true keepers of our liberty, though the most of their business will be in foreign affairs. But to prevent all mistrust, the people then will have their several ordinary assemblies (which will henceforth quite annihilate the odious power and name of committees) in the chief towns of every county, without the trouble, charge, or time lost of summoning and assembling from far in so great a number, and so long residing from their own houses, or removing of their families, to do as much at home in their several shires, entire or subdivided, toward the securing of their liberty, as a numerous assembly of them all formed and convened on purpose with the wariest rotation. Whereof I shall speak more ere the end of this discourse; for it may be referred to time, so we be still going on by degrees to perfection. The people well weighing and performing these things, I suppose would have no cause to fear, though the parliament abolishing that name, as originally signifying but the parley of our lords and commons with the Norman king when he pleased to call them, should, with certain limitations of their power, sit perpetual, if their ends be faithful and for a free commonwealth, under the name of a grand or general council.

Till this be done, I am in doubt whether our state will be ever certainly and throughly settled; never likely till then to see an end of our troubles and continual changes, or at least never the true settlement and assurance of our liberty. The grand council being thus firmly constituted to perpetuity, and still, upon the death or default of any member, supplied and kept in full number, there can be no cause alleged, why peace, justice, plentiful trade, and all prosperity should not thereupon ensue throughout the whole land; with as much assurance as can be of human things, that they shall so continue (if God favour us, and our wilful sins provoke Him not) even to the coming of our true and rightful, and only to be expected King, only worthy as He is our only Saviour, the Messiah, the Christ, the only heir of His eternal Father, the only by Him anointed and ordained since the work of our redemption finished, universal Lord of all mankind.

The way propounded is plain, easy, and open before us; without intricacies, without the introducement of new or absolute forms or terms, or exotic models; ideas that would effect nothing; but with a number of new injunctions to manacle the native liberty of mankind; turning all virtue into prescription, servitude, and necessity, to the great impairing and frustrating of Christian liberty. I say again, this way lies free and smooth before us; is not tangled with inconveniences; invents no new incumbrances; requires no perilous, no injurious alteration or circumscription of men's lands and properties; secure, that in this commonwealth, temporal and spiritual lords removed, no man or number of men can attain to such wealth or vast possession, as will need the hedge of an agrarian law (never successful, but the cause rather of sedition, save only where it began seasonably with first possession) to confine them from endangering our public liberty. To conclude, it can have no considerable objection made against it, that it is not practicable; lest it be said hereafter, that we gave up our liberty for want of a ready way or distinct form proposed of a free commonwealth. And this facility we shall have above our next neighbouring commonwealth (if we can keep us from the fond conceit of something like a duke of Venice, put lately into many men's heads, by some one or other subtly driving on under that notion his own ambitious ends to lurch a crown), that our liberty shall not be hampered or hovered over by any engagement to such a potent family as the house of Nassau, of whom to stand in perpetual doubt and suspicion, but we shall live the clearest and absolutest free nation in the world.

On the contrary, if there be a king, which the inconsiderate multitude are now so mad upon, mark how far short we are like to come of all those happinesses which in a free state we shall immediately be possessed of. First, the grand council, which, as I showed before, should sit perpetually (unless their leisure give them now and then some intermissions or vacations, easily manageable by the council of state left sitting), shall be called, by the king's good will and utmost endeavour, as seldom as may be. For it is only the king's right, he will say, to call a parliament; and this he will do most commonly about his own affairs rather than the kingdom's, as will appear plainly so soon as they are called. For what will their business then be, and the chief expense of their time, but an endless tugging between petition of right and royal prerogative, especially about the negative voice, militia, or subsidies, demanded and ofttimes extorted without reasonable cause appearing to the commons, who are the only true representatives of the people and their liberty, but will be then mingled with a court-faction; besides which, within their own walls, the sincere part of them who stand faithful to the people will again have to deal with two troublesome counter-working adversaries from without, mere creatures of the king, spiritual, and the greater part, as is likeliest of temporal lords, nothing concerned with the people's liberty.

If these prevail not in what they please, though never so much against the people's interest, the parliament shall be soon dissolved, or sit and do nothing; not suffered to remedy the least grievance, or enact aught advantageous to the people. Next, the council of state shall not be chosen by the parliament, but by the king, still his own creatures, courtiers, and favourers; who will be sure in all their counsels to set their master's grandeur and absolute power, in what they are able, far above the people's liberty. I deny not but that there may be such a king, who may regard the common good before his own, may have no vicious favourite, may hearken only to the wisest and incorruptest of his parliament: but this rarely happens in a monarchy not elective; and it behoves not a wise nation to commit the sum of their well-being, the whole state of their safety to fortune. What need they? and how absurd would it be, whenas they themselves, to whom his chief virtue will be but to hearken, may with much better management and dispatch, with much more commendation of their own worth and magnanimity, govern without a master? Can the folly be paralleled, to adore and be slaves of a single person, for doing that which it is ten thousand to one whether he can or will do, and we without him might do more easily, more effectually, more laudably ourselves? Shall we never grow old enough to be wise, to make seasonable use of gravest authorities, experiences, examples? Is it such an unspeakable joy to serve, such felicity to wear a yoke? to clink our shackles, locked on by pretended law of subjection, more intolerable and hopeless to be ever shaken off, than those which are knocked on by illegal injury and violence?

Aristotle, our chief instructor in the universities, lest this doctrine be thought sectarian, as the royalist would have it thought, tells us in the third of his Politics, that certain men at first, for the matchless excellence of their virtue above others, or some great public benefit, were created kings by the people, in small cities and territories, and in the scarcity of others to be found like them; but when they abused their power, and governments grew larger, and the number of prudent men increased, that then the people, soon deposing their tyrants, betook them, in all civilest places, to the form of a free commonwealth. And why should we thus disparage and prejudicate our own nation, as to fear a scarcity of able and worthy men united in counsel to govern us, if we will but use diligence and impartiality, to find them out and choose them, rather yoking ourselves to a single person, the natural adversary and oppressor of liberty; though good, yet far easier corruptible by the excess of his single power and exaltation, or at best, not comparably sufficient to bear the weight of government, nor equally disposed to make us happy in the enjoyment of our liberty under him?

But admit that monarchy of itself may be convenient to some nations; yet to us who have thrown it out, received back again, it cannot but prove pernicious. For kings to come, never forgetting their former ejection, will be sure to fortify and arm themselves sufficiently for the future against all such attempts hereafter from the people; who shall be then so narrowly watched and kept so low, that though they would never so fain, and at the same rate of their blood and treasure, they never shall be able to regain what they now have purchased and may enjoy, or to free themselves from any yoke imposed upon them. Nor will they dare to go about it; utterly disheartened for the future, if these their highest attempts prove unsuccessful; which will be the triumph of all tyrants hereafter over any people that shall resist oppression; and their song will then be, to others, How sped the rebellious English? to our posterity, How sped the rebels, your fathers?

This is not my conjecture, but drawn from God's known denouncement against the gentilising Israelites, who, though they were governed in a commonwealth of God's own ordaining, he only their king, they his peculiar people, yet affecting rather to resemble heathen, but pretending the misgovernment of Samuel's sons, no more a reason to dislike their commonwealth, than the violence of Eli's sons was imputable to that priesthood or religion, clamoured for a king. They had their longing, but with this testimony of God's wrath: "Ye shall cry out in that day, because of your king whom ye shall have chosen, and the Lord will not hear you in that day." Us if he shall hear now, how much less will he hear when we cry hereafter, who once delivered by him from a king, and not without wondrous acts of his providence, insensible and unworthy of those high mercies, are returning precipitantly, if he withhold us not, back to the captivity from whence he freed us!

Yet neither shall we obtain or buy at an easy rate this new

gilded yoke, which thus transports us: a new royal revenue must be found, a new episcopal; for those are individual: both which being wholly dissipated, or bought by private persons, or assigned for service done, and especially to the army, cannot be recovered without general detriment and confusion to men's estates, or a heavy imposition on all men's purses; benefit to none but to the worst and ignoblest sort of men, whose hope is to be either the ministers of court riot and excess, or the gainers by it. But not to speak more of losses and extraordinary levies on our estates, what will then be the revenges and offences remembered and returned, not only by the chief person, but by all his adherents; accounts and reparations that will be required, suits, indictments, inquiries, discoveries, complaints, informations, who knows against whom or how many, though perhaps neuters, if not to utmost infliction, yet to imprisonment, fines, banishment, or molestation? if not these, yet disfavour, discountenance, disregard, and contempt on all but the known royalist, or whom he favours, will be plenteous.

Nor let the new royalised presbyterians persuade themselves, that their old doings, though now recanted, will be forgotten; whatever conditions be contrived or trusted on. Will they not believe this; nor remember the pacification, how it was kept to the Scots; how other solemn promises many a time to us? Let them but now read the diabolical forerunning libels, the faces, the gestures, that now appear foremost and briskest in all public places, as the harbingers of those that are in expectation to reign over us; let them but hear the insolencies, the menaces, the insultings, of our newly animated common enemies, crept lately out of their holes, their hell I might say, by the language of their infernal pamphlets, the spew of every drunkard, every ribald; nameless, yet not for want of licence, but for very shame of their own vile persons, not daring to name themselves, while they traduce others by name; and give us to foresee, that they intend to second their wicked words, if ever they have power, with more wicked deeds.

Let our zealous backsliders forethink now with themselves how their necks yoked with these tigers of Bacchus, these new fanatics of not the preaching, but the sweating-tub, inspired with nothing holier than the venereal pox, can draw one way under monarchy to the establishing of church discipline with these new disgorged atheisms. Yet shall they not have the honour to yoke with these, but shall be yoked under them; these shall plough on their backs. And do they among them, who are so forward to bring in the single person, think to be by him trusted or long regarded? So trusted they shall be, and so regarded, as by kings are wont reconciled enemies; neglected, and soon after discarded, if not persecuted for old traitors; the first inciters, beginners, and more than to the third part actors, of all that followed.

It will be found also, that there must be then, as necessarily as now (for the contrary part will be still feared), a standing army; which for certain shall not be this, but of the fiercest cavaliers, of no less expense, and perhaps again under Rupert. But let this army be sure they shall be soon disbanded, and likeliest without arrear or pay; and being disbanded, not be sure but they may as soon be questioned for being in arms against their king. The same let them fear who have contributed money; which will amount to no small number; that must then take their turn to be made delinquents and compounders. They who past reason and recovery are devoted to kingship perhaps will answer, that a greater part by far of the nation will have it so, the rest therefore must yield.

Not so much to convince these, which I little hope, as to confirm them who yield not, I reply, that this greatest part have both in reason, and the trial of just battle, lost the right of their election what the government shall be. Of them who have not lost that right, whether they for kingship be the greater number, who can certainly determine? Suppose they be, yet of freedom they partake all alike, one main end of government; which if the greater part value not, but will degenerately forego, is it just or reasonable, that most voices against the main end of government should enslave the less number that would be free? More just it is, doubtless, if it come to force, that a less number compel a greater to retain, which can be no wrong to them, their liberty, than that a greater number, for the pleasure of their baseness, compel a less most injuriously to be their fellow-slaves. They who seek nothing but their own just liberty, have always right to win it and keep it, whenever they have power, be the voices never so numerous that oppose it. And how much we above others are concerned to defend it from kingship, and from them who in pursuance thereof so perniciously would betray us and themselves to most certain misery and thraldom, will be needless to repeat.

Having thus far shown with what ease we may now obtain a free commonwealth, and by it, with as much ease, all the freedom, peace, justice, plenty, that we can desire; on the other side, the difficulties, troubles, uncertainties, nay, rather impossibilities, to enjoy these things constantly under a monarch; I will now proceed to show more particularly wherein our freedom and flourishing condition will be more ample and secure to us under a free commonwealth, than under kingship.

The whole freedom of man consists either in spiritual or civil liberty. As for spiritual, who can be at rest, who can enjoy anything in this world with contentment, who hath not liberty to serve God, and to save his own soul, according to the best light which God hath planted in him to that purpose, by the reading of his revealed will, and the guidance of his Holy Spirit? That this is best pleasing to God, and that the whole protestant church allows no supreme judge or rule in matters of religion, but the Scriptures; and these to be interpreted by the Scriptures themselves, which necessarily infers liberty of conscience, I have heretofore proved at large in another treatise; and might yet further, by the public declarations, confessions, and admonitions of whole churches and states, obvious in all histories since the reformation.

This liberty of conscience, which above all other things ought to be to all men dearest and most precious, no government more inclinable not to favour only, but to protect, than a free commonwealth; as being most magnanimous, most fearless, and confident of its own fair proceedings. Whereas kingship, though looking big, yet indeed most pusillanimous, full of fears, full of jealousies, startled at every umbrage, as it hath been observed of old to have ever suspected most and mistrusted them who were in most esteem for virtue and generosity of mind, so it is now known to have most in doubt and suspicion them who are most reputed to be religious. Queen Elizabeth, though herself accounted so good a protestant, so moderate, so confident of her subjects' love, would never give way so much as to presbyterian reformation in this land, though once and again besought, as Camden relates ; but imprisoned and persecuted the very proposers thereof, alleging it as her mind and maxim unalterable, that such reformation would diminish regal authority.

What liberty of conscience can we then expect of others, far worse principled from the cradle, trained up and governed by popish and Spanish counsels, and on such depending hitherto for subsistence? Especially what can this last parliament expect, who having revived lately and published the covenant, have re-engaged themselves, never to readmit episcopacy? Which no son of Charles returning but will most certainly bring back with him, if he regard the last and strictest charge of his father, "to persevere in, not the doctrine only, but government of the church of England, not to neglect the speedy and effectual suppressing of errors and schisms ;" among which he accounted presbytery one of the chief.

Or if, notwithstanding that charge of his father, he submit to the covenant, how will he keep faith to us, with disobedience to him ; or regard that faith given, which must be founded on the breach of that last and solemnest paternal charge, and the reluctance, I may say the antipathy, which is in all kings, against presbyterian and independent discipline? For they hear the gospel speaking much of liberty ; a word which monarchy and her bishops both fear and hate, but a free commonwealth both favours and promotes ; and not the word only, but the thing itself. But let our governors beware in time, lest their hard measure to liberty of conscience be found the rock whereon they shipwreck themselves, as others have now done before them in the course wherein God was directing their steerage to a free commonwealth; and the abandoning of all those whom they call secretaries, for the detected falsehood and ambition of some, be a wilful rejection of their own chief strength and interest in the freedom of all protestant religion, under what abusive name soever calumniated.

The other part of our freedom consists in the civil rights and advancements of every person according to his merit : the enjoyment of those never more certain, and the access to these never more open, than in a free commonwealth. Both which, in my opinion, may be best and soonest obtained, if every county in the land were made a kind of subordinate commonalty or commonwealth, and one chief town or more, according as the shire is in circuit, made cities, if they be not so called already; where the nobility and chief gentry, from a proportionable compass of territory annexed to each city, may build houses or palaces befitting their quality; may bear part in the government, make their own judicial laws, or use those that are, and execute them by their own elected judicatures and judges without appeal, in all things of civil government between man and man. So they shall have justice in their own hands, law executed fully and finally in their own counties and precincts, long wished and spoken of, but never yet obtained. They shall have none then to blame but themselves, if it be not well administered; and fewer laws to expect or fear from the supreme authority; or to those that shall be made, of any great concernment to public liberty, they may, without much trouble in these commonalties, or in more general assemblies called to their cities from the whole territory on such occasion, declare and publish their assent or dissent by deputies, within a time limited, sent to the grand council; yet so as this their judgment declared shall submit to the greater number of other counties or commonalties, and not avail them to any exemption of themselves, or refusal of agreement with the rest, as it may in any of the United Provinces, being sovereign within itself, ofttimes to the great disadvantage of that union.

In these employments they may, much better than they do now, exercise and fit themselves till their lot fall to be chosen into the grand council, according as their worth and merit shall be taken notice of by the people. As for controversies that shall happen between men of several counties, they may repair, as they do now, to the capital city, or any other more commodious, indifferent place, and equal judges. And this I find to have been practised in the old Athenian commonwealth, reputed the first and ancientest place of civility in all Greece; that they had in their several cities a peculiar, in Athens a common government; and their right, as it befell them, to the administration of both.

They should have here also schools and academies at their own choice, wherein their children may be bred up in their own sight to all learning and noble education; not in grammar only, but in all liberal arts and exercises. This would soon spread much more knowledge and civility, yea, religion, through all parts of the land, by communicating the natural heat of government and culture more distributively to all extreme parts, which now lie numb and neglected; would soon make the whole nation more industrious, more ingenious at home, more potent, more honourable abroad. To this a free commonwealth will easily assent (nay, the parliament hath had already some such thing in design); for of all governments a commonwealth aims most to make the people flourishing, virtuous, noble, and high-spirited. Monarchs will never permit; whose aim is to make the people wealthy indeed perhaps, and well fleeced, for their own shearing, and the supply of regal prodigality; but otherwise softest, basest, viciousest, servilest, easiest to be kept under. And not only in fleece, but in mind also sheepishest; and will have all the benches of judicature annexed to the throne, as a gift of royal grace, that we have justice done us; whenas nothing can be more essential to the freedom of a people, than to have the administration of justice, and all public ornaments, in their own election, and within their own bounds, without long travelling or depending upon remote places to obtain their right, or any civil accomplishment; so it be not supreme, but subordinate to the general power and union of the whole republic.

In which happy firmness, as in the particular above mentioned, we shall also far exceed the United Provinces, by having not as they (to the retarding and distracting ofttimes of their counsels or urgentest occasions), many sovereignties united in one commonwealth, but many commonwealths under one united and intrusted sovereignty. And when we have our forces by sea and land either of a faithful army, or a settled militia, in our own hands, to the firm establishing of a free commonwealth, public accounts under our own inspection, general laws and taxes, with their causes in our own domestic suffrages, judicial laws, offices, and ornaments at home in our own ordering and administration, all distinction of lords and commoners, that may any way divide or sever the public interest, removed; what can a perpetual senate have then, wherein to grow corrupt, wherein to encroach upon us, or usurp? Or if they do, wherein to be formidable? Yet if all this avail not to remove the fear or envy of a perpetual sitting, it may be easily provided, to change a third part of them yearly, or every two or three years, as was above mentioned: or that it be at those times in the people's choice, whether they will change them, or renew their power, as they shall find cause.

I have no more to say at present: few words will save us, well considered; few and easy things, now seasonably done. But if the people be so affected as to prostitute religion and liberty to the vain and groundless apprehension, that nothing but kingship can restore trade, not remembering the frequent plagues and pestilences that then wasted this city, such as through God's mercy we never have felt since; and that trade flourishes nowhere more than in the free commonwealths of Italy, Germany, and the Low Countries, before their eyes at this day; yet if trade be grown so craving and importunate through the profuse living of tradesmen, that nothing can support it but the luxurious expenses of a nation upon trifles or superfluities; so as if the people generally should betake themselves to frugality, it might prove a dangerous matter, lest tradesmen should mutiny for want of trading; and that therefore we must forego and set to sale religion, liberty, honour, safety, all concernments divine or human, to keep up trading : if, lastly, after all this light among us, the same reason shall pass for current, to put our necks again under kingship, as was made use of by the Jews to return back to Egypt, and to the worship of their idol queen, because they falsely imagined that they then lived in more plenty and prosperity; our condition is not sound, but rotten, both in religion and all civil prudence; and will bring us soon, the way we are marching, to those calamities, which attend always and unavoidably on luxury, all national judgments under foreign and domestic slavery : so far we shall be from mending our condition by monarchising our government, whatever new conceit now possesses us.

However, with all hazard I have ventured what I thought my duty to speak in season, and to forewarn my country in time ; wherein I doubt not but there be many wise men in all places and degrees, but am sorry the effects of wisdom are so little seen among us. Many circumstances and particulars I could have added in those things whereof I have spoken : but a few main matters now put speedily in execution, will suffice to recover us, and set all right : and there will want at no time who are good at circumstances; but men who set their minds on main matters, and sufficiently urge them, in these most difficult times I find not many.

What I have spoken, is the language of that which is not called amiss " The good old Cause : " if it seem strange to any, it will not seem more strange, I hope, than convincing to backsliders. Thus much I should perhaps have said, though I was sure I should have spoken only to trees and stones; and had none to cry to, but with the prophet, " O, earth, earth, earth ! " to tell the very soil itself what her perverse inhabitants are deaf to. Nay, though what I have spoke should happen (which thou suffer not, who didst create mankind free ! nor thou next, who didst redeem us from being servants of men !) to be the last words of our expiring liberty. But I trust I shall have spoken persuasion to abundance of sensible and ingenuous men ; to some, perhaps, whom God may raise from these stones to become children of reviving liberty ; and may reclaim, though they seem now choosing them a captain back for Egypt, to bethink themselves a little, and consider whither they are rushing; to exhort this torrent also of the people, not to be so impetuous, but to keep their due channel; and at length recovering and uniting their better resolutions, now that they see already how open and unbounded the insolence and rage is of our common enemies, to stay these ruinous proceedings, justly and timely fearing to what a precipice of destruction the deluge of this epidemic madness would hurry us, through the general defection of a misguided and abused multitude.

FROM "REFORMATION IN ENGLAND, AND THE CAUSES THAT HITHERTO HAVE HINDERED IT."

SIR,—Amidst those deep and retired thoughts, which, with every man Christianly instructed, ought to be most frequent of God, and of His miraculous ways and works amongst men, and of our religion and works, to be performed to Him; after the story of our Saviour Christ, suffering to the lowest bent of weakness in the flesh, and presently triumphing to the highest pitch of glory in the spirit, which drew up His body also; till we in both be united to Him in the revelation of His kingdom, I do not know of anything more worthy to take up the whole passion of pity on the one side, and joy on the other, than to consider first the foul and sudden corruption, and then, after many a tedious age, the long deferred, but much more wonderful and happy reformation of the church in these latter days. Sad it is to think how that doctrine of the gospel, planted by teachers divinely inspired, and by them winnowed and sifted from the chaff of overdated ceremonies, and refined to such a spiritual height and temper of purity, and knowledge of the Creator, that the body, with all the circumstances of time and place, were purified by the affections of the regenerate soul, and nothing left impure but sin; faith needing not the weak and fallible office of the senses, to be either the ushers or interpreters of heavenly mysteries, save where our Lord Himself in His sacraments ordained; that such a doctrine should, through the grossness and blindness of her professors, and the fraud of deceivable traditions, drag so downwards, as to backslide one way into the Jewish beggary of old cast rudiments, and stumble forward another way into the new-vomited paganism of sensual idolatry, attributing purity or impurity to things indifferent, that they might bring the inward acts of the spirit to the outward and customary eye-service of the body, as if they could make God earthly and fleshly, because they could not make themselves heavenly and spiritual; they began to draw down all the divine intercourse betwixt God and the soul, yea, the very shape of God himself, into an exterior and bodily form, urgently pretending a necessity and obligement of joining the body in a formal reverence and worship circumscribed; they hallowed it, they fumed up, they sprinkled it, they bedecked it, not in robes of pure innocency, but of pure linen, with other deformed and fantastic dresses, in palls and mitres, gold, and gewgaws fetched from Aaron's old wardrobe, or the flamins vestry: then was the priest set to con his motions and his postures, his liturgies and his lurries, till the soul by this means of overbodying herself, given up justly to fleshly delights, bated her wing apace downward: and finding the ease she had from her visible and sensuous colleague, the body, in performance of religious duties, her pinions now broken, and flagging, shifted off from herself the labour of high soaring any more, forgot her heavenly flight, and left the dull and droiling carcase to plod on in the old road, and drudging trade of outward conformity. And here out of question from her perverse conceiting of God and holy things, she had fallen to believe no God at all, had not custom and the worm of conscience nipped her incredulity: hence to all the duties of evangelical grace, instead of the adoptive and cheerful boldness which our new alliance with God requires, came servile and thrallike fear: for in very deed, the superstitious man by his good will is an atheist; but being scared from thence by the pangs and gripes of a boiling conscience, all in a pudder shuffles up to himself such a God and such a worship as is most agreeable to remedy his fear; which fear of his, as also is his hope, fixed only upon the flesh, renders likewise the whole faculty of his apprehension carnal; and all the inward acts of worship, issuing from the native strength of the soul, run out lavishly to the upper skin, and there harden into a crust of formality. Hence men came to scan the Scriptures by the letter, and in the covenant of our redemption, magnified the external signs more than the quickening power of the Spirit; and yet, looking on them through their own guiltiness with a servile fear, and finding as little comfort, or rather terror from them again, they knew not how to hide their slavish approach to God's behests, by them not understood, nor worthily received, but by cloaking their servile crouching to all religious presentments, sometimes lawful, sometimes idolatrous, under the name of humility, and terming the piebald frippery and ostentation of ceremonies, decency.

Then was baptism changed into a kind of exorcism, and water, sanctified by Christ's institute, thought little enough to wash off the original spot, without the scratch or cross impression of a priest's forefinger: and that feast of free grace and adoption to which Christ invited His disciples to sit as brethren, and coheirs of the happy covenant, which at that table was to be sealed to them, even that feast of love and heavenly-admitted fellowship, the seal of filial grace, became the subject of horror, and glouting adoration, pageanted about like a dreadful idol; which sometimes deceives well-meaning men, and beguiles them of their reward, by their voluntary humility; which indeed is fleshly pride, preferring a foolish sacrifice, and the rudiments of the world, as St. Paul to the Colossians explaineth, before a savoury obedience to Christ's example. Such was Peter's unseasonable humility, as then his knowledge was small, when Christ came to wash his feet; who at an impertinent time would needs strain courtesy with his master, and falling troublesomely upon the lowly, all-wise, and unexaminable intention of Christ, in what he went with resolution to do, so provoked by his interruption the meek Lord, that He threatened to exclude him from his heavenly portion, unless he could be content to be less arrogant and stiff-necked in his humility.

But to dwell no longer in characterising the depravities of the church, and how they sprung, and how they took increase;

when I recall to mind at last, after so many dark ages, wherein the huge overshadowing train of error had almost swept all the stars out of the firmament of the church; how the bright and blissful Reformation (by divine power) struck through the black and settled night of ignorance and antichristian tyranny, methinks a sovereign and reviving joy must needs rush into the bosom of him that reads or hears; and the sweet odour of the returning gospel imbathe his soul with the fragrancy of heaven. Then was the sacred Bible sought out of the dusty corners where profane falsehood and neglect had thrown it, the schools opened, divine and human learning raked out of the embers of forgotten tongues, the princes and cities trooping apace to the new erected banner of salvation; the martyrs, with the unresistible might of weakness, shaking the powers of darkness, and scorning the fiery rage of the old red dragon.

The pleasing pursuit of these thoughts hath ofttimes led me into a serious question and debatement with myself, how it should come to pass that England (having had this grace and honour from God, to be the first that should set up a standard for the recovery of lost truth, and blow the first evangelic trumpet to the nations, holding up, as from a hill, the new lamp of saving light to all Christendom) should now be last and most unsettled in the enjoyment of that peace, whereof she taught the way to others; although indeed our Wickliffe's preaching, at which all the succeeding reformers more effectually lighted their tapers, was to his countrymen but a short blaze, soon damped and stifled by the pope and prelates for six or seven kings' reigns; yet methinks the precedency which God gave this island, to be first restorer of buried truth, should have been followed with more happy success, and sooner attained perfection; in which as yet we are amongst the last: for, albeit in purity of doctrine we agree with our brethren; yet in discipline, which is the execution and applying of doctrine home, and laying the salve to the very orifice of the wound, yea, tenting and searching to the core, without which pulpit preaching is but shooting at rovers; in this we are no better than a schism from all the Reformation, and a sore scandal to them: for while we hold ordination to belong only to bishops, as our prelates do, we must of necessity hold also their ministers to be no ministers, and shortly after their church to be no church : not to speak of those senseless ceremonies which we only retain, as a dangerous earnest of sliding back to Rome, and serving merely, either as a mist to cover nakedness where true grace is extinguished, or as an interlude to set out the pomp of prelatism. Certainly it would be worth the while therefore, and the pains, to inquire more particularly, what, and how many the chief causes have been, that have still hindered our uniform consent to the rest of the churches abroad, at this time especially when the kingdom is in a good propensity thereto, and all men in prayers, in hopes, or in disputes, either for or against it.

. . . . . .

Hitherto, sir, you have heard how the prelates have weakened and withdrawn the external accomplishments of kingly prosperity, the love of the people, their multitude, their valour, their wealth; mining and sapping the outworks and redoubts of monarchy. Now hear how they strike at the very heart and vitals.

We know that monarchy is made up of two parts, the liberty of the subject, and the supremacy of the king. I begin at the root. See what gentle and benign fathers they have been to our liberty ! Their trade being, by the same alchemy that the pope uses, to extract heaps of gold and silver out of the drossy bullion of the people's sins ; and justly fearing that the quick-sighted protestant's eye, cleared in great part from the mist of superstition, may at one time or another look with a good judgment into these their deceitful pedleries ; to gain as many associates of guiltiness as they can, and to infect the temporal magistrate with the like lawless, though not sacrilegious extortion, see awhile what they do ! they engage themselves to preach, and persuade an assertion for truth the most false, and to this monarchy the most pernicious and destructive that could be chosen. What more baneful to monarchy than a popular commotion? for the dissolution of monarchy slides aptest into a democracy; and what stirs the Englishmen, as our wisest writers have observed, sooner to rebellion, than violent and heavy hands upon their goods and purses? Yet these devout prelates, spite of our Great Charter, and the souls of our progenitors that wrested their liberties out of the Norman gripe with their dearest blood and highest prowess, for these many years have not ceased in their pulpits wrenching and spraining the text, to set at nought and trample under foot all the most sacred and lifeblood laws, statutes, and acts of parliament, that are the holy covenant of union and marriage between the king and his realm, by proscribing and confiscating from us all the right we have to our own bodies, goods, and liberties. What is this but to blow a trumpet, and proclaim a firecross to an hereditary and perpetual civil war? Thus much against the subjects' liberty hath been assaulted by them. Now how they have spared supremacy, or are likely hereafter to submit to it, remains lastly to be considered.

The emulation that under the old law was in the king towards the priest, is now so come about in the gospel, that all the danger is to be feared from the priest to the king. Whilst the priest's office in the law was set out with an exterior lustre of pomp and glory, kings were ambitious to be priests; now priests, not perceiving the heavenly brightness and inward splendour of their more glorious evangelic ministry, with as great ambition affect to be kings, as in all their courses is easy to be observed. Their eyes ever eminent upon worldly matters, their desires ever thirsting after worldly employments, instead of diligent and fervent study in the Bible, they covet to be expert in canons and decretals, which may enable them to judge and interpose in temporal causes, however pretended ecclesiastical. Do they not hoard up pelf, seek to be potent in secular strength, in state affairs, in lands, lordships, and domains, to sway and carry all before them in high courts and privy-councils, to bring into their grasp the high and principal offices of the kingdom? Have they not been told of late to check the common law, to slight and brave the indiminishable majesty of our highest court, the lawgiving and sacred parliament? Do they not plainly labour to exempt churchmen from the magistrate? Yea, so presumptuously as to question and menace officers that represent the king's person for using their authority against drunken priests? The cause of protecting murderous clergymen was the first heart-burning that swelled up the audacious Becket to the pestilent and odious vexation of Henry the Second. Nay, more: have not some of their devoted scholars begun, I need not say to nibble, but openly to argue against the king's supremacy? Is not the chief of them accused out of his own book, and his late canons, to affect a certain unquestionable patriarchate, independent, and unsubordinate to the crown? From whence having first brought us to a servile state of religion and manhood, and having predisposed his conditions with the pope, that lays claim to this land, or some Pepin of his own creating, it were all as likely for him to aspire to the monarchy among us, as that the pope could find means so on the sudden both to bereave the emperor of the Roman territory with the favour of Italy, and by an unexpected friend out of France, while he was in danger to lose his new-got purchase, beyond hope to leap into the fair exarchate of Ravenna.

A good while the pope subtly acted the lamb, writing to the emperor, "my lord Tiberius, my lord Mauritius;" but no sooner did this his lord pluck at the images and idols, but he threw off his sheep's clothing, and started up a wolf, laying his paws upon the emperor's right, as forfeited to Peter. Why may not we as well, having been forewarned at home by our renowned Chaucer, and from abroad by the great and learned Padre Paolo, from the like beginnings, as we see they are, fear the like events? Certainly a wise and provident king ought to suspect a hierarchy in his realm, being ever attended, as it is, with two such greedy purveyors, ambition and usurpation; I say, he ought to suspect a hierarchy to be as dangerous and derogatory from his crown as a tetrarchy or a heptarchy. Yet now that the prelates had almost attained to what their insolent and unbridled minds had hurried them; to thrust the laity under the despotical rule of the monarch, that they themselves might confine the monarch to a kind of pupilage under their hierarchy, observe but how their own principles combat one another, and supplant each one his fellow.

Having fitted us only for peace, and that a servile peace, by lessening our numbers, draining our estates, enfeebling our bodies, cowing our free spirits by those ways as you have heard, their impotent actions cannot sustain themselves the least moment, unless they would rouse us up to a war fit for Cain to be the leader of, an abhorred, a cursed, a fraternal war. England and Scotland, dearest brothers both in nature and in Christ, must be set to wade in one another's blood; and Ireland, our free denizen, upon the back of us both, as occasion should serve : a piece of service that the pope and all his factors have been compassing to do ever since the Reformation.

But ever blessed be He, and ever glorified, that from his high watch-tower in the heavens, discerning the crooked ways of perverse and cruel men, hath hitherto maimed and infatuated all their damnable inventions, and deluded their great wizards with a delusion fit for fools and children: had God been so minded, he could have sent a spirit of mutiny amongst us, as he did between Abimelech and the Sechemites, to have made our funerals, and slain heaps more in number than the miserable surviving remnant; but He, when we least deserved, sent out a gentle gale and message of peace from the wings of those his cherubims that fan his mercy-seat. Nor shall the wisdom, the moderation, the Christian piety, the constancy of our nobility and commons of England, be ever forgotten, whose calm and temperate connivance could sit still and smile out the stormy bluster of men more audacious and precipitant than of solid and deep reach, until their own fury had run itself out of breath, assailing by rash and heady approaches the impregnable situation of our liberty and safety, that laughed such weak enginery to scorn, such poor drifts to make a national war of a surplice brabble, a tippet scuffle, and engage the untainted honour of English knighthood to unfurl the streaming red cross, or to rear the horrid standard of those fatal guly dragons, for so unworthy a purpose, as to force upon their fellow-subjects that which themselves are weary of, the skeleton of a mass-book. Nor must the patience, the fortitude, the firm obedience of the nobles and people of Scotland, striving against manifold provocations; nor must their sincere and moderate proceedings hitherto be unremembered, to the shameful conviction of all their detractors.

Go on both hand in hand, O nations, never to be disunited; be the praise and the heroic song of all posterity; merit this, but seek only virtue, not to extend your limits; (for what needs to win a fading triumphant laurel out of the tears of wretched men?) but to settle the pure worship of God in His church, and justice in the state: then shall the hardest difficulties smooth out themselves before ye; envy shall sink to hell, craft and malice be confounded, whether it be homebred mischief or outlandish cunning: yea, other nations will then covet to serve ye, for lordship and victory are but the pages of justice and virtue. Commit securely to true wisdom the vanquishing and uncasing of craft and subtlety, which are but her two runagates: join your invincible might to do worthy and godlike deeds; and then he that seeks to break your union, a cleaving curse be his inheritance to all generations.

Sir, you have now at length this question for the time, and as my memory would best serve me in such a copious and vast theme, fully handled, and you yourself may judge whether prelacy be the only church-government agreeable to monarchy. Seeing therefore the perilous and confused state into which we are fallen, and that, to the certain knowledge of all men, through the irreligious pride and hateful tyranny of prelates (as the innumerable and grievous complaints of every shire cry out), if we will now resolve to settle affairs either according to pure religion or sound policy, we must first of all begin roundly to cashier and cut away from the public body the noisome and diseased tumour of prelacy, and come from schism to unity with our neighbour reformed sister-churches, which with the blessing of peace and pure doctrine have now long time flourished; and doubtless with all hearty joy and gratitude will meet and welcome our Christian union with them, as they have been all this while grieved at our strangeness, and little better than separation from them. And for the discipline propounded, seeing that it hath been inevitably proved, that the natural and fundamental causes of political happiness in all governments are the same, and that this church-discipline is taught in the word of God, and, as we see, agrees according to wish with all such states as have received it; we may infallibly assure ourselves that it will as well agree with monarchy, though all the tribe of Aphorismers and Politicasters would persuade us there be secret and mysterious reasons against it. For upon the settling hereof mark what nourishing and cordial restorements to the state will follow, the ministers of the gospel attending only to the work of salvation, every one within his limited charge; besides the diffusive blessings of God upon all our actions, the king shall sit without an old disturber, a daily encroacher and intruder; shall rid his kingdom of a strong sequestered and collateral power; a confronting mitre, whose potent wealth and wakeful ambition he had just cause to hold in jealousy: not to repeat the other present evils which only their removal will remove, and because things simply pure are inconsistent in the mass of nature, nor are the elements or humours in a man's body exactly homogeneal; and hence the best-founded commonwealths and least barbarous have aimed at a certain mixture and temperament, partaking the several virtues of each other state, that each part drawing to itself may keep up a steady and even uprightness in common.

There is no civil government that hath been known, no not the Spartan, not the Roman, though both for this respect so much praised by the wise Polybius, more divinely and harmoniously tuned, more equally balanced as it were by the hand and scale of justice, than is the commonwealth of England; where, under a free and untutored monarch, the noblest, worthiest, and most prudent men, with full approbation and suffrage of the people, have in their power the supreme and final determination of highest affairs. Now if conformity of church-discipline to the civil be so desired, there can be nothing more parallel, more uniform, than when under the sovereign prince, Christ's vicegerent, using the sceptre of David, according to God's law, the godliest, the wisest, the learnedest ministers in their several charges have the instructing and disciplining of God's people, by whose full and free election they are consecrated to that holy and equal aristocracy. And why should not the piety and conscience of Englishmen, as members of the church, be trusted in the election of pastors to functions that nothing concern a monarch, as well as their worldly wisdoms are privileged as members of the state in suffraging their knights and burgesses to matters that concern him nearly? And if in weighing these several offices, their difference in time and quality be cast in, I know they will not turn the beam of equal judgment the moiety of a scruple. We therefore having already a kind of apostolical and ancient church election in our state, what a perverseness would it be in us of all others to retain forcibly a kind of imperious and stately election in our church! And what a blindness to think that what is already evangelical, as it were by a happy chance in our polity, should be repugnant to that which is the same by divine command in the ministry! Thus then we see that our ecclesiastical and political choices may consent and sort as well together without any rupture in the state, as Christians and freeholders. But as for honour, that ought indeed to be different and distinct, as either office looks a several way; the minister whose calling and end is spiritual, ought to be honoured as a father and physician to the soul (if he be found to be so), with a sonlike and disciplelike reverence, which is indeed the dearest and most affectionate honour, most to be desired by a wise man, and such as will easily command a free and plentiful provision of outward necessaries, without his further care of this world.

The magistrate, whose charge is to see to our persons and estates, is to be honoured with a more elaborate and personal courtship, with large salaries and stipends, that he himself may abound in those things whereof his legal justice and watchful care give us the quiet enjoyment. And this distinction of honour will bring forth a seemly and graceful uniformity over all the kingdom.

Then shall the nobles possess all the dignities and offices of temporal honour to themselves, sole lords without the improper mixture of scholastic and pusillanimous upstarts; the parliament shall void her upper house of the same annoyances; the common and civil laws shall be both set free, the former from the control, the other from the mere vassalage and copyhold of the clergy.

And whereas temporal laws rather punish men when they have transgressed, than form them to be such as should transgress seldomest, we may conceive great hopes, through the showers of divine benediction watering the unmolested and watchful pains of the ministry, that the whole inheritance of God will grow up so straight and blameless, that the civil magistrate may with far less toil and difficulty, and far more ease and delight, steer the tall and goodly vessel of the commonwealth through all the gusts and tides of the world's mutability.

Here I might have ended, but that some objections, which I have heard commonly flying about, press me to the endeavour of an answer. We must not run, they say, into sudden extremes. This is a fallacious rule, unless understood only of the actions of virtue about things indifferent: for if it be found that those two extremes be vice and virtue, falsehood and truth, the greater extremity of virtue and superlative truth we run into, the more virtuous and the more wise we become; and he that, flying from degenerate and traditional corruption, fears to shoot himself too far into the meeting embraces of a divinely warranted reformation, had better not have run at all. And for the suddenness, it cannot be feared. Who should oppose it? The papists? They dare not. The protestants otherwise affected? They were mad. There is nothing will be removed but what to them is professedly indifferent. The long affection which the people have borne to it, what for itself, what for the odiousness of prelates, is evident: from the first year of Queen Elizabeth it hath still been more and more propounded, desired, and beseeched, yea, sometimes favourably forwarded by the parliaments themselves. Yet if it were sudden and swift, provided still it be from worse to better, certainly we ought to hie us from evil like a torrent, and rid ourselves of corrupt discipline, as we would shake fire out of our bosoms.

Speedy and vehement were the reformations of all the good kings of Judah, though the people had been nuzzled in idolatry ever so long before; they feared not the bugbear danger, nor the lion in the way that the sluggish and timorous politician thinks he sees; no more did our brethren of the reformed churches abroad, they ventured (God being their guide) out of rigid popery, into that which we in mockery call precise puritanism, and yet we see no inconvenience befell them.

Let us not dally with God when he offers us a full blessing, to take as much of it as we think will serve our ends, and turn him back the rest upon his hands, lest in his anger he snatch all from us again. Next, they allege the antiquity of episcopacy through all ages. What it was in the apostle's time, that questionless it must be still; and therein I trust the ministers will be able to satisfy the parliament. But if episcopacy be taken for prelacy, all the ages they can deduce it through, will make it no more venerable than papacy.

Most certain it is (as all our stories bear witness), that ever since their coming to the see of Canterbury, for near twelve hundred years, to speak of them in general, they have been in England to our souls a sad and doleful succession of illiterate and blind guides; to our purses and goods a wasteful band of robbers, a perpetual havoc and rapine; to our state a continual hydra of mischief and molestation, the forge of discord and rebellion; this is the trophy of their antiquity, and boasted succession through so many ages. And for those prelate-martyrs they glory of, they are to be judged what they were by the gospel, and not the gospel to be tried by them.

And it is to be noted, that if they were for bishoprics and ceremonies, it was in their prosperity and fulness of bread; but in their persecution, which purified them, and near their death, which was their garland, they plainly disliked and condemned the ceremonies, and threw away those episcopal ornaments wherein they were installed as foolish and detestable; for so the words of Ridley at his degradement, and his letter to

Hooper, expressly show. Neither doth the author of our church-history spare to record sadly the fall (for so he terms it) and infirmities of these martyrs, though we would deify them. And why should their martyrdom more countenance corrupt doctrine or discipline, than their subscriptions justify their treason to the royal blood of this realm, by diverting and entailing the right of the crown from the true heirs, to the houses of Northumberland and Suffolk? which had it took effect, this present king had, in all likelihood, never sat on this throne, and the happy union of this island had been frustrated.

Lastly, whereas they add that some the learnedst of the reformed abroad admire our episcopacy; it had been more for the strength of the argument to tell us that some of the wisest statesmen admire it, for thereby we might guess them weary of the present discipline, as offensive to their state, which is the bug we fear; but being they are churchmen, we may rather suspect them for some prelatising spirits that admire our bishoprics, not episcopacy.

The next objection vanishes of itself, propounding a doubt, whether a greater inconvenience would not grow from the corruption of any other discipline than from that of episcopacy. This seems an unseasonable foresight, and out of order, to defer and put off the most needful constitution of one right discipline, while we stand balancing the discommodities of two corrupt ones. First constitute that which is right, and of itself it will discover and rectify that which swerves, and easily remedy the pretended fear of having a pope in every parish, unless we call the zealous and meek censure of the church a popedom, which whoso does, let him advise how he can reject the pastorly rod and sheephook of Christ, and those cords of love, and not fear to fall under the iron sceptre of His anger, that will dash him to pieces like a potsherd.

At another doubt of theirs I wonder, whether this discipline which we desire be such as can be put in practice within this kingdom; they say it cannot stand with the common law nor with the king's safety, the government of episcopacy is now so weaved into the common law. In God's name let it weave out again; let not human quillets keep back divine authority. It is not the common law, nor the civil, but piety and justice that are our foundresses; they stoop not, neither change colour for aristocracy, democracy, or monarchy, nor yet at all interrupt their just courses; but far above the taking notice of these inferior niceties, with perfect sympathy, wherever they meet, kiss each other. Lastly, they are fearful that the discipline which will succeed cannot stand with the king's safety. Wherefore? it is but episcopacy reduced to what it should be: were it not that the tyranny of prelates under the name of bishops had made our ears tender and startling, we might call every good minister a bishop, as every bishop, yea, the apostles themselves, are called ministers, and the angels ministering spirits, and the ministers again angels. But wherein is this propounded government so shrewd? Because the government of assemblies will succeed. Did not the apostles govern the church by assemblies? How should it else be catholic? How should it have communion? We count it sacrilege to take from the rich prelates their lands and revenues, which is sacrilege in them to keep, using them as they do; and can we think it safe to defraud the living church of God of that right which God has given her in assemblies? O but the consequence! assemblies draw to them the supremacy of ecclesiastical jurisdiction. No, surely, they draw no supremacy, but that authority which Christ, and St. Paul in His name, confers upon them. The king may still retain the same supremacy in the assemblies, as in the parliament; here he can do nothing alone against the common law, and there neither alone, nor with consent, against the Scriptures. But is this all? No: this ecclesiastical supremacy draws to it the power to excommunicate kings; and then follows the worst that can be imagined. Do they hope to avoid this, by keeping prelates that have so often done it? Not to exemplify the malapert insolence of our own bishops in this kind towards our kings, I shall turn back to the primitive and pure times, which the objectors would have the rule of reformation to us.

Not an assembly, but one bishop alone, St. Ambrose of

Milan, held Theodosius, the most Christian emperor, under excommunication above eight months together, drove him from the church in the presence of his nobles; which the good emperor bore with heroic humility, and never ceased by prayers and tears, till he was absolved; for which coming to the bishop with supplication into the salutatory, some outporch of the church, he was charged by him with tyrannical madness against God, for coming into holy ground. At last, upon conditions absolved, and after great humiliation approaching to the altar to offer (as those thrice pure times then thought meet), he had scarce withdrawn his hand, and stood awhile, when a bold archdeacon comes in the bishop's name, and chases him from within the rails, telling him peremptorily, that the place wherein he stood was for none but the priests to enter, or to touch: and this is another piece of pure primitive divinity! Think ye, then, our bishops will forego the power of excommunication on whomsoever? No, certainly, unless to compass sinister ends, and then revoke when they see their time. And yet this most mild, though withal dreadful and inviolable prerogative of Christ's diadem, excommunication, serves for nothing with them, but to prog and pander for fees, or to display their pride, and sharpen their revenge, debarring men the protection of the law; and I remember not whether in some cases it bereave not men all right to their worldly goods and inheritances, besides the denial of Christian burial. But in the evangelical and reformed use of this sacred censure, no such prostitution, no such Iscariotical drifts are to be doubted, as that spiritual doom and sentence should invade worldly possession, which is the rightful lot and portion even of the wickedest men, as frankly bestowed upon them by the all-dispensing bounty as rain and sunshine. No, no, it seeks not to bereave or destroy the body; it seeks to save the soul by humbling the body, not by imprisonment, or pecuniary mulct, much less by stripes, or bonds, or disinheritance, but by fatherly admonishment and Christian rebuke, to cast it into godly sorrow, whose end is joy, and ingenuous bashfulness to sin: if that cannot be wrought, then as a tender mother takes her child and holds it over the pit with scaring words, that it may learn to fear where danger is; so doth excommunication as dearly and as freely, without money, use her wholesome and saving terrors; she is instant, she beseeches, by all the dear and sweet promises of salvation she entices and woos; by all the threatenings and thunders of the law, and rejected gospel, she charges and adjures: this is all her armoury, her munition, her artillery; then she awaits with long-sufferance, and yet ardent zeal. In brief, there is no act in all the errand of God's ministers to mankind wherein passes more loverlike contestation between Christ and the soul of a regenerate man lapsing, than before, and in, and after the sentence of excommunication. As for the fogging proctorage of money, with such an eye as struck Gehazi with leprosy and Simon Magus with a curse, so does she look, and so threaten her fiery whip against that banking den of thieves that dare thus baffle, and buy and sell the awful and majestic wrinkles of her brow. He that is rightly and apostolically sped with her invisible arrow, if he can be at peace in his soul, and not smell within him the brimstone of hell, may have fair leave to tell all his bags over undiminished of the least farthing, may eat his dainties, drink his wine, use his delights, enjoy his lands and liberties, not the least skin raised, not the least hair misplaced, for all that excommunication has done: much more may a king enjoy his rights and prerogatives undeflowered, untouched, and be as absolute and complete a king, as all his royalties and revenues can make him. And therefore little did Theodosius fear a plot upon his empire, when he stood excommunicate by Saint Ambrose, though it were done either with much haughty pride, or ignorant zeal. But let us rather look upon the reformed churches beyond the seas, the Grizons, the Swisses, the Hollanders, the French, that have a supremacy to live under, as well as we: where do the churches in all these places strive for supremacy? Where do they clash and justle supremacies with the civil magistrate? In France, a more severe monarchy than ours, the protestants under this church government carry the name of the best subjects the king has;

and yet presbytery, if it must be so called, does there all that
it desires to do: how easy were it, if there be such great suspicion, to give no more scope to it in England! But let us not
for fear of a scarecrow, or else through hatred to be reformed,
stand hankering and politising, when God with spread hands
testifies to us, and points us out the way to our peace.

Let us not be so over-credulous, unless God hath blinded us,
as to trust our dear souls into the hands of men that beg so
devoutly for the pride and gluttony of their own backs and
bellies, that sue and solicit so eagerly, not for the saving of
souls, the consideration of which can have here no place at all,
but for their bishoprics, deaneries, prebends, and canonries:
how can these men not be corrupt, whose very cause is the
bribe of their own pleading, whose mouths cannot open without the strong breath and loud stench of avarice, simony, and
sacrilege, embezzling the treasury of the church on painted and
gilded walls of temples, wherein God hath testified to have no
delight, warming their palace kitchens, and from thence their
unctious and epicurean paunches, with the alms of the blind,
the lame, the impotent, the aged, the orphan, the widow? for
with these the treasury of Christ ought to be, here must be His
jewels bestowed, His rich cabinet must be emptied here; as the
constant martyr St. Lawrence taught the Roman prætor. Sir,
would you know what the remonstrance of these men would
have, what their petition implies? They entreat us that we
would not be weary of those insupportable grievances that our
shoulders have hitherto cracked under; they beseech us that
we would think them fit to be our justices of peace, our lords,
our highest officers of state, though they come furnished with
no more experience than they learnt between the cook and the
manciple, or more profoundly at the college audit, or the regent
house, or to come to their deepest insight, at their patron's
table; they would request us to endure still the rustling of their
silken cassocks, and that we would burst our midriffs, rather
than laugh to see them under sail in all their lawn and sarcenet,
their shrouds and tackle, with a geometrical rhomboides upon
their heads: they would bear us in hand that we must of duty

still appear before them once a year in Jerusalem, like good circumcised males and females, to be taxed by the poll, to be sconced our head-money, our twopences, in their chandlerly shopbook of Easter. They pray us that it would please us to let them still hale us, and worry us with their bandogs and pursuivants; and that it would please the parliament that they may yet have the whipping, fleecing, and flaying of us in their diabolical courts, to tear the flesh from our bones, and into our wide wounds instead of balm, to pour in the oil of tartar, vitriol, and mercury: surely, a right reasonable, innocent, and soft-hearted petition. O the relenting bowels of the fathers! Can this be granted them, unless God have smitten us with frenzy from above, and with a dazzling giddiness at noonday? Should not those men rather be heard that come to plead against their own preferments, their worldly advantages, their own abundance; for honour and obedience to God's word, the conversion of souls, the Christian peace of the land, and union of the reformed catholic church, the unappropriating and unmonopolising the rewards of learning and industry, from the greasy clutch of ignorance and high feeding? We have tried already, and miserably felt what ambition, worldly glory, and immoderate wealth, can do; what the boisterous and contradictional hand of a temporal, earthly, and corporeal spirituality can avail to the edifying of Christ's holy church; were it such a desperate hazard to put to the venture the universal votes of Christ's congregation, and fellowly and friendly yoke of a teaching and laborious ministry, the pastorlike and apostolic imitation of meek and unlordly discipline, the gentle and benevolent mediocrity of church-maintenance, without the ignoble hucksterage of piddling tithes? Were it such an incurable mischief to make a little trial, what all this would do to the flourishing and growing up of Christ's mystical body? as rather to use every poor shift, and if that serve not, to threaten uproar and combustion, and shake the brand of civil discord?

O, sir, I do now feel myself inwrapped on the sudden into those mazes and labyrinths of dreadful and hideous thoughts, that which way to get out, or which way to end, I know not, unless I turn mine eyes, and with your help lift up my hands to that eternal and propitious throne, where nothing is readier than grace and refuge to the distresses of mortal suppliants : and it were a shame to leave these serious thoughts less piously than the heathen were wont to conclude their graver discourses.

Thou, therefore, that sittest in light and glory unapproachable, parent of angels and men ! next, thee I implore, omnipotent King, Redeemer of that lost remnant whose nature thou didst assume, ineffable and everlasting Love ! and thou, the third subsistence of divine infinitude, illumining Spirit, the joy and solace of created things ! one Tripersonal godhead ! look upon this thy poor and almost spent and expiring church, leave her not thus a prey to these importunate wolves, that wait and think long till they devour thy tender flock ; these wild boars that have broke into thy vineyard, and left the print of their polluting hoofs on the souls of thy servants. O let them not bring about their damned designs, that stand now at the entrance of the bottomless pit, expecting the watchword to open and let out those dreadful locusts and scorpions, to reinvolve us in that pitchy cloud of infernal darkness, where we shall never more see the sun of thy truth again, never hope for the cheerful dawn, never more hear the bird of morning sing. Be moved with pity at the afflicted state of this our shaken monarchy, that now lies labouring under her throes, and struggling against the grudges of more dreaded calamities.

O thou, that, after the impetuous rage of five bloody inundations, and the succeeding sword of intestine war, soaking the land in her own gore, didst pity the sad and ceaseless revolution of our swift and thick-coming sorrows ; when we were quite breathless, of thy free grace didst motion peace, and terms of covenant with us ; and having first well-nigh freed us from antichristian thraldom, didst build up this Brittanic empire to a glorious and enviable height, with all her daughter-islands about her ; stay us in this felicity, let not the obstinacy of our half-obedience and will-worship bring forth that viper of sedition, that for these fourscore years hath been breeding to eat through the entrails of our peace; but let her cast her abortive spawn without the danger of this travailing and throbbing kingdom: that we may still remember in our solemn thanksgivings, how for us, the northern ocean even to the frozen Thule was scattered with the proud shipwrecks of the Spanish armada, and the very maw of hell ransacked, and made to give up her concealed destruction, ere she could vent it in that horrible and damned blast.

O how much more glorious will those former deliverances appear, when we shall know them not only to have saved us from greatest miseries past, but to have reserved us for greatest happiness to come! Hitherto thou hast but freed us, and that not fully, from the unjust and tyrannous claim of thy foes; now unite us entirely, and appropriate us to thyself, tie us everlastingly in willing homage to the prerogative of thy eternal throne.

And now we know, O thou our most certain hope and defence, that thine enemies have been consulting all the sorceries of the great whore, and have joined their plots with that sad intelligencing tyrant that mischiefs the world with his mines of Ophir, and lies thirsting to revenge his naval ruins that have larded our seas: but let them all take counsel together, and let it come to nought; let them decree, and do thou cancel it; let them gather themselves, and be scattered; let them embattle themselves, and be broken; let them embattle, and be broken, for thou art with us.

Then, amidst the hymns and hallelujahs of saints, some one may perhaps be heard offering at high strains in new and lofty measure to sing and celebrate thy divine mercies and marvellous judgments in this land throughout all ages; whereby this great and warlike nation, instructed and inured to the fervent and continual practice of truth and righteousness, and casting far from her the rags of her whole vices, may press on hard to that high and happy emulation to be found the soberest, wisest, and most Christian people at that day, when thou, the eternal and shortly expected King, shalt open the clouds to judge the several kingdoms of the world, and distributing national honours and rewards to religious and just commonwealths, shalt put an end to all earthly tyrannies, proclaiming thy universal and mild monarchy through heaven and earth; where they undoubtedly, that by their labours, counsels, and prayers, have been earnest for the common good of religion and their country, shall receive above the inferior orders of the blessed, the regal addition of principalities, legions, and thrones into their glorious titles, and in supereminence of beatific vision, progressing the dateless and irrevoluble circle of eternity, shall clasp inseparable hands with joy and bliss, in overmeasure for ever.

But they contrary, that by the impairing and diminution of the true faith, the distresses and servitude of their country, aspire to high dignity, rule, and promotion here, after a shameful end in this life (which God grant them), shall be thrown down eternally into the darkest and deepest gulf of hell, where, under the despiteful control, the trample and spurn of all the other damned, that in the anguish of their torture, shall have no other ease than to exercise and raving and bestial tyranny over them as their slaves and negroes, they shall remain in that plight for ever, the basest, the lowermost, the most dejected, most underfoot, and downtrodden vassals of perdition.

FROM "ANIMADVERSIONS UPON THE REMONSTRANT'S DEFENCE AGAINST SMECTYMNUUS."

REMONST. *They cannot name any man in this nation, that ever contradicted episcopacy till this present age.*

ANSW. What an overworn and bedridden argument is this! the last refuge ever of old falsehood, and therefore a good sign, I trust, that your castle cannot hold out long. This was the plea of judaism and idolatry against Christ and his apostles, of papacy against reformation; and perhaps to the frailty of flesh and blood in a man destitute of better enlightening may for some while be pardonable: for what has fleshly apprehension other to subsist by than succession, custom, and visibility; which only hold, if in his weakness and blindness he be loath to lose, who can blame? But in a protestant nation, that should have thrown off these tattered rudiments long ago, after the many strivings of God's Spirit, and our fourscore years' vexation of him in this our wilderness since reformation began, to urge these rotten principles, and twit us with the present age, which is to us an age of ages wherein God is manifestly come down among us, to do some remarkable good to our church or state, is, as if a man should tax the renovating and reingendering Spirit of God with innovation, and that new creature for an upstart novelty; yea, the new Jerusalem, which, without your admired link of succession, descends from heaven, could not escape some such-like censure. If you require a further answer, it will not misbecome a Christian to be either more magnanimous or more devout than Scipio was; who, instead of other answer to the frivolous accusations of Petilius the tribune, "This day, Romans (saith he), I fought with Hannibal prosperously; let us all go and thank the gods that gave us so great a victory;" in like manner will we now say, not caring otherwise to answer this unprotestantlike objection: In this age, Britons, God hath reformed his church after many hundred years of popish corruption; in this age He hath freed us from the intolerable yoke of prelates and papal discipline; in this age He hath renewed our protestation against all those yet remaining dregs of superstition. Let us all go, every true protested Briton, throughout the three kingdoms, and render thanks to God the Father of light, and Fountain of heavenly grace, and to his Son Christ our Lord, leaving this Remonstrant and his adherents to their own designs; and let us recount even here without delay the patience and long-suffering that God hath used towards our blindness and hardness time after time. For He being equally near to his whole creation of mankind, and of free power to turn his beneficent and fatherly regard to what region or kingdom He pleases, hath yet ever had this island under the special indulgent eye of his providence; and pitying us the first of all other nations, after He had decreed to purify and renew his church that lay wallowing in idolatrous pollutions, sent first to us a healing messenger to touch softly our sores, and carry a gentle hand over our wounds: he knocked once and twice, and came again opening our drowsy eyelids leisurely by that glimmering light which Wickliff and his followers dispersed; and still taking off by degrees the inveterate scales from our nigh perished sight, purged also our deaf ears, and prepared them to attend his second warning trumpet in our grandsire's days. How else could they have been able to have received the sudden assault of his reforming Spirit, warring against human principles, and carnal sense, the pride of flesh, that still cried up antiquity, custom, canons, councils, and laws; and cried down the truth for novelty, schism, profaneness, and sacrilege? whenas we that have lived so long in abundant light, besides the sunny reflection of all the neighbouring churches, have yet our hearts riveted with those old opinions, and so obstructed and benumbed with the same fleshly reasonings, which in our forefathers soon melted and gave way, against the morning beam of reformation. If God had left undone this whole work, so contrary to flesh and blood, till these times, how should we have yielded to his heavenly call, had we been taken, as they were, in the starkness of our ignorance; that yet, after all these spiritual preparatives and purgations, have our earthly apprehensions so clammed and furred with the old leaven? O if we freeze at noon after their early thaw, let us fear lest the sun for ever hide himself, and turn his orient steps from our ingrateful horizon, justly condemned to be eternally benighted. Which dreadful judgment, O thou the ever-begotten Light and perfect Image of the Father! intercede, may never come upon us, as we trust thou hast; for thou hast opened our difficult and sad times, and given us an unexpected breathing after our long oppressions: thou hast done justice upon those that tyrannised over us, while some men wavered and admired a vain shadow of wisdom in a tongue nothing slow to utter guile, though thou hast taught us to admire only that which is good, and to count that only praiseworthy which is grounded upon thy divine precepts. Thou hast discovered the plots, and frustrated the hopes, of all the wicked in the land, and put to shame the persecutors of thy church: thou hast made our false prophets to be found a lie in the sight of all the people, and chased them with sudden confusion and amazement before the redoubled brightness of thy descending cloud, that now covers thy tabernacle. Who is there that cannot trace thee now in thy beamy walk through the midst of thy sanctuary, amidst those golden candlesticks, which have long suffered a dimness amongst us through the violence of those that had seized them, and were more taken with the mention of their gold than of their starry light; teaching the doctrine of Balaam, to cast a stumbling-block before thy servants, commanding them to eat things sacrificed to idols, and forcing them to fornication? Come therefore, O thou that hast the seven stars in thy right hand, appoint thy chosen priests according to their orders and courses of old, to minister before thee, and duly to press and pour out the consecrated oil into thy holy and ever-burning lamps. Thou hast sent out the spirit of prayer upon thy servants over all the land to this effect, and stirred up their vows as the sound of many waters about thy throne. Every one can say, that now certainly thou hast visited this land, and hast not forgotten the utmost corners of the earth, in a time when men had thought that thou wast gone up from us to the furthest end of the heavens, and hadst left to do marvellously among the sons of these last ages. O perfect and accomplish thy glorious acts! for men may leave their works unfinished, but thou art a God, thy nature is perfection: shouldst thou bring us thus far onward from Egypt to destroy us in this wilderness, though we deserve, yet thy great name would suffer in the rejoicing of thine enemies, and the deluded hope of all thy servants. When thou hast settled peace in the church, and righteous judgment in the kingdom, then shall all thy saints address their voices of joy and triumph to thee, standing on the shore of that Red Sea into which our enemies had almost driven us. And he that now for haste snatches up a plain ungarnished present as a thank-offering to thee, which could not be deferred in regard of thy so many late deliverances wrought for us one upon another, may then perhaps take up a harp, and sing thee an elaborate song to generations. In that day it shall no more be said as in scorn, this or that was never held so till this present age, when men have better learnt that the times and seasons pass along under thy feet to go and come at thy bidding: and as thou didst dignify our fathers' days with many revelations above all the foregoing ages, since thou tookest the flesh; so thou canst vouchsafe to us (though unworthy) as large a portion of thy Spirit as thou pleasest: for who shall prejudice thy all-governing will? seeing the power of thy grace is not passed away with the primitive times, as fond and faithless men imagine, but thy kingdom is now at hand, and thou standing at the door. Come forth out of thy royal chambers, O Prince of all the kings of the earth! put on the visible robes of thy imperial majesty, take up that unlimited sceptre which thy Almighty Father hath bequeathed thee; for now the voice of thy bride calls thee, and all creatures sigh to be renewed.

. . . .

In the constitution and founding of a church, that some men inspired from God should have an extraordinary calling to appoint, to order, and dispose, must needs be. So Moses, though himself no priest, sanctified and ordained Aaron and his sons; but when all needful things be set, and regulated by the writings of the apostles, whether it be not a mere folly to keep up a superior degree in the church only for ordination and jurisdiction, it will be no hurt to debate awhile. The apostles were the builders, and, as it were, the architects of the Christian church: wherein consisted their excellence above ordinary ministers? A prelate would say, In commanding, in controlling, in appointing, in calling to them, and sending from about them, to all countries, their bishops and archbishops as their deputies, with a kind of legantine power. No, no, vain prelates; this was but as the scaffolding of a new edifice, which for the time must board and overlook the highest battlements; but if the structure once finished, any passenger should fall in love with them, and pray that they might still stand, as being a singular grace and strengthening to the house, who would otherwise think, but that the man was presently to be laid hold on, and sent to his friends and kindred? The eminence of the apostles consisted in their powerful preaching, their unwearied labouring in the word, their unquenchable charity, which, above all earthly respects, like a working flame, had spun up to such a height of pure desire, as might be thought next to that love which dwells in God to save souls; which, while they did, they were contented to be the offscouring of the world, and to expose themselves willingly to all afflictions, perfecting thereby their hope through patience to a joy unspeakable. As for ordination, what is it, but the laying on of hands, an outward sign or symbol of admission? It creates nothing, it confers nothing; it is the inward calling of God that makes a minister, and his own painful study and diligence that manures and improves his ministerial gifts. In the primitive times, many, before ever they had received ordination from the apostles, had done the church noble service, as Apollos and others. It is but an orderly form of receiving a man already fitted, and committing to him a particular charge; the employment of preaching is as holy, and far more excellent; the care also and judgment to be used in the winning of souls, which is thought to be sufficient in every worthy minister, is an ability above that which is required in ordination: for many may be able to judge who is fit to be made a minister, that would not be found fit to be made ministers themselves; as it will not be denied that he may be the competent judge of a neat picture, or elegant poem, that cannot limn the like. Why, therefore, we should constitute a superior order in the church to perform an office which is not only every minister's function, but inferior also to that which he has a confessed right to, and why this superiority should remain thus usurped, some wise Epimenides tell us. Now for jurisdiction, this dear saint of the prelates, it will be best to consider, first, what it is: that sovereign Lord, who in the discharge of his holy anointment from God the Father, which made him supreme bishop of our souls, was so humble as to say, "Who made me a judge, or a divider over ye?" hath taught us that a churchman's jurisdiction is no more but to watch over his flock in season, and out of season, to deal by sweet and efficacious instructions, gentle admonitions, and sometimes rounder reproofs; against negligence or obstinacy, will be required a rousing volley of pastoral threatenings; against a persisting stubbornness, or the fear of a reprobate sense, a timely separation from the flock by that interdictive sentence, lest his conversation unprohibited, or unbranded, might breathe a pestilential murrain into the other sheep. In sum, his jurisdiction is to see the thriving and prospering of that which he hath planted: what other work the prelates have found for chancellors and suffragans, delegates and officials, with all the hell-pestering rabble of sumners and apparitors, is but an invasion upon the temporal magistrate, and affected by them as men that are not ashamed of the ensign and banner of antichrist. But true evangelical jurisdiction or discipline is no more, as was said, than for a minister to see to the thriving and prospering of that which he hath planted. And which is the worthiest work of these two, to plant as every minister's office is equally with the bishops, or to tend that which is planted, which the blind and undiscerning prelates call jurisdiction, and would appropriate to themselves as a business of higher dignity? Have patience, therefore, a little, and hear a law case. A certain man of large possessions had a fair garden, and kept therein an honest and laborious servant, whose skill and profession was to set or sow all wholesome herbs, and delightful flowers, according to every season, and whatever else was to be done in a well-husbanded nursery of plants and fruits. Now, when the time was come that he should cut his hedges, prune his trees, look to his tender slips, and pluck up the weeds that hindered their growth, he gets him up by break of day, and makes account to do what was needful in his garden: and who would think that any other should know better than he how the day's work was to be spent? Yet, for all this, there comes another strange gardener, that never knew the soil, never handled a dibble or spade to set the least potherb that grew there, much less had endured an hour's sweat or chillness, and yet challenges as his right the binding or unbinding of every flower, the clipping of every bush, the weeding and worming of every bed, both in that and all other gardens thereabout. The honest gardener, that ever since the daypeep, till now the sun was grown somewhat rank, had wrought painfully about his banks and seed-plots, at his commanding voice turns suddenly about with some wonder; and although he could have well beteemed to have thanked him for the ease he proffered, yet loving his own handywork, modestly refused him, telling him withal, that, for his part, if he had thought much of his own pains, he could for once have committed the work to one of his fellow-labourers, forasmuch as it is well known to be a matter of less skill and less labour to keep a garden handsome, than it is to plant it, or contrive it; and that he had already performed himself. No, said the stranger, this is neither for you nor your fellows to meddle with, but for me only that am for this purpose in dignity far above you; and the provision which the lord of the soil allows me in this office is, and that with good reason, tenfold your wages. The gardener smiled and shook his head; but what was determined, I cannot tell you till the end of this parliament.

REMONST. *If in time you shall see wooden chalices, and wooden priests, thank yourselves*

ANSW. It had been happy for this land if your priests had been but only wooden; all England knows they have been to this island not wood, but wormwood, that have infected the third part of our waters, like that apostate star in the Revelation, that many souls have died of their bitterness; and if you mean by wooden, illiterate or contemptible, there was no want of that sort among you; and their number increasing daily, as their laziness, their tavern-hunting, their neglect of all sound literature, and their liking of doltish and monastical schoolmen daily increased. What, should I tell you how the universities, that men look should be fountains of learning and knowledge, have been poisoned and choked under your governance? And if to be wooden be to be base, where could there be found among all the reformed churches, nay, in the church of Rome itself, a baser brood of flattering and time-serving priests? according as God pronounces by Isaiah, the prophet that teacheth lies, he is the tail. As for your young scholars, that petition for bishoprics and deaneries to encourage them in their studies, and that many gentlemen else will not put their sons to learning, away with such young mercenary striplings, and their simoniacal fathers; God has no need of such, they have no part or lot in his vineyard: they may as well sue for nunneries, that they may have some convenient stowage for their withered daughters, because they cannot give them portions answerable to the pride and vanity they have bred them in. This is the root of all our mischief, that which they allege for the encouragement of their studies should be cut away forewith as the very bait of pride and ambition, the very garbage that draws together all the fowls of prey and ravine in the land to come and gorge upon the church. How can it be but ever unhappy to the church of England, while she shall think to entice men to the pure service of God by the same means that were used to tempt our Saviour to the service of the devil, by laying before him honour and preferment? Fit professors indeed are they like to be, to teach others that godliness with content is great gain, whenas their godliness of teaching had not been but for worldly gain. The heathen philosophers thought that virtue was for its own sake inestimable, and the greatest gain of a teacher to make a soul virtuous; so Xenophon writes to Socrates, who never bargained with any for teaching them; he feared not lest those who had received so high a benefit from him would not of their own free will return him all possible thanks. Was moral virtue so lovely, and so alluring, and heathen men so enamoured of her, as to teach and study her with greatest neglect and contempt of worldly profit and advancement? And is Christian piety so homely and so unpleasant, and Christian men so cloyed with her, as that none will study and teach her but for lucre and preferment? O stale grown piety! O gospel rated as cheap as thy Master, at thirty pence, and not worth the study, unless thou canst buy those that will sell thee! O race of Capernaïtans, senseless of divine doctrine, and capable only of loaves and belly-cheer! But they will grant, perhaps, piety may thrive, but learning will decay: I would fain ask these men at whose hands they seek inferior things, as wealth, honour, their dainty fare, their lofty houses? No doubt but they will soon answer, that all these things they seek at God's hands. Do they think then that all these meaner and superfluous things come from God, and the divine gift of learning from the den of Plutus, or the cave of Mammon? Certainly never any clear spirit nursed up from brighter influences, with a soul enlarged to the dimensions of spacious art and high knowledge, ever entered there but with scorn, and thought it ever foul disdain to make pelf or ambition the reward of his studies: it being the greatest honour, the greatest fruit and proficiency of learned studies to despise these things. Not liberal science, but illiberal must that needs be, that mounts in contemplation merely for money. And what would it avail us to have a hireling clergy, though never so learned? For such can have neither true wisdom nor grace; and then in vain do men trust in learning where these be wanting. If in less noble and almost mechanic arts, according to the definitions of those authors, he is not esteemed to deserve the name of a complete architect, an excellent painter, or the like, that bears not a generous mind above the peasantly regard of wages and hire; much more must we think him a most imperfect and incomplete divine, who is so far from being a contemner of filthy lucre, that his whole divinity is moulded and bred up in the beggarly and brutish hopes of a fat prebendary, deanery, or bishopric; which poor and low-pitched desires, if they do but mix with those other heavenly intentions that draw a man to this study, it is justly expected that they should bring forth a baseborn issue of divinity, like that of those imperfect and putrid creatures that receive a crawling life from two most unlike procreants, the sun and mud. And in matters of religion, there is not anything more intolerable than a learned fool, or a learned hypocrite: the one is ever cooped up at his empty speculations, a sot, an idiot for any use that mankind can make of him, or else sowing the world with nice and idle questions, and with much toil and difficulty wading to his auditors up to the eyebrows in deep shallows that wet not the instep: a plain unlearned man that lives well by that light which he has, is better and wiser, and edifies others more towards a godly and happy life than he. The other is still using his sophisticated arts, and bending all his studies how to make his insatiate avarice and ambition seem pious and orthodoxal, by painting his lewd and deceitful principles with a smooth and glossy varnish in a doctrinal way, to bring about his wickedest purposes. Instead of the great harm therefore that these men fear upon the dissolving of prelates, what an ease and happiness will it be to us, when tempting rewards are taken away, that the cunningest and mos dangerous mercenaries will cease of themselves to frequent the fold, whom otherwise scarce all the prayers of the faithful could have kept back from devouring the flock! But a true pastor of Christ's sending hath this especial mark, that for greatest labours and greatest merits in the church, he requires either nothing, if he could so subsist, or a very common and reasonable supply of human necessaries. We cannot therefore do better than to leave this care of ours to God: He can easily send labourers into his harvest, that shall not cry, Give, give, but be contented with a moderate and beseeming allowance; nor will He suffer true learning to be wanting, where true grace and our obedience to him abounds: for if He give us to know him aright, and to practise this our knowledge in right-established discipline, how much more will he replenish us with all abilities in tongues and arts, that may conduce to his glory and our good! He can stir up rich fathers to bestow exquisite education upon their children, and so dedicate them to the service of the gospel; He can make the sons of nobles his ministers, and princes to be his Nazarites; for certainly there is no employment more honourable, more worthy to take up a great spirit, more requiring a generous and free nurture, than to be the messenger and herald of heavenly truth from God to man, and, by the faithful work of holy doctrine, to procreate a number of faithful men, making a kind of creation like to God's, by infusing his spirit and likeness into them, to their salvation, as God did into him; arising to what climate soever he turn him, like that Sun of Righteousness that sent him, with healing in his wings, and new light to break in upon the chill and gloomy hearts of his hearers, raising out of darksome barrenness a delicious and fragrant spring of saving knowledge, and good works. Can a man, thus employed, find himself discontented, or dishonoured for want of admittance to have a pragmatical voice at sessions and jail deliveries? or because he may not as a judge sit out the wrangling noise of litigious courts to shrive the purses of unconfessing and unmortified sinners, and not their souls, or be discouraged though men call him not lord, whenas the due performance of his office would gain him, even from lords and princes, the voluntary title of father? Would he tug for a barony to sit and vote in parliament, knowing that no man can take from him the gift of wisdom and sound doctrine, which leaves him free, though not to be a member, yet a teacher and persuader of the parliament? And in all wise apprehensions the persuasive power in man to win others to goodness by instruction is greater, and more divine, than the compulsive power to restrain men from being evil by terror of the law; and therefore Christ left Moses to be the lawgiver, but himself came down amongst us to be a teacher, with which office his heavenly wisdom was so well pleased, as that he was angry with those that would have put a piece of temporal judicature into his hands, disclaiming that he had any commission from above for such matters.

FROM "THE REASON OF CHURCH GOVERNMENT URGED AGAINST PRELATY."

SECOND BOOK.

How happy were it for this frail, and as it may be called mortal life of man, since all earthly things which have the name of good and convenient in our daily use, are withal so cumbersome and full of trouble, if knowledge, yet which is the best and lightsomest possession of the mind, were, as the common saying is, no burden; and that what it wanted of being a load to any part of the body, it did not with a heavy advantage overlay upon the spirit! For not to speak of that knowledge that rests in the contemplation of natural causes and dimensions, which must needs be a lower wisdom, as the object is low, certain it is, that he who hath obtained in more than the scantiest measure to know anything distinctly of God, and of his true worship, and what is infallibly good and happy in the state of man's life, what in itself evil and miserable, though vulgarly not so esteemed; he that hath obtained to know this, the only high valuable wisdom indeed, remembering also that God, even to a strictness, requires the improvement of these his entrusted gifts, cannot but sustain a sorer burden of mind, and more pressing, than any supportable toil or weight which the body can labour under, how and in what manner he shall dispose and employ those sums of knowledge and illumination, which God hath sent him into this world to trade with. And that which aggravates the burden more, is, that, having received amongst his allotted parcels certain precious truths, of such an orient lustre as no diamond can equal, which nevertheless he has in charge to put off at any cheap rate, yea, for nothing to them that will; the great merchants of this world, fearing that this course would soon discover and disgrace the false glitter of their deceitful wares, wherewith they abuse the people, like poor Indians with beads and glasses, practise by all means how they may suppress the vending of such rarities, and at such a cheapness as would undo them, and turn their trash upon their hands. Therefore by gratifying the corrupt desires of men in fleshly doctrines, they stir them up to persecute with hatred and contempt all those that seek to bear themselves uprightly in this their spiritual factory: which they foreseeing, though they cannot but testify of truth, and the excellency of that heavenly traffic which they bring, against what opposition or danger soever, yet needs must it sit heavily upon their spirits, that being, in God's prime intention and their own, selected heralds of peace, and dispensers of treasure inestimable, without price, to them that have no peace, they find in the discharge of their commission, that they are made the greatest variance and offence, a very sword and fire both in house and city over the whole earth. This is that which the sad prophet Jeremiah laments: "Woe is me, my mother, that thou hast borne me, a man of strife and contention!" And although divine inspiration must certainly have been sweet to those ancient prophets, yet the irksomeness of that truth which they brought was so unpleasant unto them, that everywhere they call it a burden. Yea, that mysterious book of revelation, which the great evangelist was bid to eat, as it had been some eye-brightening electuary of knowledge and foresight, though it were sweet in his mouth, and in the learning, it was bitter in his belly, bitter in the denouncing. Nor was this hid from the wise poet Sophocles, who in that place of his tragedy where Tiresias is called to resolve king Œdipus in a matter which he knew would be grievous, brings him in bemoaning his lot, that he knew more than other men. For surely to every good and peaceable man, it must in nature needs be a hateful thing to be the displeaser and molester of thousands; much better would it like him doubtless to be the messenger of gladness and contentment, which is his chief intended business to all mankind, but that they resist and oppose their own true happiness. But when God commands to take the trumpet, and blow a dolorous or a jarring blast, it lies not in man's will what he shall say, or what he shall conceal. If he shall think to be silent as Jeremiah did, because of the reproach and derision he met with daily, "And all his familiar friends watched for his halting," to be revenged on him for speaking the truth, he would be forced to confess as he confessed: "His word was in my heart as a burning fire shut up in my bones; I was weary with forbearing, and could not stay." Which might teach these times not suddenly to condemn all things that are sharply spoken or vehemently written as proceeding out of stomach, virulence, and ill-nature; but to consider rather, that if the prelates have leave to say the worst that can be said, or do the worst that can be done, while they strive to keep to themselves, to their great pleasure and commodity, those things which they ought to render up, no man can be justly offended with him that shall endeavour to impart and bestow, without any gain to himself, those sharp but saving words which would be a terror and a torment in him to keep back. For me, I have determined to lay up as the best treasure and solace of a good old age, if God vouchsafe it me, the honest liberty of free speech from my youth, where I shall think it available in so dear a concernment as the church's good. For if I be, either by disposition or what other cause, too inquisitive, or suspicious of myself and mine own doings, who can help it? But this I foresee, that should the church be brought under heavy oppression, and God have given me ability the while to reason against that man that should be the author of so foul a deed; or should she, by blessing from above on the industry and courage of faithful men, change this her distracted estate into better days, without the least furtherance or contribution of those few talents, which God at that present had lent me; I foresee what stories I should hear within myself, all my life after, of discourage and reproach. Timorous and ungrateful, the church of God is now again at the foot of her insulting enemies, and thou bewailest. What matters it for thee, or thy bewailing? When time was, thou couldst not find a syllable of all that thou hast read, or studied, to utter in her behalf. Yet ease and leisure was given thee for thy retired thoughts, out of the sweat of other men. Thou hast the diligence, the parts, the language of a man, if a vain subject were to be adorned or beautified; but when the cause of God and his church was to be pleaded, for which purpose that tongue was given thee which thou hast, God listened if he could hear thy voice among his zealous servants, but thou wert dumb as a beast; from henceforward be that which thine own brutish silence hath made thee. Or else I should have heard on the other ear: Slothful, and ever to be set light by, the church hath now overcome her late distresses after the unwearied labours of many her true servants that stood up in her defence; thou also wouldst take upon thee to share amongst them of their joy: but wherefore thou? Where canst thou show any word or deed of thine which might have hastened her peace? Whatever thou dost now talk, or write, or look, is the alms of other men's active prudence and zeal. Dare not now to say or do anything better than thy former sloth and infancy; or if thou darest, thou dost impudently to make a thrifty purchase of boldness to thyself, out of the painful merits of other men; what before was thy sin is now thy duty, to be abject and worthless. These, and such-like lessons as these, I know would have been my matins duly, and my even-song. But now by this little diligence, mark what a privilege I have gained with good men and saints, to claim my right of lamenting the tribulations of the church, if she should suffer, when others, that have ventured nothing for her sake, have not the honour to be admitted mourners. But if she lift up her drooping head and prosper, among those that have something more than wished her welfare, I have my charter and freehold of rejoicing to me and my heirs. Concerning therefore this wayward subject against prelaty, the touching whereof is so distasteful and disquietous to a number of men, as by what hath been said I may deserve of charitable readers to be credited, that neither envy nor gall hath entered me upon this controversy, but the enforcement of conscience only, and a preventive fear lest the omitting of this duty should be against me, when I would store up to myself the good provision of peaceful hours: so, lest it should be still imputed to me, as I have found it hath been, that some self-pleasing humour of vainglory hath incited me to contest with men of high estimation, now while green years are upon my head; from this needless surmisal I shall hope to dissuade the intelligent and equal auditor, if I can but say successfully that which in this exigent behoves me; although I would be heard only, if it might be, by the elegant and learned reader, to whom principally for a while I shall beg leave I may address myself. To him it will be no new thing, though I tell him that if I hunted after praise, by the ostentation of wit and learning, I should not write thus out of mine own season when I have neither yet completed to my mind the full circle of my private studies, although I complain not of any insufficiency to the matter in hand; or were I ready to my wishes, it were a folly to commit anything elaborately composed to the careless and interrupted listening of these tumultuous times. Next, if I were wise only to my own ends, I would certainly take such a subject as of itself might catch applause, whereas this hath all the disadvantages on the contrary, and such a subject as the publishing whereof might be delayed at pleasure, and time enough to pencil it over with all the curious touches of art, even to the perfection of a faultless picture; whenas in this argument the not deferring is of great moment to the good speeding, that if solidity have leisure to do her office, art cannot have much. Lastly, I should not choose this manner of writing, wherein knowing myself inferior to myself, led by the genial power of nature to another task, I have the use, as I may account, but of my left hand. And though I shall be foolish in saying more to this purpose, yet, since it will be such a folly, as wisest men go about to commit, having only confessed and so committed, I may trust with more reason, because with more folly, to have courteous pardon. For although a poet, soaring in the high reason of his fancies, with his garland and singing robes about him, might, without apology, speak more of himself than I mean to do; yet for me sitting here below in the cool element of prose, a mortal thing among many readers of no empyreal conceit, to venture and divulge unusual things of myself, I shall petition to the gentler sort, it may not be envy to me. I must say, therefore, that after I had for my first years, by the ceaseless diligence and care of my father (whom God recompense !), been exercised to the tongues, and some sciences, as my age would suffer, by sundry masters and teachers, both at home and at the schools, it was found that whether aught was imposed me by them that had the overlooking, or betaken to of mine own choice in English, or other tongue, prosing or versing, but chiefly by this latter, the style, by certain vital signs it had, was likely to live. But much latelier in the private academies of Italy, whither I was favoured to resort, perceiving that some trifles which I had in memory, composed at under twenty or thereabout (for the manner is, that every one must give some proof of his wit and reading there), met with acceptance above what was looked for; and other things, which I had shifted in scarcity of books and conveniences to patch up amongst them, were received with written encomiums, which the Italian is not forward to bestow on men of this side the Alps; I began thus far to assent both to them and divers of my friends here at home, and not less to an inward prompting which now grew daily upon me, that by labour and intense study (which I take to be my portion in this life), joined with the strong propensity of nature, I might perhaps leave something so written to aftertimes, as they should not willingly let it die. These thoughts at once possessed me, and these other; that if I were certain to write as men buy leases, for three lives and downward, there ought no regard be sooner had than to God's glory, by the honour and instruction of my country. For which cause, and not only for that I knew it would be hard to arrive at the second rank among the Latins, I applied myself to that resolution, which Ariosto followed against the persuasions of Bembo, to fix all the industry and art I could unite to the adorning of my native tongue; not to make verbal curiosities the end (that were a toilsome vanity), but to be an interpreter and relater of the best and sagest things among mine own citizens throughout this island in the mother dialect. That what the greatest and choicest wits of Athens, Rome, or modern Italy, and those Hebrews of old did for their country, I, in my proportion, with this over and above, of being a Christian, might do for mine; not caring to be once named abroad, though perhaps I could attain to that, but content with these British islands as my world; whose fortune hath hitherto been, that if the Athenians, as some say, made their small deeds great and renowned by their eloquent writers, England hath had her noble achievements made small by the unskilful handling of monks and mechanics.

Time serves not now, and perhaps I might seem too profuse to give any certain account of what the mind at home, in the spacious circuits of her musing, hath liberty to propose to herself, though of highest hope and hardest attempting; whether that epic form whereof the two poems of Homer, and those other two of Virgil and Tasso, are a diffuse, and the book of Job a brief model: or whether the rules of Aristotle herein are strictly to be kept, or nature to be followed, which in them that know art, and use judgment, is no transgression, but an enriching of art: and lastly, what king or knight, before the conquest, might be chosen in whom to lay the pattern of a Christian hero. And as Tasso gave to a prince of Italy his choice whether he would command him to write of Godfrey's expedition against the Infidels, or Belisarius against the Goths, or Charlemain against the Lombards; if to the instinct of nature and the emboldening of art aught may be trusted, and that there be nothing adverse in our climate, or the fate of this age, it haply would be no rashness, from an equal diligence and inclination, to present the like offer in our own ancient stories; or whether those dramatic constitutions, wherein Sophocles and Euripides reign, shall be found more doctrinal and exemplary to a nation. The Scripture also affords us a divine pastoral drama in the Song of Solomon, consisting of two persons, and a double chorus, as Origen rightly judges. And the Apocalypse of St. John is the majestic image of a high and stately tragedy, shutting up and intermingling her solemn scenes and acts with a sevenfold chorus of hallelujahs and harping symphonies: and this my opinion the grave authority of Pareus, commenting on that book, is sufficient to confirm. Or if occasion shall lead, to imitate those magnific odes and hymns, wherein Pindarus and Callimachus are in most things worthy, some others in their frame judicious, in their matter most an end faulty. But those frequent songs throughout the law and prophets beyond all these, not in their divine argument alone, but in the very critical art of composition, may be easily made appear over all the kinds of lyric poesy to be incomparable. These abilities, wheresoever they be found, are the inspired gift of God, rarely bestowed, but yet to some (though most abuse) in every nation; and are of power, beside the office of a pulpit, to imbreed and cherish in a great people the seeds of virtue and public civility, to allay the perturbations of the mind, and set the affections in right tune; to celebrate in glorious and lofty hymns the throne and equipage of God's almightiness, and what He works, and what He suffers to be wrought with high providence in His church; to sing victorious agonies of martyrs and saints, the deeds and triumphs of just and pious nations, doing valiantly through faith against the enemies of Christ; to deplore the general relapses of kingdoms and states from justice and God's true worship. Lastly, whatsoever in religion is holy and sublime, in virtue amiable or grave, whatsoever hath passion or admiration in all the changes of that which is called fortune from without, or the wily subtleties and refluxes of man's thoughts from within; all these things with a solid and treatable smoothness to paint out and describe. Teaching over the whole book of sanctity and virtue, through all the instances of example, with such delight to those especially of soft and delicious temper, who will not so much as look upon truth herself, unless they see her elegantly dressed; that whereas the paths of honesty and good life appear now rugged and difficult, though they be indeed easy and pleasant, they will then appear to all men both easy and pleasant, though they were rugged and difficult indeed. And what a benefit this would be to our youth and gentry, may be soon guessed by what we know of the corruption and bane which they suck in daily from the writings and interludes of libidinous and ignorant poetasters, who having scarce ever heard of that which is the main consistence of a true poem, the choice of such persons as they ought to introduce, and what is moral and decent to each one; do for the most part lay up vicious principles in sweet pills to be swallowed down, and make the taste of virtuous documents harsh and sour. But because the spirit of man cannot demean itself lively in this body, without some recreating intermission of labour and serious things, it were happy for the commonwealth, if our magistrates, as in those famous governments of old, would take into their care, not only the deciding of our contentious law-cases and brawls, but the managing of our public sports and festival pastimes; that they might be, not such as were authorised a while since, the provocations of drunkenness and lust, but such as may inure and harden our bodies by martial exercises to all warlike skill and performance; and may civilise, adorn, and make discreet our minds by the learned and affable meeting of frequent academies, and the procurement of wise and artful recitations, sweetened with eloquent and graceful enticements to the love and practice of justice, temperance, and fortitude, instructing and bettering the nation at all opportunities, that the call of wisdom and virtue may be heard everywhere, as Solomon saith: "She crieth without, she uttereth her voice in the streets, in the top of high places, in the chief concourse, and in the openings of the gates." Whether this may not be, not only in pulpits, but after another persuasive method, at set and solemn paneguries, in theatres, porches, or what other place or way may win most upon the people to receive at once both recreation and instruction, let them in authority consult. The thing which I had to say, and those intentions which have lived within me ever since I could conceive myself anything worth to my country, I return to crave excuse that urgent reason hath plucked from me, by an abortive and foredated discovery. And the accomplishment of them lies not but in a power above man's to promise; but that none hath by more studious ways endeavoured, and with more unwearied spirit that none shall, that I dare almost aver of myself, as far as life and free leisure will extend; and that the land had once enfranchised herself from this impertinent yoke of prelaty, under whose inquisitorious and tyrannical duncery, no free and splendid wit can flourish. Neither do I think it shame to covenant with any knowing reader, that for some few years yet I may go on trust with him toward the payment of what I am now indebted, as being a work not to be raised from the heat of youth, or the vapours of wine; like that which flows at waste from the pen of some vulgar amourist, or the trencher fury of a rhyming parasite; nor to be obtained by the invocation of dame memory and her siren daughters, but by devout prayer to that eternal Spirit, who can enrich with all utterance and knowledge, and sends out His seraphim, with the hallowed fire of His altar, to touch and purify the lips of whom He pleases: to this must be added industrious and select reading, steady observation, insight into all seemly and generous arts and affairs; till which in some measure be compassed, at mine own peril and cost, I refuse not to sustain this expectation from as many as are not loth to hazard so much credulity upon the best pledges that I can give them. Although it nothing content me to have disclosed thus much beforehand, but that I trust hereby to make it manifest with what small willingness I endure to interrupt the pursuit of no less hopes than these, and leave a calm and pleasing solitariness, fed with cheerful and confident thoughts, to embark in a troubled sea of noises and hoarse disputes, put from beholding the bright countenance of truth in the quiet and still air of delightful studies, to come into the dim reflection of hollow antiquities sold by the seeming bulk, and there be fain to club quotations with men whose learning and belief lies in marginal stuffings, who, when they have, like good sumpters, laid ye down their horse-loads of citations and fathers at your door, with a rhapsody of who and who were bishops here or there, ye may take off their packsaddles, their day's work is done, and episcopacy, as they think, stoutly vindicated. Let any gentle apprehension, that can distinguish learned pains from unlearned drudgery imagine what pleasure or profoundness can be in this, or what honour to deal against such adversaries. But were it the meanest under-service, if God by his secretary conscience enjoin it, it were sad for me if I should draw back; for me especially, now when all men offer their aid to help, ease, and lighten the difficult labours of the church, to whose service, by the intentions of my parents and friends, I was destined of a child, and in mine own resolutions: till coming to some maturity of years, and perceiving what tyranny had invaded the church, that he who would take orders must subscribe slave, and take an oath withal, which, unless he took with a conscience that would retch, he must either straight perjure, or split his faith; I thought it better to prefer a blameless silence before the sacred office of speaking, bought and begun with servitude and forswearing. Howsoever, thus church-outed by the prelates, hence may appear the right I have to meddle in these matters, as before the necessity and constraint appeared.

That prelatical Jurisdiction opposeth the Reason and End of the Gospel and of State.

The third and last consideration remains, whether the prelates in their function do work according to the gospel, practising to subdue the mighty things of this world by things weak, which St. Paul hath set forth to be the power and excellence of the gospel; or whether in more likelihood they band themselves with the prevalent things of this world, to overrun the weak things which Christ hath made choice to work by: and this will soonest be discerned by the course of their jurisdiction. But here again I find my thoughts almost in suspense betwixt yea and no, and am nigh turning mine eye which way I may best retire, and not proceed in this subject, blaming the ardency of my mind that fixed me too attentively to come thus far. For truth, I know not how, hath this unhappiness fatal to her, ere she can come to the trial and inspection of the understanding; being to pass through many little wards and limits of the several affections and desires, she cannot shift it, but must put on such colours and attire as those pathetic handmaids of the soul please

to lead her in to their queen: and if she find so much favour
with them, they let her pass in her own likeness; if not, they
bring her into the presence habited and coloured like a notorious
falsehood. And contrary, when any falsehood comes that way,
if they like the errand she brings, they are so artful to counterfeit the very shape and visage of truth, that the understanding
not being able to discern the fucus which these enchantresses
with such cunning have laid upon the feature sometimes of
truth, sometimes of falsehood interchangeably, sentences for the
most part one for the other at the first blush, according to the
subtle imposture of these sensual mistresses, that keep the ports
and passages between her and the object. So that were it not
for leaving imperfect that which is already said, I should go
near to relinquish that which is to follow. And because I see
that most men, as it happens in this world, either weakly or
falsely principled, what through ignorance, and what through
custom of licence, both in discourse and writing, by what hath
been of late written in vulgar, have not seemed to attain the
decision of this point: I shall likewise assay those wily arbi-
tresses who in most men have, as was heard, the sole ushering
of truth and falsehood between the sense and the soul, with
what loyalty they will use me in convoying this truth to my
understanding; the rather for that, by as much acquaintance as
I can obtain with them, I do not find them engaged either one
way or other. Concerning therefore ecclesiastical jurisdiction,
I find still more controversy, who should administer it, than
diligent inquiry made to learn what it is: for had the pains been
taken to search out that, it had been long ago enrolled to be
nothing else but a pure tyrannical forgery of the prelates; and
that jurisdictive power in the church there ought to be none at
all. It cannot be conceived that what men now call jurisdiction
in the church, should be other thing than a Christian censorship; and therefore it is most commonly and truly named
ecclesiastical censure. Now if the Roman censor, a civil
function, to that severe assize of surveying and controlling the
privatest and slyest manners of all men and all degrees, had no
jurisdiction, no courts of plea or indictment, no punitive force

annexed; whether it were that to this manner of correction the entanglement of suits was improper, or that the notice of those upright inquisitors extended to such the most covert and spirituous vices as would slip easily between the wider and more material grasp of the law, or that it stood more with the majesty of that office to have no other sergeants or maces about them but those invisible ones of terror and shame; or, lastly, were it their fear, lest the greatness of this authority and honour, armed with jurisdiction, might step with ease into a tyranny: in all these respects, with much more reason undoubtedly ought the censure of the church be quite divested and disentailed of all jurisdiction whatsoever. For if the course of judicature to a political censorship seem either too tedious, or too contentious, much more may it to the discipline of the church, whose definitive decrees are to be speedy, but the execution of rigour slow, contrary to what in legal proceedings is most usual; and by how much the less contentious it is, by so much will it be the more Christian. And if the Censor, in his moral episcopy being to judge most in matters not answerable by writ or action, could not use an instrument so gross and bodily as jurisdiction is, how can the minister of the gospel manage the corpulent and secular trial of bill and process in things merely spiritual? Or could that Roman office, without this juridical sword or saw, strike such a reverence of itself into the most undaunted hearts, as with one single dash of ignominy to put all the senate and knighthood of Rome into a tremble? Surely much rather might the heavenly ministry of the evangel bind herself about with far more piercing beams of majesty and awe, by wanting the beggarly help of halings and amercements in the use of her powerful keys. For when the church without temporal support is able to do her great works upon the unforced obedience of men, it argues a divinity about her. But when she thinks to credit and better her spiritual efficacy, and to win herself respect and dread by strutting in the false vizard of worldly authority, it is evident that God is not there, but that her apostolic virtue is departed from her, and hath left her keycold; which she perceiving as in a decayed nature, seeks to the outward fomentations and chafings of worldly help, and external flourishes, to fetch, if it be possible, some motion into her extreme parts, or to hatch a counterfeit life with the crafty and artificial heat of jurisdiction. But it is observable, that so long as the church, in true imitation of Christ, can be content to ride upon an ass, carrying herself and her government along in a mean and simple guise, she may be, as he is, a lion of the tribe of Judah; and in her humility all men with loud hosannas will confess her greatness. But when, despising the mighty operation of the Spirit by the weak things of this world, she thinks to make herself bigger and more considerable, by using the way of civil force and jurisdiction, as she sits upon this lion she changes into an ass, and, instead of hosannas every man pelts her with stones and dirt. Lastly, if the wisdom of the Romans feared to commit jurisdiction to an office of so high esteem and dread as was the censor's, we may see what a solecism in the art of policy it hath been, all this while through Christendom to give jurisdiction to ecclesiastical censure. For that strength, joined with religion, abused and pretended to ambitious ends, must of necessity breed the heaviest and most quelling tyranny not only upon the necks, but even to the souls of men: which if Christian Rome had been so cautelous to prevent in her church, as pagan Rome was in her state, we had not such a lamentable experience thereof as now we have from thence upon all Christendom. For although I said before, that the church coveting to ride upon the lionly form of jurisdiction, makes a transformation of herself into an ass, and becomes despicable, that is, to those whom God hath enlightened with true knowledge; but where they remain yet in the reliques of superstition, this is the extremity of their bondage and blindness, that while they think they do obeisance to the lordly vision of a lion, they do it to an ass, that through the just judgment of God is permitted to play the dragon among them because of their wilful stupidity. And let England here well rub her eyes, lest by leaving jurisdiction and church censure to the same persons, now that God hath been so long medicining her eyesight, she do not with her over-politic fetches mar all, and bring herself back again to worship this ass bestriding a lion. Having hitherto explained, that to ecclesiastical censure no jurisdictive power can be added, without a childish and dangerous oversight in policy, and a pernicious contradiction in evangelical discipline, as anon more fully, it will be next to declare wherein the true reason and force of church censure consists, which by then it shall be laid open to the root; so little is it that I fear lest any crookedness, any wrinkle or spot should be found in presbyterian government, that if Bodin, the famous French writer, though a papist, yet affirms that the commonwealth which maintains this discipline will certainly flourish in virtue and piety, I dare assure myself, that every true protestant will admire the integrity, the uprightness, the divine and gracious purposes thereof, and even for the reason of it so coherent with the doctrine of the gospel, beside the evidence of command in Scripture, will confess it to be the only true church government; and that, contrary to the whole end and mystery of Christ's coming in the flesh, a false appearance of the same is exercised by prelaty. But because some count it rigorous, and that hereby men shall be liable to a double punishment, I will begin somewhat higher, and speak of punishment; which, as it is an evil, I esteem to be of two sorts, or rather two degrees only, a reprobate conscience in this life, and hell in the other world. Whatever else men call punishment or censure, is not properly an evil, so it be not an illegal violence, but a saving medicine ordained of God both for the public and private good of man; who consisting of two parts, the inward and the outward, was by the eternal Providence left under two sorts of cure, the church and the magistrate. The magistrate hath only to deal with the outward part, I mean not of the body alone, but of the mind in all her outward acts, which in Scripture is called the outward man. So that it would be helpful to us if we might borrow such authority as the rhetoricians by patent may give us, with a kind of Promethean skill to shape and fashion this outward man into the similitude of a body, and set him visible before us; imagining the inner man only as the soul. Thus then the civil magistrate looking only upon the outward man (I say as a magistrate, for what he doth further, he doth it as a member of the church), if he find in his complexion, skin, or outward temperature the signs and marks, or in his doings the effects of injustice, rapine, lust, cruelty, or the like, sometimes he shuts up as in frenetic or infectious diseases; or confines within doors, as in every sickly estate. Sometimes he shaves by penalty or mulct, or else to cool and take down those luxuriant humours which wealth and excess have caused to abound. Otherwhiles he sears, he cauterises, he scarifies, lets blood ; and finally, for utmost remedy cuts off. The patients, which most an end are brought into his hospital, are such as are far gone, and beside themselves (unless they be falsely accused), so that force is necessary to tame and quiet them in their unruly fits, before they can be made capable of a more human cure. His general end is the outward peace and welfare of the commonwealth, and civil happiness in this life. His particular end in every man is, by the infliction of pain, damage, and disgrace, that the senses and common perceivance might carry this message to the soul within, that it is neither easeful, profitable, nor praiseworthy in this life to do evil. Which must needs tend to the good of man, whether he be to live or die; and be undoubtedly the first means to a natural man, especially an offender, which might open his eyes to a higher consideration of good and evil, as it is taught in religion. This is seen in the often penitence of those that suffer, who, had they escaped, had gone on sinning to an immeasurable heap, which is one of the extremest punishments. And this is all that the civil magistrate, as so being, confers to the healing of man's mind, working only by terrifying plasters upon the rind and orifice of the sore; and by all outward appliances, as the logicians say, *a posteriori*, at the effect, and not from the cause; not once touching the inward bed of corruption, and that hectic disposition to evil, the source of all vice and obliquity against the rule of law. Which how insufficient it is to cure the soul of man, we cannot better guess than by the art of bodily physic. Therefore God, to the intent of further healing man's depraved mind, to this power of the magistrate, which contents itself with the restraint of evil-doing in the external man, added that which we call censure, to purge it and remove it clean out of the inmost soul. In the beginning this authority seems to have been placed, as all both civil and religious rites once were, only in each father of a family; afterwards, among the heathen, in the wise men and philosophers of the age; but so as it was a thing voluntary, and no set government. More distinctly among the Jews, as being God's peculiar people, where the priests, Levites, prophets, and at last the scribes and pharisees, took charge of instructing and overseeing the lives of the people. But in the gospel, which is the straightest and the dearest covenant can be made between God and man, we being now his adopted sons, and nothing fitter for us to think on than to be like him, united to him, and, as he pleases to express it, to have fellowship with him; it is all necessity that we should expect this blessed efficacy of healing our inward man to be ministered to us in a more familiar and effectual method than ever before. God being now no more a judge after the sentence of the law, nor, as it were, a schoolmaster of perishable rites, but a most indulgent father, governing his church as a family of sons in their discreet age; and therefore, in the sweetest and mildest manner of paternal discipline, he hath committed this other office of preserving in healthful constitution the inner man, which may be termed the spirit of the soul, to his spiritual deputy the minister of each congregation; who being best acquainted with his own flock, hath best reason to know all the secretest diseases likely to be there. And look by how much the internal man is more excellent and noble than the external, by so much is his cure more exactly, more thoroughly, and more particularly to be performed. For which cause the Holy Ghost by the apostles, joined to the minister, as assistant in this great office, sometimes a certain number of grave and faithful brethren (for neither doth the physician do all in restoring his patient; he prescribes, another prepares the medicine; some tend, some watch, some visit), much more may a minister partly not see all, partly err as a man: besides, that nothing can be more for the mutual honour and love of the people to their pastor, and his to them, than

CHURCH GOVERNMENT.

when in select numbers and courses they are seen partaking and doing reverence to the holy duties of discipline by their serviceable and solemn presence, and receiving honour again from their employment, not now any more to be separated in the church by veils and partitions, as laics and unclean, but admitted to wait upon the tabernacle as the rightful clergy of Christ, a chosen generation, a royal priesthood, to offer up spiritual sacrifice in that meet place, to which God and the congregation shall call and assign them. And this all Christians ought to know, that the title of clergy St. Peter gave to all God's people, till pope Higinus and the succeeding prelates took it from them, appropriating that name to themselves and their priests only; and condemning the rest of God's inheritance to an injurious and alienate condition of laity, they separated from them by local partitions in churches, through their gross ignorance and pride imitating the old temple, and excluding the members of Christ from the property of being members, the bearing of orderly and fit offices in the ecclesiastical body; as if they had meant to sew up that Jewish veil, which Christ by his death on the cross rent in sunder. Although these usurpers could not so presently overmaster the liberties and lawful titles of God's freeborn church; but that Origen, being yet a layman, expounded the Scriptures publicly, and was therein defended by Alexander of Jerusalem, and Theoctistus of Cæsarea, producing in his behalf divers examples, that the privilege of teaching was anciently permitted to many worthy laymen: and Cyprian in his epistles professes he will do nothing without the advice and assent of his assistant laics. Neither did the first Nicene council, as great and learned as it was, think it any robbery to receive in, and require the help and presence of many learned lay-brethren, as they were then called. Many other authorities to confirm this assertion, both out of Scripture and the writings of next antiquity, Golartius hath collected in his notes upon Cyprian; whereby it will be evident that the laity, not only by apostolic permission, but by consent of many of the ancientest prelates, did participate in church offices as much as is desired any lay-elder should now do. Sometimes also not the elders alone, but the whole body of the church is interested in the work of discipline, as oft as public satisfaction is given by those that have given public scandal. Not to speak now of her right in elections. But another reason there is in it, which though religion did not commend to us, yet moral and civil prudence could not but extol. It was thought of old in philosophy, that shame, or to call it better, the reverence of our elders, our brethren, and friends, was the greatest incitement to virtuous deeds, and the greatest dissuasion from unworthy attempts that might be. Hence we may read in the *Iliad*, where Hector being wished to retire from the battle, many of his forces being routed, makes answer, that he durst not for shame, lest the Trojan knights and dames should think he did ignobly. And certain it is, that whereas terror is thought such a great stickler in a commonwealth, honourable shame is a far greater, and has more reason: for where shame is, there is fear; but where fear is, there is not presently shame. And if anything may be done to inbreed in us this generous and Christianly reverence one of another, the very nurse and guardian of piety and virtue, it cannot sooner be than by such a discipline in the church, as may use us to have in awe the assemblies of the faithful, and to count it a thing most grievous, next to the grieving of God's Spirit, to offend those whom he hath put in authority, as a healing superintendence over our lives and behaviours, both to our own happiness, and that we may not give offence to good men, who, without amends by us made, dare not, against God's command, hold communion with us in holy things. And this will be accompanied with a religious dread of being outcast from the company of saints, and from the fatherly protection of God in his church, to consort with the devil and his angels. But there is yet a more ingenuous and noble degree of honest shame, or, call it, if you will, an esteem, whereby men bear an inward reverence toward their own persons. And if the love of God, as a fire sent from heaven to be ever kept alive upon the altars of our hearts, be the first principle of all godly and virtuous actions in men, this pious and just honouring of ourselves is the second, and may be thought as the radical moisture and fountain-head, whence every laudable and worthy enterprise issues forth. And although I have given it the name of a liquid thing, yet it is not incontinent to bound itself, as humid things are, but hath in it a most restraining and powerful abstinence to start back, and glob itself upward from the mixture of any ungenerous and unbeseeming motion, or any soil wherewith it may peril to stain itself. Something I confess it is to be ashamed of evil-doing in the presence of any; and to reverence the opinion and the countenance of a good man rather than a bad, fearing most in his sight to offend, goes so far as almost to be virtuous; yet this is but still the fear of infamy, and many such, when they find themselves alone, saving their reputation, will compound with other scruples, and come to a close treaty with their dearer vices in secret. But he that holds himself in reverence and due esteem, both for the dignity of God's image upon him, and for the price of his redemption, which he thinks is visibly marked upon his forehead, accounts himself both a fit person to do the noblest and godliest deeds, and much better worth than to deject and defile, with such a debasement, and such a pollution as sin is, himself so highly ransomed and ennobled to a new friendship and filial relation with God. Nor can he fear so much the offence and reproach of others, as he dreads and would blush at the reflection of his own severe and modest eye upon himself, if it should see him doing or imagining that which is sinful, though in the deepest secrecy. How shall a man know to do himself this right, how to perform his honourable duty of estimation and respect towards his own soul and body? which way will lead him best to this hill-top of sanctity and goodness, above which there is no higher ascent but to the love of God, which from this self-pious regard cannot be asunder? No better way doubtless, than to let him duly understand, that as he is called by the high calling of God, to be holy and pure, so is he by the same appointment ordained, and by the church's call admitted, to such offices of discipline in the church, to which his own spiritual gifts, by the example of apostolic institution, have authorised him. For we have learned that the scornful term of laic, the consecrating of temples, carpets, and tablecloths, the railing in of a repugnant and contradictive mount Sinai in the gospel, as if the touch of a lay-christian, who is nevertheless God's living temple, could profane dead judaisms, the exclusion of Christ's people from the offices of holy discipline through the pride of a usurping clergy, causes the rest to have an unworthy and abject opinion of themselves, to approach to holy duties with a slavish fear, and to unholy doings with a familiar boldness. For seeing such a wide and terrible distance between religious things and themselves, and that in respect of a wooden table, and the perimeter of holy ground above it, a flagon pot, and a linen corporal, the priest esteems their layships unhallowed and unclean, they fear religion with such a fear as loves not, and think the purity of the gospel too pure for them, and that any uncleanness is more suitable to their unconsecrated estate. But when every good Christian, thoroughly acquainted with all those glorious privileges of sanctification and adoption, which render him more sacred than any dedicated altar or element, shall be restored to his right in the church, and not excluded from such place of spiritual government, as his Christian abilities, and his approved good life in the eye and testimony of the church shall prefer him to, this and nothing sooner will open his eyes to a wise and true valuation of himself (which is so requisite and high a point of Christianity), and will stir him up to walk worthy the honourable and grave employment wherewith God and the church hath dignified him; not fearing lest he should meet with some outward holy thing in religion, which his lay-touch or presence might profane; but lest something unholy from within his own heart should dishonour and profane in himself that priestly unction and clergy-right whereto Christ hath entitled him. Then would the congregation of the Lord soon recover the true likeness and visage of what she is indeed, a holy generation, a royal priesthood, a saintly communion, the household and city of God. And this I hold to be another considerable reason why the functions of church government ought to be free and open to any Christian man, though never so laic, if his capacity, his faith, and prudent demeanour, commend him. And this the apostles warrant us to do. But the prelates object, that this will bring profaneness into the church: to whom may be replied, that none have brought that in more than their own irreligious courses, nor more driven holiness out of living into lifeless things. For whereas God, who hath cleansed every beast and creeping worm, would not suffer St. Peter to call them common or unclean, the prelate bishops, in their printed orders hung up in churches, have proclaimed the best of creatures, mankind, so unpurified and contagious, that for him to lay his hat or his garment upon the chancel-table, they have defined it no less heinous, in express words, than to profane the table of the Lord. And thus have they by their Canaanitish doctrine (for that which was to the Jew but Jewish, is to the Christian no better than Canaanitish), thus have they made common and unclean, thus have they made profane that nature which God hath not only cleansed, but Christ also hath assumed. And now that the equity and just reason is so perspicuous, why in ecclesiastic censure the assistance should be added of such as whom not the vile odour of gain and fees (forbid it, God, and blow it with a whirlwind out of our land!), but charity, neighbourhood, and duty to church government hath called together, where could a wise man wish a more equal, gratuitous, and meek examination of any offence, that he might happen to commit against Christianity, than here? Would he prefer those proud simoniacal courts? Thus therefore the minister assisted attends his heavenly and spiritual cure : where we shall see him both in the course of his proceeding, and first in the excellency of his end, from the magistrate far different, and not more different than excelling. His end is to recover all that is of man, both soul and body, to an everlasting health; and yet as for worldly happiness, which is the proper sphere wherein the magistrate cannot but confine his motion without a hideous exorbitancy from law, so little aims the minister, as his intended scope, to procure the much prosperity of this life, that ofttimes he may have cause to wish much of it away, as a diet puffing up the soul with a slimy fleshiness, and weakening her principal organic parts. Two heads of evil he has to cope with, ignorance and malice. Against the former he provides the daily manna of incorruptible doctrine, not at those set meals only in public, but as oft as he shall know that each infirmity or constitution requires. Against the latter with all the branches thereof, not meddling with that restraining and styptic surgery, which the law uses, not indeed against the malady, but against the eruptions, and outermost effects thereof; he on the contrary, beginning at the prime causes and roots of the disease, sends in those two divine ingredients of most cleansing power to the soul, admonition and reproof; besides which two there is no drug or antidote that can reach to purge the mind, and without which all other experiments are but vain, unless by accident. And he that will not let these pass into him, though he be the greatest king, as Plato affirms, must be thought to remain impure within, and unknowing of those things wherein his pureness and his knowledge should most appear. As soon therefore as it may be discerned that the Christian patient, by feeding otherwise on meats not allowable, but of evil juice, hath disordered his diet, and spread an ill-humour through his veins, immediately disposing to a sickness, the minister, as being much nearer both in eye and duty than the magistrate, speeds him betimes to overtake that diffused malignance with some gentle potion of admonishment; or if aught be obstructed, puts in his opening and discussive confections. This not succeeding after once or twice, or oftener, in the presence of two or three his faithful brethren appointed thereto, he advises him to be more careful of his dearest health, and what it is that he so rashly hath let down into the divine vessel of his soul, God's temple. If this obtain not, he then, with the counsel of more assistants, who are informed of what diligence hath been already used, with more speedy remedies lays nearer siege to the entrenched causes of his distemper, not sparing such fervent and well-aimed reproofs as may best give him to see the dangerous estate wherein he is. To this also his brethren and friends entreat, exhort, adjure; and all these endeavours, as there is hope left, are more or less repeated. But if neither the regard of himself, nor the reverence of his elders and friends prevail with him to leave his vicious appetite, then as the time urges, such engines of terror God hath given into the hand of his minister, as to search the tenderest angles of the heart : one while he shakes his stubbornness with racking convulsions nigh despair ; otherwhiles with deadly corrosives he gripes the very roots of his faulty liver to bring him to life through the entry of death. Hereto the whole church beseech him, beg of him, deplore him, pray for him. After all this performed with what patience and attendance is possible, and no relenting on his part, having done the utmost of their cure, in the name of God and of the church they dissolve their fellowship with him, and holding forth the dreadful sponge of excommunion, pronounce him wiped out of the list of God's inheritance, and in the custody of Satan till he repent. Which horrid sentence, though it touch neither life nor limb, nor any worldly possession, yet has it such a penetrating force, that swifter than any chemical sulphur, or that lightning which harms not the skin, and rifles the entrails, it scorches the inmost soul. Yet even this terrible denouncement is left to the church for no other cause but to be as a rough and vehement cleansing medicine, where the malady is obdurate, a mortifying to life, a kind of saving by undoing. And it may be truly said, that as the mercies of wicked men are cruelties, so the cruelties of the church are mercies. For if repentance sent from Heaven meet this lost wanderer, and draw him out of that steep journey wherein he was hasting towards destruction, to come and reconcile to the church, if he bring with him his bill of health, and that he is now clear of infection, and of no danger to the other sheep ; then with incredible expressions of joy all his brethren receive him, and set before him those perfumed banquets of Christian consolation; with precious ointments bathing and fomenting the old, and now to be forgotten stripes, which terror and shame had inflicted ; and thus with heavenly solaces they cheer up his humble remorse, till he regain his first health and felicity. This is the approved way, which the gospel prescribes, these are the "spiritual weapons of holy censure, and ministerial warfare, not carnal, but mighty through God to the pulling down of strong holds, casting down imaginations, and every high thing that exalteth itself against the knowledge of God, and bringing into captivity every thought to the obedience of Christ." What could be done more for the healing and reclaiming that divine particle of God's breathing, the soul? and what could be done less? he that would hide his faults from such a wholesome curing as this, and count it a twofold punishment, as some do, is like a man that having foul diseases about him, perishes for shame, and the fear he has of a rigorous incision to come upon his flesh. We shall be able by this time to discern whether prelatical jurisdiction be contrary to the gospel or no. First, therefore, the government of the gospel being economical and parental, that is, of such a family where there be no servants, but all sons in obedience, not in servility, as cannot be denied by him that lives but within the sound of Scripture; how can the prelates justify to have turned the fatherly orders of Christ's household, the blessed meekness of his lowly roof, those ever-open and inviting doors of his dwelling-house, which delight to be frequented with only filial accesses; how can they justify to have turned these domestic privileges into the bar of a proud judicial court, where fees and clamours keep shop and drive a trade, where bribery and corruption solicits, paltering the free and moneyless power of discipline with a carnal satisfaction by the purse? Contrition, humiliation, confession, the very sighs of a repentant spirit, are there sold by the penny. That undeflowered and unblemishable simplicity of the gospel, not she herself, for that could never be, but a false-whited, a lawny resemblance of her, like that airborn Helena in the fables, made by the sorcery of prelates, instead of calling her disciples from the receipt of custom, is now turned publican herself; and gives up her body to a mercenary whoredom under those fornicated arches, which she calls God's house, and in the sight of those her altars, which she hath set up to be adored, makes merchandise of the bodies and souls of men. Rejecting purgatory for no other reason, as it seems, than because her greediness cannot defer, but had rather use the utmost extortion of redeemed penances in this life. But because these matters could not be thus carried without a begged and borrowed force from worldly authority, therefore prelaty, slighting the deliberate and chosen council of Christ in his spiritual government, whose glory is in the weakness of fleshly things, to tread upon the crest of the world's pride and violence by the power of spiritual ordinances, hath on the contrary made these her friends and champions, which are Christ's enemies in this his high design, smothering and extinguishing the spiritual force of his bodily weakness in the discipline of his church with the boisterous and carnal tyranny of an undue, unlawful, and ungospel-like jurisdiction. And thus prelaty, both in her fleshly supportments, in her carnal doctrine of ceremony and tradition, in her violent and secular power, going quite counter to the prime end of Christ's coming in the flesh, that is, to reveal his truth, his glory, and his might, in a clean contrary manner than prelaty seeks to do, thwarting and defeating the great mystery of God; I do not conclude that prelaty is antichristian, for what need I? the things themselves conclude it. Yet if such-like practices, and not many worse than these of our prelates, in that great darkness of the Roman church, have not exempted both her and her present members from being judged to be antichristian in all orthodoxal esteem; I cannot think but that it is the absolute voice of truth and all her children to pronounce this prelaty, and these her dark deeds in the midst of this great light wherein we live, to be more antichristian than antichrist himself.

FROM "AN APOLOGY FOR SMECTYMNUUS."

BECAUSE as well by this upbraiding to me the bordelloes, as by other suspicious glancings in his book, he would seem privily to point me out to his readers, as one whose custom of life were not honest, but licentious, I shall entreat to be borne with, though I digress; and in a way not often trod, acquaint ye with the sum of my thoughts in this matter, through the course of my years and studies: although I am not ignorant how hazardous it will be to do this under the nose of the envious, as it were in skirmish to change the compact order, and instead of outward actions, to bring inmost thoughts into front. And I must tell ye, readers, that by this sort of men I have been already bitten at; yet shall they not for me know how slightly they are esteemed, unless they have so much learning as to read what in Greek ἀπειροκαλία is, which, together with envy, is the common disease of those who censure books that are not for their reading. With me it fares now, as with him whose outward garment hath been injured and ill-bedighted; for having no other shift, what help but to turn the inside outwards, especially if the lining be of the same, or, as it is sometimes, much better? So if my name and outward demeanour be not evident enough to defend me, I must make trial if the discovery of my inmost thoughts can: wherein of two purposes, both honest and both sincere, the one perhaps I shall not miss; although I fail to gain belief with others, of being such as my perpetual thoughts shall here disclose me, I may yet not fail of success in persuading some to be such really themselves, as they cannot believe me to be more than what I feign.

I had my time, readers, as others have, who have good learning bestowed upon them, to be sent to those places where, the opinion was, it might be soonest attained; and as the manner is, was not unstudied in those authors which are most commended. Whereof some were grave orators and historians, whose matter methought I loved indeed, but as my age then was, so I understood them; others were the smooth elegiac poets, whereof the schools are not scarce, whom both for the pleasing sound of their numerous writing, which in imitation I found most easy, and most agreeable to nature's part in me, and for their matter, which what it is, there be few who know not, I was so allured to read, that no recreation came to me better welcome. For that it was then those years with me which are excused, though they be least severe, I may be saved the labour to remember ye. Whence having observed them to account it the chief glory of their wit, in that they were ablest to judge, to praise, and by that could esteem themselves worthiest to love those high perfections, which under one or other name they took to celebrate; I thought with myself by every instinct and presage of nature, which is not wont to be false, that what emboldened them to this task, might with such diligence as they used embolden me; and that what judgment, wit, or elegance was my share, would herein best appear, and best value itself, by how much more wisely, and with more love of virtue I should choose (let rude ears be absent) the object of not unlike praises. For albeit these thoughts to some will seem virtuous and commendable, to others only pardonable, to a third sort perhaps idle; yet the mentioning of them now will end in serious.

Nor blame it, readers, in those years to propose to themselves such a reward, as the noblest dispositions above other things in this life have sometimes preferred: whereof not to be sensible when good and fair in one person meet, argues both a gross and shallow argument, and withal an ungentle and swainish breast. For by the firm settling of these persuasions,

I became, to my best memory, so much a proficient, that if I found those authors anywhere speaking unworthy things of themselves, or unchaste of those names which before they had extolled; this effect it wrought with me, from that time forward their art I still applauded, but the men I deplored; and above them all, preferred the two famous renowners of Beatrice and Laura, who never write but honour of them to whom they devote their verse, displaying sublime and pure thoughts, without transgression. And long it was not after, when I was confirmed in this opinion, that he who would not be frustrate of his hope to write well hereafter in laudable things, ought himself to be a true poem; that is, a composition and pattern of the best and honourablest things; not presuming to sing high praises of heroic men, or famous cities, unless he have in himself the experience and the practice of all that which is praiseworthy. These reasonings, together with a certain niceness of nature, an honest haughtiness, and self-esteem either of what I was, or what I might be (which let envy call pride), and lastly that modesty, whereof, though not in the title-page, yet here I may be excused to make some beseeming profession; all these uniting the supply of their natural aid together, kept me still above those low descents of mind, beneath which he must deject and plunge himself, that can agree to saleable and unlawful prostitutions.

Next (for hear me out now, readers), that I may tell ye whither my younger feet wandered; I betook me among those lofty fables and romances, which recount in solemn cantos the deeds of knighthood founded by our victorious kings, and from hence had in renown over all Christendom. There I read it in the oath of every knight, that he should defend to the expense of his best blood, or of his life, if it so befell him, the honour and chastity of virgin or matron; from whence even then I learned what a noble virtue chastity sure must be, to the defence of which so many worthies, by such a dear adventure of themselves, had sworn. And if I found in the story afterward, any of them, by word or deed, breaking that oath, I judged it the same fault of the poet, as that which is attributed to Homer, to have written indecent things of the gods. Only this my mind gave me, that every free and gentle spirit, without that oath, ought to be born a knight, nor needed to expect the gilt spur, or the laying of a sword upon his shoulder to stir him up both by his counsel and his arms, to secure and protect the weakness of any attempted chastity. So that even these books, which to many others have been the fuel of wantonness and loose living, I cannot think how, unless by divine indulgence, proved to me so many incitements, as you have heard, to the love and steadfast observation of that virtue which abhors the society of bordelloes.

Thus, from the laureat fraternity of poets, riper years and the ceaseless round of study and reading led me to the shady spaces of philosophy; but chiefly to the divine volumes of Plato, and his equal Xenophon: where, if I should tell ye what I learnt of chastity and love, I mean that which is truly so, whose charming cup is only virtue, which she bears in her hand to those who are worthy (the rest are cheated with a thick intoxicating potion, which a certain sorceress, the abuser of love's name, carries about); and how the first and chiefest office of love begins and ends in the soul, producing those happy twins of her divine generation, knowledge and virtue. With such abstracted sublimities as these, it might be worth your listening, readers, as I may one day hope to have ye in a still time, when there shall be no chiding; not in these noises, the adversary, as ye know, barking at the door, or searching for me at the bordelloes, where it may be has lost himself, and raps up without pity the sage and rheumatic old prelates, with all her young Corinthian laity, to inquire for such a one.

Last of all, not in time, but as perfection is last, that care was ever had of me, with my earliest capacity, not to be negligently trained in the precepts of the Christian religion: this that I have hitherto related, hath been to show, that though Christianity had been but slightly taught me, yet a certain reservedness of natural disposition, and moral discipline, learnt out of the noblest philosophy, was enough to keep me in disdain of far less incontinences than this of the bordello. But having had the doctrine of Holy Scripture unfolding those chaste and high mysteries, with timeliest care infused, that "the body is for the Lord, and the Lord for the body;" thus also I argued to myself, that if unchastity in a woman, whom St. Paul terms the glory of man, be such a scandal and dishonour, then certainly in a man, who is both the image and glory of God, it must, though commonly not so thought, be much more deflouring and dishonourable; in that he sins both against his own body, which is the perfecter sex, and his own glory, which is in the woman; and, that which is worst, against the image and glory of God, which is in himself. Nor did I slumber over that place expressing such high rewards of ever accompanying the Lamb, with those celestial songs to others inapprehensible, but not to those who were not defiled with women, which doubtless means fornication; for marriage must not be called a defilement.

Thus large I have purposely been, that if I have been justly taxed with this crime, it may come upon me, after all this my confession, with a tenfold shame: but if I have hitherto deserved no such opprobrious word, or suspicion, I may hereby engage myself now openly to the faithful observation of what I have professed.

. . . .

But to the end that nothing may be omitted, which may farther satisfy any conscionable man, who, notwithstanding what I could explain before the Animadversions, remains yet unsatisfied concerning that way of writing which I there defended, but this confuter, whom it pinches, utterly disapproves; I shall assay once again, and perhaps with more success. If therefore the question were in oratory, whether a vehement vein throwing out indignation or scorn upon an object that merits it, were among the aptest *ideas* of speech to be allowed, it were my work, and that an easy one, to make it clear both by the rules of best rhetoricians, and the famousest examples of the Greek and Roman orations. But since the religion of it is disputed, and not the art, I shall make use only of such reasons and authorities as religion cannot except against. It will be harder to gainsay, than for me to evince, that in the teaching of men diversely tempered, different ways are to be tried. The Baptist, we know, was a strict man, remarkable for austerity and set order of life. Our Saviour, who had all gifts in him, was Lord to express his indoctrinating power in what sort him best seemed; sometimes by a mild and familiar converse; sometimes with plain and impartial home-speaking, regardless of those whom the auditors might think he should have had in more respect; otherwhile, with bitter and ireful rebukes, if not teaching, yet leaving excuseless those his wilful impugners.

What was all in him, was divided among many others the teachers of his church; some to be severe and ever of a sad gravity, that they may win such, and check sometimes those who be of nature over-confident and jocund; others were sent more cheerful, free, and still as it were at large, in the midst of an untrespassing honesty; that they who are so tempered, may have by whom they might be drawn to salvation, and they who are too scrupulous, and dejected of spirit, might be often strengthened with wise consolations and revivings: no man being forced wholly to dissolve that groundwork of nature which God created in him, the sanguine to empty out all his sociable liveliness, the choleric to expel quite the unsinning predominance of his anger; but that each radical humour and passion, wrought upon and corrected as it ought, might be made the proper mould and foundation of every man's peculiar gifts and virtues. Some also were indued with a staid moderation and soundness of argument, to teach and convince the rational and sober-minded; yet not therefore that to be thought the only expedient course of teaching, for in times of opposition, when either against new heresies arising, or old corruptions to be reformed, this cool unpassionate mildness of positive wisdom is not enough to damp and astonish the proud resistance of carnal and false doctors, then (that I may have leave to soar awhile as the poets use) Zeal, whose substance is ethereal, arming in complete diamond, ascends his fiery chariot, drawn with two blazing meteors, figured like beasts, but of a higher breed than any the zodiac yields, resembling two of those four which Ezekiel and St. John saw; the one visaged like a lion, to express power, high authority, and indignation; the other of countenance like a man, to cast derision and scorn upon perverse and fraudulent seducers: with these the invincible warrior, Zeal, shaking loosely the slack reins, drives over the heads of scarlet prelates, and such as are insolent to maintain traditions, bruising their stiff necks under his flaming wheels.

DEDICATION TO "THE DOCTRINE AND DISCIPLINE OF DIVORCE."

TO THE PARLIAMENT OF ENGLAND, WITH THE ASSEMBLY.

'IF it were seriously asked (and it would be no untimely question), renowned parliament, select assembly! who of all teachers and masters, that have ever taught, hath drawn the most disciples after him, both in religion and in manners? it might be not untruly answered, custom. Though virtue be commended for the most persuasive in her theory, and conscience in the plain demonstration of the spirit finds most evincing; yet whether it be the secret of divine will, or the original blindness we are born in, so it happens for the most part that custom still is silently received for the best instructor, Except it be, because her method is so glib and easy, in some manner like to that vision of Ezekiel rolling up her sudden book of implicit knowledge, for him that will to take and swallow down at pleasure; which proving but of bad nourishment in the concoction, as it was heedless in the devouring, puffs up unhealthily a certain big face of pretended learning, mistaken among credulous men for the wholesome habit of soundness and good constitution, but is indeed no other than that swoln visit of counterfeit knowledge and literature, which not only in private mars our education, but also in public is the common climber into every chair, where either religion is preached, or law reported; filling each estate of life and profession with abject and servile principles, depressing the high and heaven-born spirit of man, far beneath the condition wherein either God created him, or sin hath sunk him. To pursue the allegory, custom being but a mere face, as echo is a mere voice, rests not in her unaccomplishment, until by secret inclination she accorporate herself with error, who being a blind and serpentine body without a head, willingly accepts what he wants, and supplies what her incompleteness went seeking. 'Hence it is, that error supports custom, custom countenances error; and these two between them would persecute and chase away all truth and solid wisdom out of human life, were it not that God, rather than man, once in many ages calls together the prudent and religious counsels of men, deputed to repress the incroachments, and to work off the inveterate blots and obscurities wrought upon our minds by the subtle insinuating of error and custom; who, with the numerous and vulgar train of their followers, make it their chief design to envy and cry down the industry of free reasoning, under the terms of humour and innovation; as if the womb of teeming truth were to be closed up, if she presume to bring forth aught that sorts not with their unchewed notions and suppositions. Against which notorious injury and abuse of man's free soul, to testify and oppose the utmost that study and true labour can attain, heretofore the incitement of men reputed grave hath led me among others; and now the duty and the right of an instructed Christian calls me through the chance of good or evil report, to be the sole advocate of a discountenanced truth: a high enterprise, lords and commons! a high enterprise and a hard, and such as every seventh son of a seventh son does not venture on. Nor have I amidst the clamour of so much envy and impertinence whither to appeal, but to the concourse of so much piety and wisdom here assembled. Bringing in my hands an ancient and most necessary, most charitable, and yet most injured statute of Moses: not repealed ever by him who only had the authority, but thrown aside with much inconsiderate neglect, under the rubbish of canonical ignorance; as once the whole law was by some such-like conveyance in Josiah's time. And he who shall endeavour the amendment of any old neglected grievance in church or state, or in the daily course of life, if he be gifted with abilities of mind, that may raise him to so high an undertaking, I grant he hath already much whereof not to repent him; yet let me aread him, not to be the foreman of any misjudged opinion, unless his resolutions be firmly seated in a square and constant mind, not conscious to itself of any deserved blame, and regardless of ungrounded suspicions. For this let him be sure, he shall be boarded presently by the ruder sort, but not by discreet and well-nurtured men, with a thousand idle descants and surmises. Who when they cannot confute the least joint or sinew of any passage in the book; yet God forbid that truth should be truth, because they have a boisterous conceit of some pretences in the writer. But were they not more busy and inquisitive than the apostle commends, they would hear him at least, "rejoicing so the truth be preached, whether of envy or other pretence whatsoever:" for truth is as impossible to be soiled by any outward touch, as the sunbeam; though this ill hap wait on her nativity, that she never comes into the world, but like a bastard, to the ignominy of him that brought her forth; till time, the midwife rather than the mother of truth, have washed and salted the infant, declared her legitimate, and churched the father of his young Minerva, from the needless causes of his purgation. Yourselves can best witness this, worthy patriots! and better will, no doubt hereafter: for who among ye of the foremost that have travailed in her behalf to the good of church or state, hath not been often traduced to be the agent of his own by-ends, under pretext of reformation? So much the more I shall not be unjust to hope, that however infamy or envy may work in other men to do her fretful will against this discourse, yet that the experience of your own uprightness misinterpreted will put ye in mind, to give it free audience and generous construction. What though the brood of Belial, the draff of men, to whom no liberty is pleasing, but unbridled and vagabond lust without pale or partition, will laugh broad perhaps, to see so great a strength of Scripture mustering up in favour, as they suppose, of their debaucheries; they will know better when they shall hence learn, that honest liberty is the greatest foe to dishonest licence. And what though others, out of a waterish and queasy conscience, because ever crazy and never yet sound, will rail and fancy to themselves that injury and licence is the best of this book? Did not the distemper of their own stomachs affect them with a dizzy megrim, they would soon tie up their tongues and discern themselves like that Assyrian blasphemer, all this while reproaching not man, but the Almighty, the Holy One of Israel, whom they do not deny to have belawgiven his own sacred people with this very allowance, which they now call injury and licence, and dare cry shame on, and will do yet awhile, till they get a little cordial sobriety to settle their qualming zeal. But this question concerns not us perhaps: indeed man's disposition, though prone to search after vain curiosities, yet when points of difficulty are to be discussed, appertaining to the removal of unreasonable wrong and burden from the perplexed life of our brother, it is incredible how cold, how dull, and far from all fellow-feeling we are, without the spur of self-concernment. Yet if the wisdom, the justice, the purity of God be to be cleared from foulest imputations, which are not yet avoided; if charity be not to be degraded and trodden down under a civil ordinance; if matrimony be not to be advanced like that exalted perdition written of to the Thessalonians, "above all that is called God," or goodness, nay, against them both; then I dare affirm, there will be found in the contents of this book that which may concern us all. You it concerns chiefly, worthies in parliament! on whom, as on our deliverers, all our grievances and cares, by the merit of your eminence and fortitude, are devolved. Me it concerns next, having with much labour and faithful diligence first found out, or at least with a fearless and communicative candour first published, to the manifest good of Christendom, that which, calling to witness everything mortal and immortal, I believe unfeignedly to be true. Let not other men think their conscience bound to search continually after truth, to pray for enlightening from above, to publish what they think they have so obtained, and debar me from conceiving myself tied by the same duties. Ye have now, doubtless, by the favour and appointment of God, ye have now in your hands a great and populous nation to reform; from what corruption, what blindness in religion, ye know well; in what a degenerate and fallen spirit from the apprehension of native liberty, and true manliness, I am sure ye find; with what unbounded licence rushing to whoredoms and adulteries, needs not long inquiry: insomuch that the fears, which men have of too strict a discipline, perhaps exceed the hopes that can be in others of ever introducing it with any great success. What if I should tell ye now of dispensations and indulgences, to give a little the reins, to let them play and nibble with the bait awhile; a people as hard of heart as that Egyptian colony that went to Canaan. This is the common doctrine that adulterous and injurious divorces were not connived only, but with eye open allowed of old for hardness of heart. But that opinion, I trust, by then this following argument hath been well read, will be left for one of the mysteries of an indulgent Antichrist to farm out incest by, and those his other tributary pollutions. What middle way can be taken then, may some interrupt, if we must neither turn to the right, nor to the left, and that the people hate to be reformed? Mark then, judges and lawgivers, and ye whose office it is to be our teachers, for I will utter now a doctrine, if ever any other, though neglected or not understood, yet of great and powerful importance to the governing of mankind. He who wisely would restrain the reasonable soul of man within due bounds, must first himself know perfectly, how far the territory and dominion extends of just and honest liberty. As little must he offer to bind that which God hath loosened, as to loosen that which he hath bound. The ignorance and mistake of this high point hath heaped up one huge half of all the misery that hath been since Adam. In the gospel we shall read a supercilious crew of masters, whose holiness, or rather whose evil eye, grieving that God should be so facile to man, was to set straiter limits to obedience than God hath set, to enslave the dignity of man, to put a garrison upon his neck of empty and over-dignified precepts: and we shall read our Saviour never more grieved and troubled than to meet with such a peevish madness among men against their own freedom. How can we expect him to be less offended with us, when much of the same folly shall be found yet remaining where it least ought, to the perishing of thousands? The greatest burden in the world is superstition, not only of ceremonies in the church, but of imaginary and scarecrow sins at home.' What greater weakening, what more subtle stratagem against our Christian warfare, when besides the gross body of real transgressions to encounter, we shall be terrified by a vain and shadowy menacing of faults that are not? When things indifferent shall be set to overfront us under the banners of sin, what wonder if we be routed, and by this art of our adversary, fall into the subjection of worst and deadliest offences? The superstition of the papist is, "Touch not, taste not," when God bids both; and ours is, "Part not, separate not," when God and charity both permits and commands. "Let all your things be done with charity," saith St. Paul; and his master saith, "She is the fulfilling of the law." Yet now a civil, an indifferent, a sometime dissuaded law of marriage, must be forced upon us to fulfil, not only without charity but against her. No place in heaven or earth, except hell, where charity may not enter: yet marriage, the ordinance of our solace and contentment, the remedy of our loneliness, will not admit now either of charity or mercy, to come in and mediate, or pacify the fierceness of this gentle ordinance, the unremedied loneliness of this remedy. Advise ye well, supreme senate, if charity be thus excluded and expulsed, how ye will defend the untainted honour of your own actions and proceedings. He who marries, intends as little to conspire his own ruin, as he that swears allegiance: and as a whole people is in proportion to an ill government, so is one man to an ill marriage. If they, against any authority, covenant, or statute, may, by the sovereign edict of charity, save not only their lives but honest liberties from unworthy bondage, as well may he against any private covenant, which he never entered to his mischief, redeem himself from unsupportable disturbances to honest peace and just contentment. And much the rather, for that to resist the highest magistrate though tyrannising, God never gave us express allowance, only he gave us reason, charity, nature, and good example to bear us out; but in this economical misfortune thus to demean ourselves, besides the warrant of those four great directors, which doth as justly belong hither, we have an express law of God, and such a law, as whereof our Saviour with a solemn threat forbade the abrogating. For no effect of tyranny can sit more heavy on the commonwealth, than this household unhappiness on the family. And farewell all hope of true reformation in the state, while such an evil as this lies undiscerned or unregarded in the house: on the redress whereof depends not only the spiritful and orderly life of our grown men, but the willing and careful education of our children. Let this therefore be new examined, this tenure and freehold of mankind, this native and domestic charter given us by a greater lord than that Saxon king the Confessor. Let the statutes of God be turned over, be scanned anew, and considered not altogether by the narrow intellectuals of quotationists and common places, but (as was the ancient right of councils) by men of what liberal profession soever, of eminent spirit and breeding, joined with a diffuse and various knowledge of divine and human things; able to balance and define good and evil, right and wrong, throughout every state of life; able to show us the ways of the Lord straight and faithful as they are, not full of cranks and contradictions, and pitfalling dispenses, but with divine insight and benignity measured out to the proportion of each mind and spirit, each temper and disposition created so different each from other, and yet by the skill of wise conducting, all to become uniform in virtue. To expedite these knots, were worthy a learned and memorable synod; while our enemies expect to see the expectation of the church tired out with dependencies and independencies, how they will compound and in what calends. Doubt not, worthy senators! to vindicate the sacred honour and judgment of Moses your predecessor, from the shallow commenting of scholastics and canonists. Doubt not after him to reach out your steady hands to the misinformed and wearied life of man; to restore this his lost heritage, into the household state: wherewith be sure that peace and love, the best subsistence of a Christian family, will return home from whence they are now banished; places of prostitution will be less haunted, the neighbour's bed less attempted, the yoke of prudent and manly discipline will be generally submitted to; sober and well-ordered living will soon spring up in the commonwealth. Ye have an author great beyond exception, Moses; and one yet greater, he who hedged in from abolishing every smallest jot and tittle of precious equity contained in that law, with a more accurate and lasting Masoreth, than either the synagogue of Ezra or the Galilæan school at Tiberias hath left us. Whatever else ye can enact, will scarce concern a third part of the British name: but the benefit and good of this your magnanimous example, will easily spread far beyond the banks of Tweed and the Norman isles. It would not be the first or second time, since our ancient druids, by whom this island was the cathedral of philosophy to France, left off their pagan rights, that England hath had this honour vouchsafed from heaven, to give out reformation to the world. Who was it but our English Constantine that baptised the Roman empire? Who but the Northumbrian Willibrode, and Winifride of Devon, with their followers, were the first apostles of Germany? Who but Alcuin and Wickliffe our countrymen, opened the eyes of Europe, the one in arts, the other in religion? Let not England forget her precedence of teaching nations how to live.

Know, worthies; and exercise the privilege of your honoured country. A greater title I here bring ye than is either in the power or in the policy of Rome to give her monarchs; this glorious act will style ye the defenders of charity. Nor is this yet the highest inscription that will adorn so religious and so holy a defence as this; behold here the pure and sacred law of God, and His yet purer and more sacred name, offering themselves to you, first of all, Christian reformers, to be acquitted from the long-suffered ungodly attribute of patronising adultery. Defer not to wipe off instantly these imputative blurs and stains cast by rude fancies upon the throne and beauty itself of inviolable holiness: lest some other people more devout and wise than we bereave us this offered immortal glory, our wonted prerogative, of being the first asserters in every great vindication. For me, as far as my part leads me, I have already my greatest gain, assurance and inward satisfaction to have done in this nothing unworthy of an honest life, and studies well employed. With what event, among the wise and right understanding handful of men, I am secure. But how among the drove of custom and prejudice this will be relished by such whose capacity, since their youth run ahead into the easy creek of a system or a medulla, sails there at will under the blown physiognomy of their unlaboured rudiments; for them, what their taste will be, I have also surety sufficient, from the entire league that hath ever been between formal ignorance and grave obstinacy. Yet when I remember the little that our Saviour could prevail about this doctrine of charity against the crabbed textuists of his time, I make no wonder, but rest confident, that whoso prefers either matrimony or other ordinance before the good of man and the plain exigence of charity, let him profess papist, or protestant, or what he will, he is no better than a pharisee, and understands not the gospel: whom as a misinterpreter of Christ I openly protest against; and provoke him to the trial of this truth before all the world: and let him bethink him withal how he will sodder up the shifting flaws of his ungirt permissions, his venial and unvenial dispenses, wherewith the law of God pardoning and unpardoning hath been shamefully branded for want of heed in glossing, to have eluded and baffled out all faith and chastity from the marriage-bed of that holy seed, with politic and judicial adulteries. I seek not to seduce the simple and illiterate; my errand is to find out the choicest and the learnedest, who have this high gift of wisdom to answer solidly, or to be convinced. I crave it from the piety, the learning, and the prudence which is housed in this place. It might perhaps more fitly have been written in another tongue: and I had done so, but that the esteem I have of my country's judgment, and the love I bear to my native language to serve it first with what I endeavour, make me speak it thus, ere I assay the verdict of outlandish readers. And perhaps also here I might have ended nameless, but that the address of these lines chiefly to the parliament of England might have seemed ingrateful not to acknowledge by whose religious care, unwearied watchfulness, courageous and heroic resolutions, I enjoy the peace and studious leisure to remain,

      The Honourer and Attendant of their
         noble Worth and Virtues,

                    JOHN MILTON.

All ingenuous men will see that the dignity and blessing of marriage is placed rather in the mutual enjoyment of that which the wanting soul needfully seeks, than of that which the plenteous body would joyfully give away. Hence it is that Plato in his festival discourse brings in Socrates relating what he feigned to have learned from the prophetess Diotima, how Love was the son of Penury, begot of Plenty in the garden of Jupiter. Which divinely sorts with that which in effect Moses tells us, that Love was the son of Loneliness, begot in Paradise by that sociable and helpful aptitude which God implanted between man and woman toward each other. The same, also, is that burning mentioned by St. Paul, whereof marriage ought to be the remedy: the flesh hath other mutual and easy curbs which are in the power of any temperate man. When, therefore, this original and sinless penury, or loneliness of the soul, cannot lay itself down by the side of such a meet and acceptable union as God ordained in marriage, at least in some proportion, it cannot conceive and bring forth love, but remains utterly unmarried under a former wedlock, and still burns in the proper meaning of St. Paul. Then enters Hate; not that hate that sins, but that which only is natural dissatisfaction, and the turning aside from a mistaken object: if that mistake have done injury, it fails not to dismiss with recompense; for to retain still, and not be able to love, is to heap up more injury. Thence this wise and pious law of dismission now defended took beginning: he, therefore, who lacking of his due in the most native and humane end of marriage, thinks it better to part than to live sadly and injuriously to that cheerful covenant (for not to be beloved, and yet

THE DOCTRINE OF DIVORCE.

retained, is the greatest injury to a gentle spirit), he, I say, who therefore seeks to part, is one who highly honours the married life and would not stain it: and the reasons which now move him to divorce are equal to the best of those that could first warrant him to marry; for, as was plainly shown, both the hate which now diverts him, and the loneliness which leads him still powerfully to seek a fit help, hath not the least grain of a sin in it, if he be worthy to understand himself.

Yet it is next to be feared, if he must be still bound without reason by a deaf rigour, that when he perceives the just expectance of his mind defeated, he will begin even against law to cast about where he may find his satisfaction more complete, unless he be a thing heroically virtuous; and that are not the common lump of men, for whom chiefly the laws ought to be made; though not to their sins, yet to their unsinning weaknesses, it being above their strength to endure the lonely estate, which while they shunned they are fallen into. And yet there follows upon this a worse temptation: for if he be such as hath spent his youth unblamably, and laid up his chiefest earthly comforts in the enjoyments of a contented marriage, nor did neglect that furtherance which was to be obtained therein by constant prayers; when he shall find himself bound fast to an uncomplying discord of nature, or, as it oft happens, to an image of earth and phlegm, with whom he looked to be the copartner of a sweet and gladsome society, and sees withal that his bondage is now inevitable; though he be almost the strongest Christian, he will be ready to despair in virtue, and mutiny against Divine Providence: and this doubtless is the reason of those lapses, and that melancholy despair, which we see in many wedded persons, though they understand it not, or pretend other causes, because they know no remedy; and is of extreme danger: therefore when human frailty surcharged it at such a loss, charity ought to venture much, and use bold physic, lest an overtossed faith endanger to shipwreck.

Marriage is a covenant, the very being whereof consists not in a forced cohabitation, and counterfeit performance of duties, but in unfeigned love and peace: and of matrimonial love, no doubt but that was chiefly meant, which by the ancient sages was thus parabled ; that Love, if he be not twin born, yet hath a brother wondrous like him, called Anteros; whom while he seeks all about, his chance is to meet with many false and feigning desires, that wander singly up and down in his likeness : by them in their borrowed garb, Love, though not wholly blind, as poets wrong him, yet having but one eye, as being born an archer aiming, and that eye not the quickest in this dark region here below, which is not Love's proper sphere, partly out of the simplicity and credulity which is native to him, often deceived, embraces and consorts him with these obvious and suborned striplings, as if they were his mother's own sons ; for so he thinks them, while they subtily keep themselves most on his blind side. But after a while, as his manner is, when soaring up into the high tower of his Apogæum, above the shadow of the earth, he darts out the direct rays of his then most piercing eyesight upon the impostures and trim disguises that were used with him, and discerns that this is not his genuine brother, as he imagined ; he has no longer the power to hold fellowship with such a personated mate : for straight his arrows lose their golden heads, and shed their purple feathers, his silken braids untwine, and slip their knots, and that original and fiery virtue given him by fate all on a sudden goes out, and leaves him undeified and despoiled of all his force ; till finding Anteros at last, he kindles and repairs the almost-faded ammunition of his deity by the reflection of a coequal and homogeneal fire. Thus mine author sung it to me : and by the leave of those who would be counted the only grave ones, this is no mere amatorious novel (though to be wise and skilful in these matters, men heretofore of greatest name in virtue have esteemed it one of the highest arcs, that human contemplation circling upwards can make from the globy sea whereon she stands) ; but this is a deep and serious verity, showing us that love in marriage cannot live nor subsist unless it be mutual ; and where love cannot be, there can be left of wedlock nothing but the empty husk of an outside matrimony, as undelightful and unpleasing to God as any other kind of hypocrisy. So far is his command from tying men to the observance of duties which there is no help for, but they must be dissembled. If Solomon's advice be not over-frolic, "Live joyfully," saith he, "with the wife whom thou lovest, all thy days, for that is thy portion:" how then, where we find it impossible to rejoice or to love, can we obey this precept? How miserably do we defraud ourselves of that comfortable portion, which God gives us, by striving vainly to glue an error together, which God and nature will not join, adding but more vexation and violence to that blissful society by our importunate superstition, that will not hearken to St. Paul, 1 Cor. vii., who, speaking of marriage and divorce, determines plain enough in general, that God therein "hath called us to peace, and not to bondage!" Yea, God himself commands in his law more than once, and by his prophet Malachi, as Calvin and the best translations read, that "he who hates, let him divorce," that is, he who cannot love. Hence it is that the rabbins, and Maimonides, famous among the rest, in a book of his set forth by Buxtorfius, tells us, that "divorce was permitted by Moses to preserve peace in marriage, and quiet in the family." Surely the Jews had their saving peace about them as well as we; yet care was taken that this wholesome provision for household peace shall also be allowed them: and must this be denied to Christians? O perverseness! that the law should be made more provident of peace-making than the gospel! that the gospel should be put to beg a most necessary help of mercy from the law, but must not have it! and that to grind in the mill of an undelighted and servile copulation, must be the only forced work of a Christian marriage, ofttimes with such a yokefellow, from whom both love and peace, both nature and religion mourns to be separated. I cannot therefore be so diffident, as not securely to conclude, that he who can receive nothing of the most important helps in marriage, being thereby disenabled to return that duty which is his, with a clear and hearty countenance, and thus continues to grieve whom he would not, and is no less grieved; that man ought even for love's sake and peace to move divorce upon good and liberal conditions to the divorced. And it is a less breach of wedlock to part with wise and quiet consent betimes, than still to foil and profane that mystery of joy and union with a polluting sadness and perpetual distemper: for it is not the outward continuing of marriage that keeps whole that covenant, but whatsoever does most according to peace and love, whether in marriage or in divorce, he it is that breaks marriage least; it being so often written, that "Love only is the fulfilling of every commandment."

. . . .

Another act of papal encroachment it was to pluck the power and arbitrement of divorce from the master of the family, into whose hands God and the law of all nations had put it, and Christ so left it, preaching only to the conscience, and not authorising a judicial court to toss about and divulge the unaccountable and secret reason of disaffection between man and wife, as a thing most improperly answerable to any such kind of trial. But the popes of Rome, perceiving the great revenue and high authority it would give them even over princes, to have the judging and deciding of such a main consequence in the life of man as was divorce, wrought so upon the superstition of those ages, as to divest them of that right, which God from the beginning had entrusted to the husband: by which means they subjected that ancient aud naturally domestic prerogative to an external and unbefitting judicature. For although differences in divorce about dowries, jointures, and the like, besides the punishing of adultery, ought not to pass without referring, if need be, to the magistrate; yet that the absolute and final hindering of divorce cannot belong to any civil or earthly power, against the will and consent of both parties, or of the husband alone, some reasons will be here urged as shall not need to decline the touch. But first I shall recite what hath been already yielded by others in favour of this opinion. Grotius and many more agree, that notwithstanding what Christ spake therein to the conscience, the magistrate is not thereby enjoined aught against the preservation of civil peace, of equity, and of convenience. And among these Fagius is most remarkable, and gives the same liberty of pronouncing divorce to the

Christian magistrate as the Mosaic had. "For whatever," saith he, "Christ spake to the regenerate, the judge hath to deal with the vulgar: if therefore any through hardness of heart will not be a tolerable wife to her husband, it will be lawful as well now as of old to pass the bill of divorce, not by private but by public authority. Nor doth man separate them then, but God by his law of divorce given by Moses. What can hinder the magistrate from so doing, to whose government all outward things are subject, to separate and remove from perpetual vexation, and no small danger, those bodies whose minds are already separate; it being his office to procure peaceable and convenient living in the commonwealth; and being as certain also, that they so necessarily separated cannot all receive a single life?" And this I observe, that our divines do generally condemn separation of bed and board, without the liberty of second choice: if that therefore in some cases be most purely necessary (as who so blockish to deny?), then is this also as needful. Thus far by others is already well stepped, to inform us that divorce is not a matter of law, but of charity; if there remain a furlong yet to end the question, these following reasons may serve to gain it with any apprehension not too unlearned or too wayward. First, because ofttimes the causes of seeking divorce reside so deeply in the radical and innocent affections of nature, as is not within the diocese of law to tamper with. Other relations may aptly enough be held together by a civil and virtuous love: but the duties of man and wife are such as are chiefly conversant in that love which is most ancient and merely natural, whose two prime statutes are to join itself to that which is good, and acceptable, and friendly; and to turn aside and depart from what is disagreeable, displeasing, and unlike: of the two this latter is the strongest, and most equal to be regarded; for although a man may often be unjust in seeking that which he loves, yet he can never be unjust or blamable in retiring from his endless trouble and distaste, whenas his tarrying can redound to no true content on either side. Haste is of all things the mightiest divider; nay, is division itself. To couple hatred therefore, though wedlock try all her golden links, and borrow to her aid all the iron manacles and fetters of law, it does but seek to twist a rope of sand, which was a task they say that posed the devil: and that sluggish fiend in hell, Ocnus, whom the poems tell of, brought his idle cordage to as good effect, which never served to bind with, but to feed the ass that stood at his elbow. And that the restrictive law against divorce attains as little to bind anything truly in a disjointed marriage, or to keep it bound, but serves only to feel the ignorance and definitive impertinence of a doltish canon, were no absurd illusion. To hinder therefore those deep and serious regresses of nature in a reasonable soul, parting from that mistaken help, which he justly seeks in a person created for him, recollecting himself from an unmeet help which was never meant, and to detain him by compulsion in such an unpredestined misery as this, is in diameter against both nature and institution: but to interpose a jurisdictive power over the inward and irremediable disposition of man, to command love and sympathy, to forbid dislike against the guiltless instinct of nature, is not within the province of any law to reach; and were indeed an uncommodious rudeness, not a just power: for that law may bandy with nature, and traverse her sage motions, was an error in Callicles the rhetorician, whom Socrates from high principles confutes in Plato's Gorgias. If therefore divorce may be so natural, and that law and nature are not to go contrary; then to forbid divorce compulsively, is not only against nature but against law.

Next, it must be remembered, that all law is for some good, that may be frequently attained without the admixture of a worse inconvenience; and therefore many gross faults, as ingratitude and the like, which are too far within the soul to be cured by constraint of law, are left only to be wrought on by conscience and persuasion. Which made Aristotle, in the 10th of his Ethics to Nicomachus, aim at a kind of division of law into private or persuasive, and public or compulsive. Hence it is, that the law forbidding divorce never attains to any good end of such prohibition, but rather multiplies evil. For if nature's resistless sway in love or hate be once compelled, it grows careless of itself, vicious, useless to friends, unserviceable and spiritless to the commonwealth. Which Moses rightly foresaw, and all wise lawgivers that ever knew man, what kind of creature he was. The parliament also and clergy of England were not ignorant of this, when they consented that Harry VIII. might put away his queen Anne of Cleve, whom he could not like after he had been wedded half a year; unless it were that, contrary to the proverb, they made a necessity of that which might have been a virtue in them to do; for even the freedom and eminence of man's creation gives him to be a law in this matter to himself, being the head of the other sex which was made for him: whom therefore though he ought not to injure, yet neither should he be forced to retain in society to his own overthrow, nor to hear any judge therein above himself: it being also an unseemly affront to the sequestered and veiled modesty of that sex, to have her unpleasingness and other concealments bandied up and down, and aggravated in open court by those hired masters of tongue-fence. Such uncomely exigencies it befell no less a majesty than Henry VIII. to be reduced to, who, finding just reason in his conscience to forego his brother's wife, after many indignities of being deluded, and made a boy of by those his two cardinal judges, was constrained at last, for want of other proof that she had been carnally known by prince Arthur, even to uncover the nakedness of that virtuous lady, and to recite openly the obscene evidence of his brother's chamberlain. Yet it pleased God to make him see all the tyranny of Rome, by discovering this which they exercised over divorce, and to make him the beginner of a reformation to this whole kingdom, by first asserting into his familiary power the right of just divorce. It is true, an adulteress cannot be shamed enough by any public proceeding; but the woman whose honour is not appeached is less injured by a silent dismission, being otherwise not illiberally dealt with, than to endure a clamouring debate of utterless things, in a business of that civil secrecy and difficult discerning as not to be overmuch questioned by nearest friends. Which drew that answer from the greatest and worthiest Roman of his time, Paulus Emilius, being demanded why he would put away his wife for no visible reason? "This shoe," said he, and held it out on his foot, "is a neat shoe, a new shoe, and yet none of you know where it wrings me:" much less by the unfamiliar cognisance of a feed gamester can such a private difference be examined, neither ought it.

Again, if law aim at the firm establishment and preservation of matrimonial faith, we know that cannot thrive under violent means, but is the more violated. It is not when two unfortunately met are by the canon forced to draw in that yoke an unmerciful day's work of sorrow till death unharness them, that then the law keeps marriage most unviolated and unbroken; but when the law takes order that marriage be accountant and responsible to perform that society, whether it be religious, civil, or corporal, which may be conscionably required and claimed therein, or else to be dissolved if it cannot be undergone. This is to make marriage most indissoluble, by making it a just and equal dealer, a performer of those due helps, which instituted the covenant; being otherwise a most unjust contract, and no more to be maintained under tuition of law, than the vilest fraud, or cheat, or theft, that may be committed. But because this is such a secret kind of fraud or theft, as cannot be discerned by law but only by the plaintiff himself; therefore to divorce was never counted a political or civil offence, neither to Jew nor Gentile, nor by any judicial intendment of Christ, further than could be discerned to transgress the allowance of Moses, which was of necessity so large, that it doth all one as if it sent back the matter undeterminable at law, and intractible by rough dealing, to have instructions and admonitions bestowed about it by them whose spiritual office is to adjure and to denounce, and so left to the conscience. The law can only appoint the just and equal conditions of divorce; and is to look how it is an injury to the divorced, which in truth it can be none, as a mere separation; for if she consent, wherein has the law to right her? or consent not, then is it either just, and so deserved; or if unjust, such in all likelihood was the divorcer: and to part from an unjust man is a happiness, and no injury to be lamented. But suppose it to be an injury, the law is not able to amend it, unless she think it other than a miserable redress, to return back from whence she was expelled, or but entreated to be gone, or else to live apart still married without marriage, a married widow. Last, if it be to chasten the divorcer, what law punishes a deed which is not moral but natural, a deed which cannot certainly be found to be an injury; or how can it be punished by prohibiting the divorce, but that the innocent must equally partake both in the shame and in the smart? So that which way soever we look, the law can to no rational purpose forbid divorce; it can only take care that the conditions of divorce be not injurious. Thus then we see the trial of law, how impertinent it is to the question of divorce, how helpless next, and then how hurtful.

Therefore the last reason, why it should not be, is the example we have, not only from the noblest and wisest commonwealths, guided by the clearest light of human knowledge, but also from the divine testimonies of God himself, lawgiving in person to a sanctified people. That all this is true, whoso desires to know at large with least pains, and expects not here overlong rehearsals of that which is by others already so judiciously gathered, let him hasten to be acquainted with that noble volume written by our learned Selden, *Of the Law of Nature and of Nations*, a work more useful and more worthy to be perused by whosoever studies to be a great man in wisdom, equity, and justice, than all those "decretals and sumless sums," which the pontifical clerks have doted on, ever since that unfortunate mother famously sinned thrice, and died impenitent of her bringing into the world those two misbegotten infants, and for ever infants, Lombard and Gratian, him the compiler of canon iniquity, the other the Tubalcain of scholastic sophistry, whose overspreading barbarism hath not only infused their own bastardy upon the fruitfulest part of human learning, not only dissipated and dejected the clear light of nature in us, and of nations, but hath tainted also the fountains of divine doctrine, and rendered the pure and solid law of God unbeneficial to us by their calumnious dunceries. Yet this law, which their unskilfulness hath made liable to all ignominy, the purity and wisdom of this law shall be the buckler of our dispute. Liberty of divorce we claim not, we think not but from this law; the dignity, the faith, the authority thereof is now grown among Christians, O astonishment! a labour of no mean difficulty and envy to defend. That it should not be counted a faltering dispense, a flattering permission of sin, the bill of adultery, a snare, is the expense of all this apology. And all that we solicit is, that it may be suffered to stand in the place where God set it, amidst the firmament of his holy laws, to shine, as it was wont, upon the weaknesses and errors of men, perishing else in the sincerity of their honest purposes: for certain there is no memory of whoredoms and adulteries left among us now, when this warranted freedom of God's own giving is made dangerous and discarded for a scroll of licence. It must be your suffrages and votes, O Englishmen, that this exploded decree of God and Moses may scape and come off fair, without the censure of a shameful abrogating: which, if yonder sun ride sure, and means not to break word with us to-morrow, was never yet abrogated by our Saviour. Give sentence if you please, that the frivolous canon may reverse the infallible judgment of Moses and his great director. Or if it be the reformed writers, whose doctrine persuades this rather, their reasons I dare affirm are all silenced, unless it be only this. Paræus, on the Corinthians, would prove, that hardness of heart in divorce is no more now to be permitted, but to be amerced with fine and imprisonment. I am not willing to discover the forgettings of reverend men, yet here I must: what article or clause of the whole new covenant can Paræus bring, to exasperate the judicial law upon any infirmity under the gospel? I say infirmity, for if it were the high hand of sin, the law as little would have endured it as the gospel; it would not stretch to the dividing of an inheritance; it refused to condemn adultery, not that these things should not be done at law, but to show that the gospel hath not the least influence upon judicial courts, much less to make them sharper and more heavy, least of all to arraign before a temporal judge that which the law without summons acquitted. "But," saith he, "the law was the time of youth, under violent affections; the gospel in us is mature age, and ought to subdue affections." True, and so ought the law too, if they be found inordinate, and not merely natural and blameless. Next I distinguish, that the time of the law is compared to youth and pupilage in respect of the ceremonial part, which led the Jews as children through corporal and garish rudiments, until the fulness of time should reveal to them the higher lessons of faith and redemption. This is not meant of the moral part; therein it soberly concerned them not to be babies, but to be men in good earnest: the sad and awful majesty of that law was not to be jested with: to bring a bearded nonage with lascivious dispensations before that throne, had been a lewd affront, as it is now a gross mistake. But what discipline is this, Paræus, to nourish violent affections in youth, by cockering and wanton indulgencies, and to chastise them in mature age with a boyish rod of correction? How much more coherent is it to Scripture, that the law, as a strict schoolmaster, should have punished every trespass without indulgence so baneful to youth, and that the gospel should now correct that by admonition and reproof only, in free and mature age, which was punished with stripes in the childhood and bondage of the law? What, therefore, it allowed them so fairly, much less is to be whipped now, especially in penal courts: and if it ought now to trouble the conscience, why did that angry accuser and condemner law reprieve it? So then, neither from Moses nor from Christ hath the magistrate any authority to proceed against it. But what, shall then the disposal of that power return again to the master of a family? Wherefore not, since God there put it, and the presumptuous canon thence bereft it? This only must be provided, that the ancient manner be observed in the presence of the minister and other grave selected elders, who after they shall have admonished and pressed upon him the words of our Saviour, and he shall have protested in the faith of the eternal gospel, and the hope he has of happy resurrection, that otherwise than thus he cannot do, and thinks himself and this his case not contained in that prohibition of divorce which Christ pronounced, the matter not being of malice, but of nature, and so not capable of reconciling; to constrain him further were to unchristian him, to unman him, to throw the mountain of Sinai upon him, with the weight of the whole law to boot, flat against the liberty and essence of the gospel; and yet nothing available either to the sanctity of marriage, the good of husband, wife, or children, nothing profitable either to church or commonwealth, but hurtful and pernicious in all these respects. But this will bring in confusion: yet these cautious mistrusters might consider, that what they thus object lights not upon this book, but upon that which I engage against them, the book of God and Moses, with all the wisdom and providence which had forecast the worst of confusion that could succeed, and yet thought fit of such a permission. But let them be of good cheer, it wrought so little disorder among the Jews, that from Moses till after the captivity, not one of the prophets thought it worth rebuking; for that of Malachi well looked into will appear to be not against divorcing, but rather against keeping strange concubines, to the vexation of their Hebrew wives. If, therefore, we Christians may be thought as good and tractable as the Jews were (and certainly the prohibitors of divorce presume us to be better), then less confusion is to be feared for this among us than was among them. If we be worse, or but as bad, which lamentable examples confirm we are, then have we more, or at least as much, need of this permitted law, as they to whom God therefore gave it (as they say) under a harsher covenant. Let not, therefore, the frailty of man go on thus inventing needless troubles to itself, to groan under the false imagination of a strictness never imposed from above; enjoining that for duty which is an impossible and vain supererogating. "Be not righteous overmuch," is the counsel of Ecclesiastes; "why shouldst thou destroy thyself?" Let us not be thus over-curious to strain at atoms, and yet to stop every vent and cranny of permissive liberty, lest nature, wanting those needful pores and breathing-places, which God hath not debarred our weakness, either suddenly break out into some wide rupture of open vice and frantic heresy, or else inwardly fester with repining and blasphemous thoughts, under an unreasonable and fruitless rigour of unwarranted law. Against which evils nothing can more beseem the religion of the church, or the wisdom of the state, than to consider timely and provide. And in so doing let them not doubt but they shall vindicate the misreputed honour of God and his great lawgiver, by suffering him to give his own laws according to the condition of man's nature best known to him, without the unsufferable imputation of dispensing legally with many ages of ratified adultery. They shall recover the misattended words of Christ to the sincerity of their true sense from manifold contradictions, and shall open them with the key of charity. Many helpless Christians they shall raise from the depth of sadness and distress, utterly unfitted as they are to serve God or man: many they shall reclaim from obscure and giddy sects, many regain from dissolute and brutish licence, many from desperate hardness, if ever that were justly pleaded. They shall set free many daughters of Israel not wanting much of her sad plight whom "Satan had bound eighteen years." Man they shall restore to his just dignity and prerogative in nature, preferring the soul's free peace before the promiscuous draining of a carnal rage. Marriage, from a perilous hazard and snare, they shall reduce to be a more certain haven and retirement of happy society; when they shall judge according to God and Moses (and how not then according to Christ), when they shall judge it more wisdom and goodness to break that covenant seemingly, and keep it really, than by compulsion of law to keep it seemingly, and by compulsion of blameless nature to break it really, at least if it were ever truly joined. The vigour of discipline they may then turn with better success upon the prostitute looseness of the times, when men, finding in themselves the infirmities of former ages, shall not be constrained above the gift of God in them to unprofitable and impossible observances, never required from the civilest, the wisest, the holiest nations, whose other excellencies in moral virtue they never yet could equal. Last of all, to those whose mind is still to maintain textual restrictions, whereof the bare sound cannot consist sometimes with humanity, much less with charity; I would ever answer, by putting them in remembrance of a command above all commands, which they seem to have forgot, and who spake it: in comparison whereof, this which they so exalt is but a petty and subordinate precept. "Let them go," therefore, with whom I am loath to couple them, yet they will needs run into the same blindness with the Pharisees; "let them go therefore," and consider well what this lesson means, "I will have mercy and not sacrifice:" for on that "saying all the law and prophets depend;" much more the gospel, whose end and excellence is mercy and peace. Or if they cannot learn that, how will they hear this? which yet I shall not doubt to leave with them as a conclusion, that God the Son hath put all other things under his own feet, but his commandments he hath left all under the feet of charity.

DEDICATION TO "A TREATISE ON CHRISTIAN DOCTRINE."

JOHN MILTON,

TO ALL THE CHURCHES OF CHRIST

And to all who profess the Christian Faith throughout the World, Peace, and the Recognition of the Truth, and Eternal Salvation in God the Father, and in our Lord Jesus Christ.

SINCE the commencement of the last century, when religion began to be restored from the corruptions of more than thirteen hundred years to something of its original purity, many treatises of theology have been published, conducted according to sounder principles, wherein the chief heads of Christian doctrine are set forth sometimes briefly, sometimes in a more enlarged and methodical order. I think myself obliged, therefore, to declare in the first instance why, if any works have already appeared as perfect as the nature of the subject will admit, I have not remained contented with them—or, if all my predecessors have treated it unsuccessfully, why their failure has not deterred me from attempting an undertaking of a similar kind.

If I were to say that I had devoted myself to the study of the Christian religion because nothing else can so effectually rescue the lives and minds of men from those two detestable curses, slavery and superstition, I should seem to have acted rather from a regard to my highest earthly comforts, than from a religious motive.

But since it is only to the individual faith of each that the

Deity has opened the way of eternal salvation, and as he requires that he who would be saved should have a personal belief of his own, I resolved not to repose on the faith or judgment of others in matters relating to God; but on the one hand, having taken the grounds of my faith from divine revelation alone, and on the other, having neglected nothing which depended on my own industry, I thought fit to scrutinise and ascertain for myself the several points of my religious belief, by the most careful perusal and meditation of the Holy Scriptures themselves.

If therefore I mention what has proved beneficial in my own practice, it is in the hope that others, who have a similar wish of improving themselves, may be thereby invited to pursue the same method. I entered upon an assiduous course of study in my youth, beginning with the books of the Old and New Testament in their original languages, and going diligently through a few of the shorter systems of divines, in imitation of whom I was in the habit of classing under certain heads whatever passages of Scripture occurred for extraction, to be made use of hereafter as occasion might require. At length I resorted with increased confidence to some of the more copious theological treatises, and to the examination of the arguments advanced by the conflicting parties respecting certain disputed points of faith. But, to speak the truth with freedom as well as candour, I was concerned to discover in many instances adverse reasonings either evaded by wretched shifts, or attempted to be refuted, rather speciously than with solidity, by an affected display of formal sophisms, or by a constant recourse to the quibbles of the grammarians; while what was most pertinaciously espoused as the true doctrine, seemed often defended, with more vehemence than strength of argument, by misconstructions of Scripture, or by the hasty deduction of erroneous inferences. Owing to these causes, the truth was sometimes as strenuously opposed as if it had been an error or a heresy—while errors and heresies were substituted for the truth, and valued rather from deference to custom and the spirit of party than from the authority of Scripture.

According to my judgment, therefore, neither my creed nor

my hope of salvation could be safely trusted to such guides; and yet it appeared highly requisite to possess some methodical tractate of Christian doctrine, or at least to attempt such a disquisition as might be useful in establishing my faith or assisting my memory. I deemed it therefore safest and most advisable to compile for myself, by my own labour and study, some original treatise which should be always at hand, derived solely from the word of God itself, and executed with all possible fidelity, seeing that I could have no wish to practise any imposition on myself in such a matter.

After a diligent perseverance in this plan for several years, I perceived that the strong holds of the reformed religion were sufficiently fortified, as far as it was in danger from the Papists, —but neglected in many other quarters; neither competently strengthened with works of defence, nor adequately provided with champions. It was also evident to me, that, in religion as in other things, the offers of God were all directed, not to an indolent credulity, but to constant diligence, and to an unwearied search after truth; and that more than I was aware of still remained which required to be more rigidly examined by the rule of Scripture, and reformed after a more accurate model. I so far satisfied myself in the prosecution of this plan as at length to trust that I had discovered, with regard to religion, what was matter of belief, and what only matter of opinion. It was also a great solace to me to have compiled, by God's assistance, a precious aid for my faith,—or rather to have laid up for myself a treasure which would be a provision for my future life, and would remove from my mind all grounds for hesitation, as often as it behoved me to render an account of the principles of my belief.

If I communicate the result of my inquiries to the world at large; if, as God is my witness, it be with a friendly and benignant feeling towards mankind, that I readily give as wide a circulation as possible to what I esteem my best and richest possession, I hope to meet with a candid reception from all parties, and that none at least will take unjust offence, even though many things should be brought to light which will at once be seen to differ from certain received opinions. I earnestly beseech all lovers of truth, not to cry out that the Church is thrown into confusion by that freedom of discussion and inquiry which is granted to the schools, and ought certainly to be refused to no believer, since we are ordered "to prove all things," and since the daily progress of the light of truth is productive far less of disturbance to the Church than of illumination and edification. Nor do I see how the Church can be more disturbed by the investigation of truth, than were the Gentiles by the first promulgation of the gospel; since so far from recommending or imposing anything on my own authority, it is my particular advice that every one should suspend his opinion on whatever points he may not feel himself fully satisfied, till the evidence of Scripture prevail, and persuade his reason into assent and faith. Concealment is not my object; it is to the learned that I address myself, or if it be thought that the learned are not the best umpires and judges of such things, I should at least wish to submit my opinions to men of a mature and manly understanding, possessing a thorough knowledge of the doctrines of the gospel; no whose judgments I should rely with far more confidence, than on those of novices in these matters. And whereas the greater part of those who have written most largely on these subjects have been wont to fill whole pages with explanations of their own opinions, thrusting into the margin the texts in support of their doctrine with a summary reference to the chapter and verse, I have chosen, on the contrary, to fill my pages even to redundance with quotations from Scripture, that so as little space as possible might be left for my own words, even when they arise from the context of revelation itself.

It has also been my object to make it appear from the opinions I shall be found to have advanced, whether new or old, of how much consequence to the Christian religion is the liberty not only of winnowing and sifting every doctrine, but also of thinking and even writing respecting it, according to our individual faith and persuasion; an inference which will be stronger in proportion to the weight and importance of those opinions, or rather in proportion to the authority of Scripture, on the abundant testimony of which they rest. Without this liberty there is neither religion nor gospel—force alone prevails,—by which it is disgraceful for the Christian religion to be supported. Without this liberty we are still enslaved, not indeed, as formerly, under the divine law, but, what is worst of all, under the law of man, or to speak more truly, under a barbarous tyranny. But I do not expect from candid and judicious readers a conduct so unworthy of them,—that like certain unjust and foolish men, they should stamp with the invidious name of heretic or heresy whatever appears to them to differ from the received opinions, without trying the doctrine by a comparison with Scripture testimonies. According to their notions, to have branded any one at random with this opprobrious mark, is to have refuted him without any trouble, by a single word. By the simple imputation of the name of heretic, they think that they have despatched their man at one blow. To men of this kind I answer, that in the time of the apostles, ere the New Testament was written, whenever the charge of heresy was applied as a term of reproach, that alone was considered as heresy which was at variance with their doctrine orally delivered,—and that those only were looked upon as heretics, who according to Rom. xvi. 17, 18, "caused divisions and offences contrary to the doctrine" of the apostles, ... "serving not our Lord Jesus Christ, but their own belly." By parity of reasoning therefore, since the compilation of the New Testament, I maintain that nothing but what is in contradiction to it can properly be called heresy.

For my own part, I adhere to the Holy Scriptures alone—I follow no other heresy or sect. I had not even read any of the works of heretics, so called, when the mistakes of those who are reckoned for orthodox, and their incautious handling of Scripture first taught me to agree with their opponents whenever those opponents agreed with Scripture. If this be heresy, I confess with St. Paul, Acts xxiv. 14, "that after the way which they call heresy, so worship I the God of my fathers, believing all things which are written in the law and the prophets"—to which I add, whatever is written in the New Testament. Any other judges or paramount interpreters of the Christian belief, together with all implicit faith, as it is called, I, in common with the whole Protestant Church, refuse to recognise.

For the rest, brethren, cultivate truth with brotherly love. Judge of my present undertaking according to the admonishing of the Spirit of God—and neither adopt my sentiments nor reject them, unless every doubt has been removed from your belief by the clear testimony of revelation. Finally, live in the faith of our Lord and Saviour Jesus Christ. Farewell.

THE WORLD'S LITERARY MASTERPIECES.

THE SCOTT LIBRARY.

Maroon Cloth, Gilt. Price 1s. net per Volume.

VOLUMES ALREADY ISSUED—

1 MALORY'S ROMANCE OF KING ARTHUR AND THE Quest of the Holy Grail. Edited by Ernest Rhys.

2 THOREAU'S WALDEN. WITH INTRODUCTORY NOTE by Will H. Dircks.

3 THOREAU'S "WEEK." WITH PREFATORY NOTE BY Will H. Dircks.

4 THOREAU'S ESSAYS. EDITED, WITH AN INTRO-duction, by Will H. Dircks.

5 CONFESSIONS OF AN ENGLISH OPIUM-EATER, ETC. By Thomas De Quincey. With Introductory Note by William Sharp.

6 LANDOR'S IMAGINARY CONVERSATIONS. SELECTED, with Introduction, by Havelock Ellis.

7 PLUTARCH'S LIVES (LANGHORNE). WITH INTRO-ductory Note by B. J. Snell, M.A.

8 BROWNE'S RELIGIO MEDICI, ETC. WITH INTRO-duction by J. Addington Symonds.

9 SHELLEY'S ESSAYS AND LETTERS. EDITED, WITH Introductory Note, by Ernest Rhys.

10 SWIFT'S PROSE WRITINGS. CHOSEN AND ARRANGED, with Introduction, by Walter Lewin.

11 MY STUDY WINDOWS. BY JAMES RUSSELL LOWELL. With Introduction by R. Garnett, LL.D.

12 LOWELL'S ESSAYS ON THE ENGLISH POETS. WITH a new Introduction by Mr. Lowell.

13 THE BIGLOW PAPERS. BY JAMES RUSSELL LOWELL. With a Prefatory Note by Ernest Rhys.

14 GREAT ENGLISH PAINTERS. SELECTED FROM Cunningham's *Lives*. Edited by William Sharp.

THE WALTER SCOTT PUBLISHING COMPANY, LIMITED,
LONDON AND FELLING-ON-TYNE.

THE SCOTT LIBRARY—continued.

15 BYRON'S LETTERS AND JOURNALS. SELECTED, with Introduction, by Mathilde Blind.

16 LEIGH HUNT'S ESSAYS. WITH INTRODUCTION AND Notes by Arthur Symons.

17 LONGFELLOW'S "HYPERION," "KAVANAGH," AND "The Trouveres." With Introduction by W. Tirebuck.

18 GREAT MUSICAL COMPOSERS. BY G. F. FERRIS. Edited, with Introduction, by Mrs. William Sharp.

19 THE MEDITATIONS OF MARCUS AURELIUS. EDITED by Alice Zimmern.

20 THE TEACHING OF EPICTETUS. TRANSLATED FROM the Greek, with Introduction and Notes, by T. W. Rolleston.

21 SELECTIONS FROM SENECA. WITH INTRODUCTION by Walter Clode.

22 SPECIMEN DAYS IN AMERICA. BY WALT WHITMAN. Revised by the Author, with fresh Preface.

23 DEMOCRATIC VISTAS, AND OTHER PAPERS. BY Walt Whitman. (Published by arrangement with the Author.)

24 WHITE'S NATURAL HISTORY OF SELBORNE. WITH a Preface by Richard Jefferies.

25 DEFOE'S CAPTAIN SINGLETON. EDITED, WITH Introduction, by H. Halliday Sparling.

26 MAZZINI'S ESSAYS: LITERARY, POLITICAL, AND Religious. With Introduction by William Clarke.

27 PROSE WRITINGS OF HEINE. WITH INTRODUCTION by Havelock Ellis.

28 REYNOLDS'S DISCOURSES. WITH INTRODUCTION by Helen Zimmern.

29 PAPERS OF STEELE AND ADDISON. EDITED BY Walter Lewin.

30 BURNS'S LETTERS. SELECTED AND ARRANGED, with Introduction, by J. Logie Robertson, M.A.

31 VOLSUNGA SAGA. WILLIAM MORRIS. WITH INTRO-duction by H. H. Sparling.

THE WALTER SCOTT PUBLISHING COMPANY, LIMITED,
LONDON AND FELLING-ON-TYNE.

THE SCOTT LIBRARY—continued.

32 SARTOR RESARTUS. BY THOMAS CARLYLE. WITH Introduction by Ernest Rhys.

33 SELECT WRITINGS OF EMERSON WITH INTROduction by Percival Chubb.

34 AUTOBIOGRAPHY OF LORD HERBERT. EDITED, with an Introduction, by Will H. Dircks.

35 ENGLISH PROSE, FROM MAUNDEVILLE TO Thackeray. Chosen and Edited by Arthur Galton.

36 THE PILLARS OF SOCIETY, AND OTHER PLAYS. BY Henrik Ibsen. Edited, with an Introduction, by Havelock Ellis.

37 IRISH FAIRY AND FOLK TALES. EDITED AND Selected by W. B. Yeats.

38 ESSAYS OF DR. JOHNSON, WITH BIOGRAPHICAL Introduction and Notes by Stuart J. Reid.

39 ESSAYS OF WILLIAM HAZLITT. SELECTED AND Edited, with Introduction and Notes, by Frank Carr.

40 LANDOR'S PENTAMERON, AND OTHER IMAGINARY Conversations. Edited, with a Preface, by H. Ellis.

41 POE'S TALES AND ESSAYS. EDITED, WITH INTROduction, by Ernest Rhys.

42 VICAR OF WAKEFIELD. BY OLIVER GOLDSMITH. Edited, with Preface, by Ernest Rhys.

43 POLITICAL ORATIONS, FROM WENTWORTH TO Macaulay. Edited, with Introduction, by William Clarke.

44 THE AUTOCRAT OF THE BREAKFAST-TABLE. BY Oliver Wendell Holmes.

45 THE POET AT THE BREAKFAST-TABLE. BY OLIVER Wendell Holmes.

46 THE PROFESSOR AT THE BREAKFAST-TABLE. BY Oliver Wendell Holmes.

47 LORD CHESTERFIELD'S LETTERS TO HIS SON. Selected, with Introduction, by Charles Sayle.

48 STORIES FROM CARLETON. SELECTED, WITH INTROduction, by W. Yeats.

THE WALTER SCOTT PUBLISHING CO., LTD.,
LONDON AND FELLING-ON-TYNE.

THE SCOTT LIBRARY—continued.

49 JANE EYRE. BY CHARLOTTE BRONTË. EDITED BY Clement K. Shorter.

50 ELIZABETHAN ENGLAND. EDITED BY LOTHROP Withington, with a Preface by Dr. Furnivall.

51 THE PROSE WRITINGS OF THOMAS DAVIS. EDITED by T. W. Rolleston.

52 SPENCE'S ANECDOTES. A SELECTION. EDITED, with an Introduction and Notes, by John Underhill.

53 MORE'S UTOPIA, AND LIFE OF EDWARD V. EDITED, with an Introduction, by Maurice Adams.

54 SADI'S GULISTAN, OR FLOWER GARDEN. TRANSlated, with an Essay, by James Ross.

55 ENGLISH FAIRY AND FOLK TALES. EDITED BY E. Sidney Hartland.

56 NORTHERN STUDIES. BY EDMUND GOSSE. WITH a Note by Ernest Rhys.

57 EARLY REVIEWS OF GREAT WRITERS. EDITED BY E. Stevenson.

58 ARISTOTLE'S ETHICS. WITH GEORGE HENRY Lewes's Essay on Aristotle prefixed.

59 LANDOR'S PERICLES AND ASPASIA. EDITED, WITH an Introduction, by Havelock Ellis.

60 ANNALS OF TACITUS. THOMAS GORDON'S TRANSlation. Edited, with an Introduction, by Arthur Galton.

61 ESSAYS OF ELIA. BY CHARLES LAMB. EDITED, with an Introduction, by Ernest Rhys.

62 BALZAC'S SHORTER STORIES. TRANSLATED BY William Wilson and the Count Stenbock.

63 COMEDIES OF DE MUSSET. EDITED, WITH AN Introductory Note, by S. L. Gwynn.

64 CORAL REEFS. BY CHARLES DARWIN. EDITED, with an Introduction, by Dr. J. W. Williams.

65 SHERIDAN'S PLAYS. EDITED, WITH AN INTROduction, by Rudolf Dircks.

THE WALTER SCOTT PUBLISHING CO., LTD.,
LONDON AND FELLING-ON-TYNE.

THE SCOTT LIBRARY—continued.

66 OUR VILLAGE. BY MISS MITFORD. EDITED, WITH an Introduction, by Ernest Rhys.

67 MASTER HUMPHREY'S CLOCK, AND OTHER STORIES. By Charles Dickens. With Introduction by Frank T. Marzials.

68 OXFORD MOVEMENT, THE. BEING A SELECTION from "Tracts for the Times." Edited, with an Introduction, by William G. Hutchison.

69 ESSAYS AND PAPERS BY DOUGLAS JERROLD. EDITED by Walter Jerrold.

70 VINDICATION OF THE RIGHTS OF WOMAN. BY Mary Wollstonecraft. Introduction by Mrs. E. Robins Pennell.

71 "THE ATHENIAN ORACLE." A SELECTION. EDITED by John Underhill, with Prefatory Note by Walter Besant.

72 ESSAYS OF SAINTE-BEUVE. TRANSLATED AND Edited, with an Introduction, by Elizabeth Lee.

73 SELECTIONS FROM PLATO. FROM THE TRANSlation of Sydenham and Taylor. Edited by T. W. Rolleston.

74 HEINE'S ITALIAN TRAVEL SKETCHES, ETC. TRANSlated by Elizabeth A. Sharp. With an Introduction from the French of Theophile Gautier.

75 SCHILLER'S MAID OF ORLEANS. TRANSLATED, with an Introduction, by Major-General Patrick Maxwell.

76 SELECTIONS FROM SYDNEY SMITH. EDITED, WITH an Introduction, by Ernest Rhys.

77 THE NEW SPIRIT. BY HAVELOCK ELLIS.

78 THE BOOK OF MARVELLOUS ADVENTURES. FROM the "Morte d'Arthur." Edited by Ernest Rhys. (This, together with No. 1, forms the complete "Morte d'Arthur.")

79 ESSAYS AND APHORISMS. BY SIR ARTHUR HELPS. With an Introduction by E. A. Helps.

80 ESSAYS OF MONTAIGNE. SELECTED, WITH A Prefatory Note, by Percival Chubb.

81 THE LUCK OF BARRY LYNDON. BY W. M. Thackeray. Edited by F. T. Marzials.

82 SCHILLER'S WILLIAM TELL. TRANSLATED, WITH an Introduction, by Major-General Patrick Maxwell.

THE WALTER SCOTT PUBLISHING CO., LTD.,
LONDON AND FELLING-ON-TYNE

THE SCOTT LIBRARY—continued.

83 CARLYLE'S ESSAYS ON GERMAN LITERATURE.
With an Introduction by Ernest Rhys.

84 PLAYS AND DRAMATIC ESSAYS OF CHARLES LAMB.
Edited, with an Introduction, by Rudolf Dircks.

85 THE PROSE OF WORDSWORTH. SELECTED AND
Edited, with an Introduction, by Professor William Knight.

86 ESSAYS, DIALOGUES, AND THOUGHTS OF COUNT
Giacomo Leopardi. Translated, with an Introduction and Notes, by Major-General Patrick Maxwell.

87 THE INSPECTOR-GENERAL. A RUSSIAN COMEDY.
By Nikolai V. Gogol. Translated from the original, with an Introduction and Notes, by Arthur A. Sykes.

88 ESSAYS AND APOTHEGMS OF FRANCIS, LORD BACON.
Edited, with an Introduction, by John Buchan.

89 PROSE OF MILTON. SELECTED AND EDITED, WiTH
an Introduction, by Richard Garnett, LL.D.

90 THE REPUBLIC OF PLATO. TRANSLATED BY
Thomas Taylor, with an Introduction by Theodore Wratislaw.

91 PASSAGES FROM FROISSART. WITH AN INTRO-
duction by Frank T. Marzials.

92 THE PROSE AND TABLE TALK OF COLERIDGE.
Edited by Will H. Dircks.

93 HEINE IN ART AND LETTERS. TRANSLATED BY
Elizabeth A. Sharp.

94 SELECTED ESSAYS OF DE QUINCEY. WITH AN
Introduction by Sir George Douglas, Bart.

95 VASARI'S LIVES OF ITALIAN PAINTERS. SELECTED
and Prefaced by Havelock Ellis.

96 LAOCOON, AND OTHER PROSE WRITINGS OF
LESSING. A new Translation by W. B. Rönnfeldt.

97 PELLEAS AND MELISANDA, AND THE SIGHTLESS
Two Plays by Maurice Maeterlinck. Translated from the French by Laurence Alma Tadema.

98 THE COMPLETE ANGLER OF WALTON AND COTTON.
Edited, with an Introduction, by Charles Hill Dick.

THE WALTER SCOTT PUBLISHING CO., LTD.,
LONDON AND FELLING-ON-TYNE.

THE SCOTT LIBRARY—continued.

99 LESSING'S NATHAN THE WISE. TRANSLATED BY
Major-General Patrick Maxwell.

100 THE POETRY OF THE CELTIC RACES, AND OTHER
Essays of Ernest Renan. Translated by W. G. Hutchison.

101 CRITICISMS, REFLECTIONS, AND MAXIMS OF GOETHE.
Translated, with an Introduction, by W. B. Rönnfeldt.

102 ESSAYS OF SCHOPENHAUER. TRANSLATED BY
Mrs. Rudolf Dircks. With an Introduction.

103 RENAN'S LIFE OF JESUS. TRANSLATED, WITH AN
Introduction, by William G. Hutchison.

104 THE CONFESSIONS OF SAINT AUGUSTINE. EDITED,
with an Introduction, by Arthur Symons.

105 THE PRINCIPLES OF SUCCESS IN LITERATURE.
By George Henry Lewes. Edited by T. Sharper Knowlson.

106 THE LIVES OF DR. JOHN DONNE, SIR HENRY WOTTON,
Mr. Richard Hooker, Mr. George Herbert, and Dr. Robert Sanderson.
By Izaac Walton. Edited, with an Introduction, by Charles Hill Dick.

108 RENAN'S ANTICHRIST. TRANSLATED, WITH AN
Introduction, by W. G. Hutchison.

109 ORATIONS OF CICERO. SELECTED AND EDITED,
with an Introduction, by Fred. W. Norris.

110 REFLECTIONS ON THE REVOLUTION IN FRANCE.
By Edmund Burke. With an Introduction by George Sampson.

111 THE LETTERS OF THE YOUNGER PLINY. SERIES I.
Translated, with an Introductory Essay, by John B. Firth, B.A., Late
Scholar of Queen's College, Oxford.

112 THE LETTERS OF THE YOUNGER PLINY. SERIES II.
Translated by John B. Firth, B.A.

THE WALTER SCOTT PUBLISHING COMPANY, LIMITED,
LONDON AND FELLING-ON-TYNE.

THE SCOTT LIBRARY—continued.

113 SELECTED THOUGHTS OF BLAISE PASCAL. TRANSlated, with an Introduction and Notes, by Gertrude Burford Rawlings.

114 SCOTS ESSAYISTS: FROM STIRLING TO STEVENSON.
Edited, with an Introduction, by Oliphant Smeaton.

115 ON LIBERTY. BY JOHN STUART MILL. WITH AN Introduction by W. L. Courtney.

116 THE DISCOURSE ON METHOD AND METAPHYSICAL
Meditations of René Descartes. Translated, with Introduction, by Gertrude B. Rawlings.

117 KÂLIDÂSA'S SAKUNTALÂ, Etc. EDITED, WITH AN Introduction, by T. Holme.

118 NEWMAN'S UNIVERSITY SKETCHES. EDITED, WITH Introduction, by George Sampson.

119 NEWMAN'S SELECT ESSAYS. EDITED, WITH AN Introduction, by George Sampson.

120 RENAN'S MARCUS AURELIUS. TRANSLATED, WITH an Introduction, by William G. Hutchison.

121 FROUDE'S NEMESIS OF FAITH. WITH AN INTROduction by William G. Hutchison.

122 WHAT IS ART? BY LEO TOLSTOY. TRANSLATED from the Original Russian MS., with Introduction, by Alymer Maude.

123 HUME'S POLITICAL ESSAYS. EDITED, WITH AN Introduction, by W. B. Robertson.

OTHER VOLUMES IN PREPARATION.

THE WALTER SCOTT PUBLISHING COMPANY, LIMITED,
LONDON AND FELLING-ON-TYNE.

IN ONE VOLUME.

Crown 8vo, Cloth, Richly Gilt. Price 3s. 6d.

Musicians' Wit, Humour, and Anecdote:

BEING

ON DITS OF COMPOSERS, SINGERS, AND INSTRUMENTALISTS OF ALL TIMES.

By FREDERICK J. CROWEST,

Author of "The Great Tone Poets," "The Story of British Music"; Editor of "The Master Musicians" Series, etc., etc.

Profusely Illustrated with Quaint Drawings by J. P. DONNE.

WHAT THE REVIEWERS SAY:—

"It is one of those delightful medleys of anecdote of all times, seasons, and persons, in every page of which there is a new specimen of humour, strange adventure, and quaint saying."—T. P. O'CONNOR in *T. P.'s Weekly*.

"A remarkable collection of good stories which must have taken years of perseverance to get together."—*Morning Leader.*

"A book which should prove acceptable to two large sections of the public—those who are interested in musicians and those who have an adequate sense of the comic."—*Globe.*

THE WALTER SCOTT PUBLISHING COMPANY, LIMITED,
LONDON AND FELLING-ON-TYNE.

The Makers of British Art.

A NEW SERIES OF MONOGRAPHS OF BRITISH PAINTERS.

Each volume illustrated with Twenty Full-page Reproductions and a Photogravure Portrait.

Square Crown 8vo, Cloth, Gilt Top, Deckled Edges, 3s. 6d. net.

VOLUMES READY.

LANDSEER, SIR EDWIN. By the EDITOR.
"This little volume may rank as the most complete account of Landseer that the world is likely to possess."—*Times.*

REYNOLDS, SIR JOSHUA. By ELSA D'ESTERRE-KEELING.
"To the series entitled 'The Makers of British Art' Miss Elsa d'Esterre-Keeling contributes an admirable little volume on Sir Joshua Reynolds. Miss Keeling's style is sprightly and epigrammatic, and her judgments are well considered."—*Daily Telegraph.*

TURNER, J. M. W. By ROBERT CHIGNELL, Author of "The Life and Paintings of Vicat Cole, R.A."

ROMNEY, GEORGE. By SIR HERBERT MAXWELL, Bart., F.R.S., M.P.
"Likely to remain the best account of the painter's life."—*Athenæum.*

WILKIE, SIR DAVID. By Professor BAYNE.

CONSTABLE, JOHN. By the Right Hon. LORD WINDSOR.

RAEBURN, SIR HENRY. By EDWARD PINNINGTON.

GAINSBOROUGH, THOMAS. By A. E. FLETCHER.

HOGARTH, WILLIAM. By Prof. G. BALDWIN BROWN.

MOORE, HENRY. By FRANK J. MACLEAN.

IN PREPARATION.
MILLAIS—LEIGHTON—MORLAND.

THE WALTER SCOTT PUBLISHING COMPANY, LIMITED,
LONDON AND FELLING-ON-TYNE.

Crown 8vo, about 350 pp. each, Cloth Cover, 2/6 per Vol.;
Half-Polished Morocco, Gilt Top, 5s.

Count Tolstoy's Works.

The following Volumes are already issued—

A RUSSIAN PROPRIETOR.
THE COSSACKS.
IVAN ILYITCH, AND OTHER STORIES.
MY RELIGION.
LIFE.
MY CONFESSION.
CHILDHOOD, BOYHOOD, YOUTH.
THE PHYSIOLOGY OF WAR.
ANNA KARÉNINA. 3/6.

WHAT TO DO?
WAR AND PEACE. (4 vols.)
THE LONG EXILE, ETC.
SEVASTOPOL.
THE KREUTZER SONATA, AND FAMILY HAPPINESS.
THE KINGDOM OF GOD IS WITHIN YOU.
WORK WHILE YE HAVE THE LIGHT.
THE GOSPEL IN BRIEF.

Uniform with the above—
IMPRESSIONS OF RUSSIA. By Dr. GEORG BRANDES.

Post 4to, Cloth, Price 1s.
PATRIOTISM AND CHRISTIANITY.
To which is appended a Reply to Criticisms of the Work.
By COUNT TOLSTOY.

1/- Booklets by Count Tolstoy.

Bound in White Grained Boards, with Gilt Lettering.

WHERE LOVE IS, THERE GOD IS ALSO.
THE TWO PILGRIMS.
WHAT MEN LIVE BY.

THE GODSON.
IF YOU NEGLECT THE FIRE, YOU DON'T PUT IT OUT.
WHAT SHALL IT PROFIT A MAN?

2/- Booklets by Count Tolstoy.

NEW EDITIONS, REVISED.

Small 12mo, Cloth, with Embossed Design on Cover, each containing Two Stories by Count Tolstoy, and Two Drawings by H. R. Millar. In Box, Price 2s. each.

Volume I. contains—
WHERE LOVE IS, THERE GOD IS ALSO.
THE GODSON.

Volume II. contains—
WHAT MEN LIVE BY.
WHAT SHALL IT PROFIT A MAN?

Volume III. contains—
THE TWO PILGRIMS.
IF YOU NEGLECT THE FIRE, YOU DON'T PUT IT OUT.

Volume IV. contains—
MASTER AND MAN.

Volume V. contains—
TOLSTOY'S PARABLES.

THE WALTER SCOTT PUBLISHING CO., LTD.,
LONDON AND FELLING-ON-TYNE

Crown 8vo, Cloth, 3s. 6d. each; some vols., 6s.

The Contemporary Science Series.

EDITED BY HAVELOCK ELLIS.

Illustrated Vols. between 300 and 400 pp. each.

EVOLUTION OF SEX. By Professors GEDDES and THOMSON. 6s.
ELECTRICITY IN MODERN LIFE. By G. W. DE TUNZELMANN.
THE ORIGIN OF THE ARYANS. By Dr. TAYLOR.
PHYSIOGNOMY AND EXPRESSION. By P. MANTEGAZZA.
EVOLUTION AND DISEASE. By J. B. SUTTON.
THE VILLAGE COMMUNITY. By G. L. GOMME.
THE CRIMINAL. By HAVELOCK ELLIS. New Edition. 6s.
SANITY AND INSANITY. By Dr. C. MERCIER.
HYPNOTISM. By Dr. ALBERT MOLL (Berlin).
MANUAL TRAINING. By Dr. WOODWARD (St. Louis).
SCIENCE OF FAIRY TALES. By E. S. HARTLAND.
PRIMITIVE FOLK. By ELIE RECLUS.
EVOLUTION OF MARRIAGE. By CH. LETOURNEAU.
BACTERIA AND THEIR PRODUCTS. By Dr. WOODHEAD.
EDUCATION AND HEREDITY. By J. M. GUYAU.
THE MAN OF GENIUS. By Prof. LOMBROSO.
PROPERTY: ITS ORIGIN. By CH. LETOURNEAU.
VOLCANOES PAST AND PRESENT. By Prof. HULL.
PUBLIC HEALTH PROBLEMS. By Dr. J. F. SYKES.
MODERN METEOROLOGY. By FRANK WALDO, Ph.D.
THE GERM-PLASM. By Professor WEISMANN. 6s.
THE INDUSTRIES OF ANIMALS. By F. HOUSSAY.
MAN AND WOMAN. By HAVELOCK ELLIS. 6s.

THE WALTER SCOTT PUBLISHING COMPANY, LIMITED,
LONDON AND FELLING-ON-TYNE.

CONTEMPORARY SCIENCE SERIES—*continued.*

MODERN CAPITALISM. By John A. Hobson, M.A.
THOUGHT-TRANSFERENCE. By F. Podmore, M.A.
COMPARATIVE PSYCHOLOGY. By Prof. C. L. Morgan, F.R.S. 6s.
THE ORIGINS OF INVENTION. By O. T. Mason.
THE GROWTH OF THE BRAIN. By H. H. Donaldson.
EVOLUTION IN ART. By Prof. A. C. Haddon, F.R.S.
HALLUCINATIONS AND ILLUSIONS. By E. Parish. 6s.
PSYCHOLOGY OF THE EMOTIONS. By Prof. Ribot. 6s.
THE NEW PSYCHOLOGY. By Dr. E. W. Scripture. 6s.
SLEEP: Its Physiology, Pathology, Hygiene, and Psychology. By Marie de Manacéïne.
THE NATURAL HISTORY OF DIGESTION. By A. Lockhart Gillespie, M.D., F.R.C.P. Ed., F.R.S. Ed. 6s.
DEGENERACY: Its Causes, Signs, and Results. By Prof. Eugene S. Talbot, M.D., Chicago. 6s.
THE HISTORY OF THE EUROPEAN FAUNA. By R. F. Scharff, B.Sc., Ph.D., F.Z.S. 6s.
THE RACES OF MAN: A Sketch of Ethnography and Anthropology. By J. Deniker. 6s.
THE PSYCHOLOGY OF RELIGION. By Prof. Starbuck. 6s.
THE CHILD. By Alexander Francis Chamberlain, M.A., Ph.D. 6s.
THE MEDITERRANEAN RACE. By Prof. Sergi. 6s.
THE STUDY OF RELIGION. By Morris Jastrow, Jun., Ph.D. 6s.
HISTORY OF GEOLOGY AND PALÆONTOLOGY. By Prof. Karl Alfred von Zittel, Munich. 6s.
THE MAKING OF CITIZENS: A Study in Comparative Education. By R. E. Hughes, M.A. 6s.
MORALS: A Treatise on the Psycho-Sociological Bases of Ethics. By Prof. G. L. Duprat.
EARTHQUAKES, A STUDY OF RECENT. By Prof. Charles Davison, D.Sc., F.G.S. 6s.

The Walter Scott Publishing Company, Limited,
London and Felling-on-Tyne.

SPECIAL EDITION OF THE

CANTERBURY POETS.

Square 8vo, Cloth, Gilt Top Elegant, Price 2s.

Each Volume with a Frontispiece in Photogravure.

CHRISTIAN YEAR. With Portrait of John Keble.
LONGFELLOW. With Portrait of Longfellow.
SHELLEY. With Portrait of Shelley.
WORDSWORTH. With Portrait of Wordsworth.
WHITTIER. With Portrait of Whittier.
BURNS. Songs } With Portrait of Burns, and View of "The
BURNS. Poems } Auld Brig o' Doon."
KEATS. With Portrait of Keats.
EMERSON. With Portrait of Emerson.
SONNETS OF THIS CENTURY. Portrait of P. B. Marston.
WHITMAN. With Portrait of Whitman.
LOVE LETTERS OF A VIOLINIST. Portrait of Eric Mackay.
SCOTT. Lady of the Lake, } With Portrait of Sir Walter Scott,
etc. } and View of "The Silver
SCOTT. Marmion, etc. } Strand, Loch Katrine."
CHILDREN OF THE POETS. With an Engraving of "The Orphans," by Gainsborough.
SONNETS OF EUROPE. With Portrait of J. A. Symonds.
SYDNEY DOBELL. With Portrait of Sydney Dobell.
HERRICK. With Portrait of Herrick.
BALLADS AND RONDEAUS. Portrait of W. E. Henley.
IRISH MINSTRELSY. With Portrait of Thomas Davis.
PARADISE LOST. With Portrait of Milton.
FAIRY MUSIC. Engraving from Drawing by C. E. Brock.
GOLDEN TREASURY. With Engraving of Virgin Mother.
AMERICAN SONNETS. With Portrait of J. R. Lowell.
IMITATION OF CHRIST. With Engraving, "Ecce Homo."
PAINTER POETS. With Portrait of Walter Crane.
WOMEN POETS. With Portrait of Mrs. Browning.
POEMS OF HON. RODEN NOEL. Portrait of Hon. R. Noel.
AMERICAN HUMOROUS VERSE. Portrait of Mark Twain.
SONGS OF FREEDOM. With Portrait of William Morris.
SCOTTISH MINOR POETS. With Portrait of R. Tannahill.
CONTEMPORARY SCOTTISH VERSE. With Portrait of Robert Louis Stevenson.
PARADISE REGAINED. With Portrait of Milton.
CAVALIER POETS. With Portrait of Suckling.
HUMOROUS POEMS. With Portrait of Hood.
HERBERT. With Portrait of Herbert.
POE. With Portrait of Poe.
OWEN MEREDITH. With Portrait of late Lord Lytton.
LOVE LYRICS. With Portrait of Raleigh.
GERMAN BALLADS. With Portrait of Schiller.
CAMPBELL. With Portrait of Campbell.
CANADIAN POEMS. With View of Mount Stephen.
EARLY ENGLISH POETRY. With Portrait of Earl of Surrey.
ALLAN RAMSAY. With Portrait of Ramsay.
SPENSER. With Portrait of Spenser.

THE WALTER SCOTT PUBLISHING COMPANY, LIMITED,
LONDON AND FELLING-ON-TYNE.

CHATTERTON. With Engraving, "The Death of Chatterton."
COWPER. With Portrait of Cowper.
CHAUCER. With Portrait of Chaucer.
COLERIDGE. With Portrait of Coleridge.
POPE. With Portrait of Pope.
BYRON. Miscellaneous } With Portraits of Byron.
BYRON. Don Juan
JACOBITE SONGS. With Portrait of Prince Charlie.
BORDER BALLADS. With View of Neidpath Castle.
AUSTRALIAN BALLADS. With Portrait of A. L. Gordon.
HOGG. With Portrait of Hogg.
GOLDSMITH. With Portrait of Goldsmith.
MOORE. With Portrait of Moore.
DORA GREENWELL. With Portrait of Dora Greenwell.
BLAKE. With Portrait of Blake.
POEMS OF NATURE. With Portrait of Andrew Lang.
PRAED. With Portrait.
SOUTHEY. With Portrait.
HUGO. With Portrait.
GOETHE. With Portrait.
BERANGER. With Portrait.
HEINE. With Portrait.
SEA MUSIC. With View of Corbière Rocks, Jersey.
SONG-TIDE. With Portrait of Philip Bourke Marston.
LADY OF LYONS. With Portrait of Bulwer Lytton.
SHAKESPEARE: Songs and Sonnets. With Portrait.
BEN JONSON. With Portrait.
HORACE. With Portrait.
CRABBE. With Portrait.
CRADLE SONGS. With Engraving from Drawing by T. E. Macklin.
BALLADS OF SPORT. Do. do.
MATTHEW ARNOLD. With Portrait.
AUSTIN'S DAYS OF THE YEAR. With Portrait.
CLOUGH'S BOTHIE, and other Poems. With View.
BROWNING'S Pippa Passes, etc.
BROWNING'S Blot in the 'Scutcheon, etc. } With Portrait.
BROWNING'S Dramatic Lyrics.
MACKAY'S LOVER'S MISSAL. With Portrait.
KIRKE WHITE'S POEMS. With Portrait.
LYRA NICOTIANA. With Portrait.
AURORA LEIGH. With Portrait of E. B. Browning.
NAVAL SONGS. With Portrait of Lord Nelson.
TENNYSON: In Memoriam, Maud, etc. With Portrait.
TENNYSON: English Idyls, The Princess, etc. With View of Farringford House.
WAR SONGS. With Portrait of Lord Roberts.
JAMES THOMSON. With Portrait.
ALEXANDER SMITH. With Portrait.

THE WALTER SCOTT PUBLISHING COMPANY, LIMITED,
LONDON AND FELLING-ON-TYNE.

The Music Story Series.

A SERIES OF LITERARY-MUSICAL MONOGRAPHS.

Edited by FREDERICK J. CROWEST,
Author of "The Great Tone Poets," etc., etc.

Illustrated with Photogravure and Collotype Portraits, Half-tone and Line Pictures, Facsimiles, etc.

Square Crown 8vo, Cloth, 3s. 6d. net.

VOLUMES NOW READY.

THE STORY OF ORATORIO. By ANNIE W. PATTERSON, B.A., Mus. Doc.

THE STORY OF NOTATION. By C. F. ABDY WILLIAMS, M.A., Mus. Bac.

THE STORY OF THE ORGAN. By C. F. ABDY WILLIAMS, M.A., Author of "Bach" and "Handel" ("Master Musicians' Series").

THE STORY OF CHAMBER MUSIC. By N. KILBURN, Mus. Bac. (Cantab.), Conductor of the Middlesbrough, Sunderland, and Bishop Auckland Musical Societies.

THE STORY OF THE VIOLIN. By PAUL STOEVING, Professor of the Violin, Guildhall School of Music, London.

THE STORY OF THE HARP. By WILLIAM H. GRATTAN FLOOD, Author of "History of Irish Music."

THE STORY OF ORGAN MUSIC. By C. F. ABDY WILLIAMS, M.A., Mus. Bac.

IN PREPARATION.

THE STORY OF THE PIANOFORTE. By ALGERNON S. ROSE, Author of "Talks with Bandsmen."

THE STORY OF ENGLISH MINSTRELSY. By EDMONDSTOUNE DUNCAN.

THE STORY OF THE ORCHESTRA. By STEWART MACPHERSON, Fellow and Professor, Royal Academy of Music.

THE STORY OF MUSICAL SOUND. By CHURCHILL SIBLEY, Mus. Doc.

THE STORY OF CHURCH MUSIC. By THE EDITOR.

ETC., ETC., ETC.

THE WALTER SCOTT PUBLISHING COMPANY, LIMITED,
LONDON AND FELLING-ON-TYNE.

www.ingramcontent.com/pod-product-compliance
Lightning Source LLC
Chambersburg PA
CBHW031330230426
43670CB00006B/296